AN INTRODUCTION TO

THE PHILOSOPHY OF METHODOLOGY

SAGE has been part of the global academic community since 1965, supporting high quality research and learning that transforms society and our understanding of individuals, groups, and cultures. SAGE is the independent, innovative, natural home for authors, editors and societies who share our commitment and passion for the social sciences.

Find out more at: **www.sagepublications.com**

Connect, Debate, Engage on Methodspace

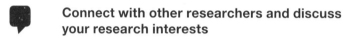 **Connect with other researchers and discuss your research interests**

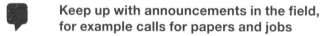 **Keep up with announcements in the field, for example calls for papers and jobs**

 **Discover and review resources**

 **Engage with featured content such as key articles, podcasts and videos**

 **Find out about relevant conferences and events**

www.methodspace.com

brought to you by

AN INTRODUCTION TO

THE PHILOSOPHY OF METHODOLOGY

KERRY E. HOWELL

Los Angeles | London | New Delhi
Singapore | Washington DC

Los Angeles | London | New Delhi
Singapore | Washington DC

SAGE Publications Ltd
1 Oliver's Yard
55 City Road
London EC1Y 1SP

SAGE Publications Inc.
2455 Teller Road
Thousand Oaks, California 91320

SAGE Publications India Pvt Ltd
B 1/I 1 Mohan Cooperative Industrial Area
Mathura Road
New Delhi 110 044

SAGE Publications Asia-Pacific Pte Ltd
3 Church Street
#10-04 Samsung Hub
Singapore 049483

© Kerry E. Howell 2013

First published 2013

Library of Congress Control Number: 2011945825

British Library Cataloguing in Publication data

A catalogue record for this book is available from
the British Library

Editor: Katie Metzler
Assistant editor: Anna Horvai
Production editor: Ian Antcliff
Copyeditor: Jeremy Toynbee
Proofreader: Jacque Woolley
Indexer: Henson Editorial Services
Marketing manager: Ben Griffin-Sherwood
Cover design: Lisa Harper
Typeset by: C&M Digitals (P) Ltd, Chennai, India
Printed in India at Replika Press Pvt Ltd

ISBN 978-1-4462-0298-2
ISBN 978-1-4462-0299-9 (pbk)

For April Mam and Poppy.

Contents

About the author

Professor Howell holds the Chair of Governance and Leadership and is Director of Research at Plymouth University Business School. Through his research Professor Howell has developed scholarly expertise in areas relating to the philosophy of research, methodology, methods and governance and written research texts with Nova Science Press, Palgrave Macmillan Press and Sage. Professor Howell has produced refereed articles for peer reviewed academic journals and managed funded research projects for various institutions. He is currently an active member of the Public Administration Committee, a member of the Association of Business Schools Research Steering Committee and sits on a number of editorial boards. Professor Howell teaches methodology and methods modules on research degree programmes and has successfully supervised numerous doctorates. He is programme leader for the Plymouth Business School (PBS) Professional Doctorate Programme and Post Graduate Certificate in Research Methodology. Professor Howell developed the PBS research strategy and Research Assessment Exercise (RAE) submission for Business and Management. Over the past five years he has continued to augment and reinforce the PBS research strategy, which informs and embeds a maturing academic culture and environment. Professor Howell is committed to securing innovative knowledge development and dissemination underpinned by rigorously deployed methodological approaches and methods.

Preface

This text covers a number of distinct areas and draws together philosophical positions relating to paradigms of inquiry that underpin methodologies, which in turn identify rationales for specific methods of data collection. The main objective of this text is to clarify the similarities and distinctions between philosophical positions and outline the difference between methodology and methods. These terms are regularly used to denote methods when the term methodology is required or methodology when the writer actually means methods. In this text, methodology is defined as the research strategy that outlines the way one goes about undertaking a research project, whereas methods identify means or modes of data collection. When clarifying the distinction between philosophy and paradigms of inquiry the situation is a little more opaque; there is a distinction between rationalism and empiricism as well as between phenomenology and positivism. This study takes phenomenology and positivism to incorporate extensions of the rationalist/empiricist debate and the paradigms of inquiry that arise out of this extension to include post-positivism, critical theory, constructivism and participatory. Three further philosophical positions also underpin the methodological approaches identified and provide some comprehension of the 'self'/'other' divide; Hegelian recognition, pragmatism and symbolic interaction inform methodological approaches in terms of the relationship between objective/subjective stances regarding self and community.

Paradigms of inquiry incorporate clear indications of how ontology (what reality is) and epistemology (the relationship between the researcher and researched) are intrinsic to each methodological approach and consequent plan for data collection. The ontological perspective identifies the epistemology that provides a strategic assessment of the methodology and methods best suited for the research programme, thesis or dissertation.

The main objective of this text is to assist in the production of rigorous academic research projects and even though research students form the primary audience it is a useful text for more experienced researchers using mixed methodological approaches who wish to have a comprehension of the underlying issues when applying interdisciplinary research positions. This book draws on a number of methodological texts and through a synthesis of these attempted to simplify some complex ideas. In some instances it is realised that further depth could have been included in the coverage of certain ideas, e.g. phenomenology. However, the rationale for this text is to provide a comprehension of how philosophical perspectives inform methodology and theory and not give an in-depth discussion of all the nuances relating to philosophical ideas; what we give here is a broad comprehension of philosophical issues. For example, an in-depth study of any one of the phenomenologist's identified would necessitate many tomes and such is well beyond the beyond the scope of this text. Hopefully, this book will reach its intended audience and provide a useful tool for all those involved in research at whatever level these endeavours may be undertaken.

ONE

Introduction: Problems Identified

Introduction

The objective of this text is to provide sound underpinning for dissertations, theses, research projects and, where necessary, more advanced interdisciplinary research programmes. This book draws together a diverse set of material that gives a comprehensive assessment, understanding and application of philosophical positions, paradigms of inquiry, ontology, epistemology, methodology and methods or data collection. Indeed, this text recognises the difficulties regarding philosophy, theory, truth, knowledge, reality, when developing understanding, and the absolute minefield these issues engender for individual researchers and larger interdisciplinary research programmes and projects. This book involves an original perspective on other similar texts because, even though distinct works exist regarding these individual areas, there has been limited coverage of the relationship between philosophical issues in general and through methodological approaches the impacts these have on researchers, participants and data collection procedures. For example, considerations regarding the nature of reality and the role of theory in the pursuit of knowledge will have implications for the methodology and methods pursued in a research project. Methodology will impact on methods and have considerable influence on what knowledge is considered to be and the consequent outcomes of the investigation. If one considers that knowledge or reality exists external to individuals then the researcher is required to undertake data collection procedures in an empirical and distanced manner; usually this perspective pursues an objective detached stance. However, if one considers there is a relationship between reality and mind then such a stance is impossible to attain and subjective tendencies will resonate throughout the research process. Consequently, this text explores these issues and begins with an assessment of notions regarding reality that were identified, discussed and debated in antiquity and further developed through Enlightenment and the thoughts of among others David Hume, Immanuel Kant, Georg Hegel and Arthur Schopenhaur.

Chapter 1 provides explanations regarding theory and practice and identifies correlations between ideas relating to knowledge, truth and reality. Knowledge, truth or reality can either involve abstract conceptualisation or be grounded and developed through practical situations and data. Indeed, these areas may be considered reflections of human relations and stances regarding levels of subjectivity and objectivity. Furthermore, this chapter introduces problems regarding ideas about knowledge, reality, truth and how these may be reflected through different ontological perspectives (conceptualisations of reality or truth) as well as the relationship between the observer and observed (epistemology). Kant considered that knowledge could be developed through critical thinking, which involved both application of received doctrines and systems as well as one's inherited thoughts, prejudices and traditions. To obtain a non-biased position or objectivity one must take the thoughts of others into account. Objectivity was not some higher standpoint but the very fact of understanding the social and subjective nature of self and others. Objects need to be viewed from different perspectives through, which one's point of view may expand. Thought is extended by taking into account the thoughts of others. We compare and contrast the possible judgements of others by putting ourselves in their place through the concept of imagination (Kant, 1952).

Definition Box

Reality, Truth, Knowledge and Theory

Reality: Related to knowledge and can be totally separate from or a construction of the mind. Positivist perspectives of reality differ from phenomenological notions of reality; positivism sees reality as totally independent of humanity whereas the latter considers them to be intrinsically linked.

Truth: Truth is a difficult concept to pin down and may be interpreted as reflections of reality based on evidence which is determined by an understanding of reality; that is ontological and epistemological positions. Truth provides an understanding of reality at a given point in time; truths like theories do not hold for eternity, when truth and/or theories change so does the nature of reality.

Knowledge: Knowledge incorporates our stock of explanations and understanding of why reality and the truth and theories that reflect this are as they are; knowledge involves interpretations of facts derived from data as well as abstract comprehensions of phenomenon.

Theory: Theory provides ways of explaining or giving meaning to understandings extrapolated from data. Theory can be expressed through immutable laws at one extreme and social or constructions at the other. Theory is a means of reflecting reality, truth or knowledge.

Each relates to the distinction between clear objective external realities that can be understood perfectly by human beings and solipsistic comprehensions of the world which consider phenomenon to be determined by the subjective mind.

Ontology and Epistemology: Does an External Reality Exist?

For empirical science and positivism a real external world exists, which focuses on empirical occurrences and concentrates on the precise nature and rules of events. Conversely, in the *Critique of Pure Reason* Kant states that 'all objects of any experience possible to us are nothing but appearances that are mere representations which ... have no independent existence outside our thoughts' (1992: 519). Transcendental idealism identifies an ordinary means of awareness which may not perceive objects as they truly exist. We only have access to reality through our perceptual capabilities, consequently it is not possible to say whether what we see is accurate; the mind constructs an understanding of phenomenon. So phenomenon as perceived or experienced involves representation; thought may initially consider that it is capable of describing an existing reality, but, all it may provide is a means of making actions transparent to self. However, the idea of an objective reality has been accepted for many years and such a notion is difficult to dispel. That said, this idea should not be taken as gospel and the pursuit of objective reality our only goal; especially in contexts where none may be realised. Indeed, once this is taken on board then other means or ways of understanding may refocus our thoughts and expand our pursuits of knowledge and truth. A distinction exists between a posteriori knowledge, which can be understood through direct awareness of phenomenon (empirically) and a priori knowledge that is known through propositions (non-empirically). Normally, a posteriori knowledge depends on support from sensory experience whereas a priori knowledge depends on intellectual processes or pure reason. Fundamentally, Kant distinguished between things that exist in themselves and the appearances of phenomenon; we know the world through the projection of pre-existing categories apparent within the mind and are not able to access things in themselves. That is, we can only have an interpretation of entities or objects as they appear to us once they have been categorised and edited by the means at our disposal for understanding the given phenomenon.

Kant (1992) argued that elements of occurrences and events are initially 'phenomenon of the brain' and made up of 'subjective conditions' (Schopenhaur, 1966: 3). As soon as someone comprehends that the 'world is my representation' it should be recognised by all as a truism. However, it is not a proposition that everyone understands and becomes or turns into an assessment of the relationship between the ideal and the real (realism and idealism); 'the world in the head (ideal) and the world outside the head (real)'. Schopenhaur, argued that understanding was 'limited to the facts of consciousness; in other words philosophy is essentially idealistic' (Schopenhaur, 1966: 5) and because it denies that the world is not primarily representation, realism is nothing but an illusion. Knowledge of truth 'is rendered more difficult only by the fact ... that not everyone has sufficient power of reflection to go back to the first elements of his consciousness of things' (Schopenhaur, 1966: 5). This is because the idea of the objective has its embryonic existence in the subjective; that is consciousness.

| Question Box |

Knowledge

Socrates saw virtue as knowledge and to be virtuous was to both know oneself and understand what one ought to do. One would consider that because virtue is knowledge and knowledge can be taught then so can virtue. However, on the one hand, Socrates argues that there are no experts of virtue while on the other hand he considers that virtue may be taught. But what if there are no experts to teach virtue? Indeed, he attempts to overcome this problem by considering that 'the soul ... has learned everything that there is. So we need not be surprised if it can recall the knowledge of virtue or anything else which ... it once possessed' (Plato, 1976: 129–30). When we learn a basic principle, if we persevere, the rest will follow. The soul remembers what it forgot at birth 'for seeking and learning are in fact nothing but recollection' (Plato, 1976: 130). Knowledge is already present and only requires recollection.

Express your considerations regarding this understanding of knowledge and learning from first principles. Does knowledge or what is sought pre-exist the research process?

Given that the starting point is the subjective self, would the objective world exist without consciousness (without idealism or the subjective)? Indeed, if we imagine an objective world without a knowing subject we actually achieve the opposite of what we intended. 'We become aware that what we are imagining at that moment is in truth the opposite of what we intended, namely nothing but just the process in the intellect of a knowing being that perceives an objective world' (Schopenhaur, 1966: 5). The real world is phenomenon of the mind and the assumption that an external world exist no more than a contradiction. When we undertake a research project we approach the world with pre-conceptions about the relationship between mind and external reality; such will affect the methodological approach, research programme and methods of data collection. If one considers reality to be an external entity then it is likely that the research will pursue objectivity and test or falsify hypotheses or null hypotheses through data, experimentation and or statistical analysis. If we consider the world and mind to be intrinsically linked a more interpretive approach would be appropriate.

Kant considered that space and time themselves were due to the intuition or perception of the subject and were consequently not things-in-themselves. Subsequently, that which exists in time and space is not objective and things-in themselves that can only be subjective and an objective world representation. Through our 'mind we represent to ourselves objects as outside us ... Space is not an empirical concept ... derived from outer experience ... Space is a necessary ... representation' (Kant, 1992: 67–8). Furthermore, time is also 'a necessary representation that underlies all intuitions' (Kant, 1992: 74). All things involve reflections of the mind continually interacting in relation to time and space; who and where we are in the era we exist will determine our notions and understanding of things, while at the same time things impact on our notions of time and space.

In many contexts, idealism is misinterpreted as denying the existence of empirical reality and the external world. However, idealism transcends realism and leaves the external world untouched but at the same time considers that the object and the empirical real is conditioned by the subject in two ways: first it is 'conditioned materially or as object in general, since an objective existence is conceivable only in the face of the subject'. Second 'it is conditioned formally, since the mode and manner of the object's existence, in other words, of it being represented (space, time, causality) proceed from the subject and are predisposed in the subject' (Schopenhaur, 1966: 8). Indeed, this links Berkeley's concept of idealism (the object in general) with Kantian (special mode and manner of objective existence).

Reflection Box

George Berkeley

In his *Treatise Concerning the Principles of Human Knowledge* (1710) George Berkeley (1658–1753) argued that the external world were no more than collections of ideas. This was a striking proposal and many dismiss the idea with some indignation. However, Berkeley was a serious philosopher and considered that God produced sensations or ideas within our mind. He further argued that if his ideas were fully understood he would be identified as a philosopher that defended truth against 'the mob' or 'the vulgar'.

Consider Berkeley's position and the implications this has for the relationship between object and subject.

Fundamentally, time and space which underpin the notion of an objective reality are themselves subjective-based entities. Kant dealt with this but does not use the notion of brain or mind. Indeed Kant based his subjective stance on the 'faculty of knowledge'. The intellect creates the order of things 'and exists only for things, but … things also exist only for it' (Kant, 1992: 9).

Realism considers that the world exists independently of the subject. However, let us remove the subject and leave only the object and then return the subject to the world; the world then repeats itself to the subject exactly (as a perfect mirror image of that which exists). 'Thus for the first world a second has been added, which, although completely separated from the first resembles it to a nicety. Now the subjective world of this perception is constituted in subjective, known space exactly as the objective world is in infinite space' (Kant, 1992: 9).

The question becomes the extent to which an external world corresponds to our subjective interpretation? Which returns to the question; is the world of subjective or objective origin? John Locke and David Hume assumed an objective or external origin because they argued understanding was drawn or developed from experience; it is a posteriori. Whereas, Kant and Schopenhaur considered the world to be a priori and subjective in origin because the 'only thing actually given empirically in the case of perception is the occurrence of a sensation in the organ of the sense' (Schopenhaur, 1966: 11). No one can doubt that 'knowledge begins with experience ... Nevertheless it ... may well be that even our empirical knowledge is made up of what we receive through impressions and of what our own faculty of knowledge ... supplies from itself' (Kant, 1992: 41–2).

Realism identified that the object existed without the subject. However, it is difficult to clearly conceive of such an object. Through knowledge and representation it is not possible to know things from within because the knowledge of all things comes from without. We may only understand from within if we are capable of getting inside things 'so that the inside would be known directly' (Schopenhaur, 1966: 12). Furthermore, knowledge of the world remains 'a mere representation since no path is here possible which leads beyond this' (Schopenhaur, 1966: 12).

Idealism and Materialism

There also exists a distinction between idealism and materialism, which may be investigated through assessing the existence of matter. Is matter real or an ideal? Is matter a representation or is it independent of the mind? If independent then matter is a thing-in-itself, if a representation then idealistic. Locke asserted the unquestionable existence of matter whereas Berkeley denied this assertion.

Materialism points out that the 'knower is a product of matter as that matter is a mere representation; but is also as one sided; for materialism is the philosophy of the subject who forgets to take account of himself' (Schopenhaur, 1966: 13). Furthermore, no less correct is the assertion that all matter exists as representation (*Materia menacium verax*): Matter is a lie and yet true. The world is more than mere representation and that the object is conditioned by the subject. Indeed a 'consciousness without object is no consciousness at all. A thinking subject has concepts for its objects: a sensuously perceiving subject has objects with the qualities corresponding to its organisation' (Schopenhaur, 1966: 15).

Reflection Box

Subject and Object

Subject: World is my representation only I exist.

Object: Without me there is nothing. You are a part of me and quite accidental.

Subject: You and your form are conditioned by me and neither would exist without me. You are represented by me and I am the locality of your existence; I am the basis of your existence.

Object: You are transitory and last but a moment I on the other hand remain from millennium to millennium. I am eternal.

Subject: Eternal time and space is merely representation which I carry within me you simply manifest yourself in this a priori conditioning. It is in this way that you first exist. If I am transitory then so are you. Only the individual is transitory who is my bearer and which like everything else is my representation.

Object: Even if I accept your existence beyond the fleeting moments of individuals your existence is still dependent on mine. You are subject only so long as you have an object. I am the object that holds all together without which incoherency would reign.

Subject: As I am tied to individuals you are tied to form. No one has seen either of us in abstraction or naked. 'At bottom it is one entity that perceives itself and is perceived by itself , but it's being-in itself cannot consist either in perceiving or being perceived as these are divided between us' (Schopenhaur, 1966: 18).

Both: We are necessary elements of a whole. Necessary to one another's existence. Only misunderstanding can set us up as enemies in opposition to each other.

Each encapsulates the world as representation or the phenomenon. Subtract this and one is left with the purely metaphysical (the thing-in-itself). Consider this conversation between the object and subject.

Overall, representation and the objective world encompass two extremes. The one extreme is the knowing subject without world the other external world without subject; they are in fact really one and the same thing considered from two opposite points view' (Schopenhaur, 1966: 15–16). Kant (1997) alludes to a similar position when he explained the consciousness of his existence. First from the place he occupied in the 'external world of sense and extends the connection in which I stand in unbounded magnitude with worlds upon worlds and systems upon systems'. Whereas the second, 'begins from the invisible self, my personality and presents me in a world which has true infinity but which can be discovered only by the understanding, and I cognise that my connection with that world (and thereby with all those visible worlds as well) is not merely contingent, as in the first case, but universal and necessary' (Kant 1997: 133). When undertaking research one takes self to the given problem; self defines perceptions of the problem and the same difficulty defines the questions self will ask. The process is interactive and iterative and involves the researcher recognising both subjective and objective tendencies in developing research strategies and programmes.

Identifying Others in the World

The distinction between subject and object may also be considered when we identify others in the world. We know we exist and the existence of others follows from this; in the social sciences if we do not analyse others what do we actually

Table 1.1 Subject and object

Subject	Object
Represented and conditioned by humanity.	Exists prior to humanity and is eternal.
Eternity and reality merely representations of the subject.	The existence of the subject is reliant on the existence of the object.
Reliant on individuals for existence to be represented.	Reliant on form for existence to be represented.
Subject reliant on the existence of object.	Object reliant on existence of the subject.

investigate? Through undertaking data collection we accept the existence of others in the world. 'Even my own person is object for another and is therefore that other's representation, and yet I know certainly that I should exist even without the other representing me in his mind' (Kant, 1997: 6). One may deal with this in the following way; the other whose object I am is not an absolute subject, but initially a knowing entity. 'Therefore if he too did not exist' or any other person exist other than myself 'this would still by no means be the elimination of the subject in whose representation alone all objects exist' (Kant, 1997: 6). For other people are only known indirectly by me.

> I know my body only in perception of my brain. This perception is brought about through the senses and on their data the perceiving understanding carries out its function ... It follows from this that the existence of my body as an extended and acting thing always presupposes a knowing being different from it, since it is essentially an existence in the apprehension, in the representation and hence an existence for another being. (Kant, 1997: 6)

The starting point for dealing with this issue could be Hegel (1977) and the naïve mind's emergent comprehension of external reality. Mind becomes aware of itself through subjective and objective self-consciousness. Subjective awareness of self is not enough to enable self-consciousness because this is unable to sufficiently inform human beings about what they are like in the world. Humans need a complimentary objective stance. Self needs an objective recognition of its own consciousness to provide an understanding of its own reality. Only another human being can provide this; through reflecting for consciousness a sense of its own external being.

In this context, objective truth lies in mutual recognition; that is the recognition of 'others' in the world. Others define 'self' and 'self' defines 'self' in relation to the definition of 'others'. Community defines 'self' and 'self' defines community. 'The savage lives in himself; sociable man outside himself, in the opinion of other ... and so to speak, derives the sentiments of his own existence solely from their judgement' (Rousseau, cited in Pippin, 1997: 93). The objective 'self' accepts Rousseau's identification of the situation and provides a potential means of dealing with it (Pippin, 1997). Hegel argued that the transition is not that straightforward because initially the existence of the 'other' will be perceived as a threat to being and a negation of 'self'. Before the subject is confronted by another he/she existed in a world of things. Consequently, the subject deals with the 'other' by treating it as a thing and validates its own image as an entity in control of a sea of things. Because the subject does not yet see itself in an objective form, it treats other consciousness as entities to be controlled. In a research context, initially the other is something to be analysed and assessed in an external fashion; a positivist position initially exists. However, through recognition of other and community a form of unity prevails and the study may shift to more constructivist ontological and epistemological positions. Indeed, through recognition we may map changes in comprehensions of research and the role of others in the knowledge generation process.

Subduing 'other' leads to conflict and enslavement and undermines opportunities to enable full self-consciousness (early anthropology and ethnographic studies reflected such positions). The form of 'recognition' initially understood is subordination or reduction of the 'other' and through a life-death struggle in the pursuit of recognition, social life and political union emerge. Death of 'other' does not solve the problem of 'recognition'. Victory must be attained and 'recognition' accepted before the death of 'other'. Indeed, a master-slave relationship arises, which underpins the emergence of 'recognition', self-consciousness and social life. Hegel does not mean that all relationships are enslaving but that this was the dialectical basis for political, economic, social relationships. The struggle for 'recognition' involves an ongoing process and a continuing feature of social life. For Hegel the master-slave relationship was not an early form of social structure; 'the development of social relationships … is not … simply … one leading from one to another, but self inclusive, each earlier stage incorporating a higher form than the earlier ones, the master-slave relationship is a protean source of the various relationships, political, economic, social and sexual' (Hampsher-Monk, 1992: 426).

Initially, it looks like the master has realised 'the peak of human existence, being the man who is fully satisfied (befriedigt) in and by his real existence, by what he is' (Kojeve, 1980: 46). Indeed, through victory the master seems to have ensured 'recognition'. However, to ensure self-awareness consciousness needs the recognition of an equal. The master has only won by reducing the 'other' to the status of a thing in the world. Because the master existed in a world of things there had been no progression of consciousness. 'His consciousness has progressed no further than its existence in a world of unconscious objects' (Kojeve, 1980: 427). Recognition is required from someone (another human being) of equal status.

On the other hand, the slave is conscious of another independent mind in the world. Although forced to recognise the master or 'other' the slave progresses from a subjective conceptualisation of 'self' toward an objective awareness of 'self'. Through synthesising a consciousness experienced subjectively in 'self', and a consciousness experienced objectively, in another, the slave is able to have an objective awareness of 'self' subjectivity. The positive aspect of enslavement relates to an understanding of the futility of ego, which clears the consciousness and identifies the importance of labour.

Reality for the master is defined by consumption whereas through work 'the slave … increases his awareness of himself and his relationship to an initially intractable Nature in the course of transforming it for his master' (Hampsher-Monk, 1992: 427). As noted above, this transition is not easy, as the individual primarily perceives others as a threat to 'self' (Hampsher-Monk, 1992: 427). However, Hegel continually indicated that humans are unable to organise a total concept of 'self' unless this is in relation to 'others'. Without recognition the Master is unsatisfied with his existence and only a satisfied consciousness is able to complete history and arrive at ultimate truth. 'If History must be completed if absolute knowledge must be possible' (Kojere, 1980: 47) through becoming satisfied only the slave can realise this. This is why Hegel considered that truth was revealed in the master/slave dichotomy; 'The human ideal, born in the Master can be realised and revealed, can become Wahrheit (truth) only in and by slavery' (Kojeve, 1980: 47). Self and other become intrinsically linked and work and study lead to emancipation and truth. True self and understanding of self is formed through critical thinking and making judgements about self, other and the world in which we exist. Self and other are defined and social science rendered explicit; we may only fully comprehend ourselves through analysis and critique in communities.

Critical Thinking and Judgements

Critical thinking is only possible when community and the judgements of others are brought into the equation with standpoints or opinions of each individual open to inspection. Consequently, although critical thinking is done alone the individual thinker is not isolated; as noted research and thought as well as knowledge development is undertaken through community. When people can form no idea of distant and unfamiliar things they judge them by what is present and familiar' (Vico, 1999: 76). Individuals use theoretical abstraction and generalisation to comprehend issues beyond experience. Things are assessed in terms of common sense or an 'unreflecting judgement shared by … human-kind' (Vico, 1999: 80). In his early writing, Husserl considered that day to day life encompassed 'bric-a-brac that has to be cleared away in order to reveal subjectivity' (Giddens, 1977: 25). However, Heidegger and Schultz considered that commonality or daily existence should not be cleared away and bracketed but embraced as the field which the student of social phenomena should never abandon. This is the lifeworld, which 'includes everything that is taken for granted and normally not reflected upon in the attitude of common sense' (Bauman, 1978: 175). Research is a generalisation of non-experiential thought though the comprehension of everyday thought; there exists a relationship between experienced practical existence and more abstract theoretical frameworks. For social sciences the relationship between theory and practice (praxis) provides the basis for knowledge generation and in-depth understanding.

Critical Thinking

Critical thinking does not indicate extensive empathy through which one understands what goes on in the minds of others. For Kant, Enlightenment meant to think for one's self. To liberate one's self from prejudice. This means abstracting from what is usually perceived as self-interest and moving to a more general standpoint. Not the generality of a concept but a general impartial view point. However viewing human affairs does not tell one how to act nor apply wisdom appropriated through occupying a general stand-point to the particulars of policy and politics.

Is the general standpoint simply the position of the observer?

One must have an untroubled mind to accomplish true cognition. Kant (1992) argued that the body interfered with the speed of thought which consequently limited the mind and that the philosopher remained a human being and existed in a social context not a lofty position from which to observe. He argued that every human can provide good sense following reflection. 'Do you really require that a kind of knowledge which concerns all men should transcend the common understanding and should only be revealed to you by philosophers?' (1992: 651–2). There should exist within the social sciences a relationship between philosophical/theoretical and empirical/practical positions; the rational and empirical co-exist in the formation and generation of knowledge.

Kant (1952) indicated that he had 'a consuming thirst for knowledge, the unrest which goes with desire to progress in it, and satisfaction in every advance in it … if I did not believe that (what I am doing) can give worth to all others in establish-ing the rights of mankind' (cited in Adredt, 1982: 27–8). For Kant, Enlightenment meant the liberation from prejudices and the authorities and incorporated a purify-ing event which was realised through critical thinking and critique; Enlightenment involved a new way of thinking. Enlightenment needed human beings to mature and have confidence in 'one's own understanding without the guidance of another' (Kant, 1995: 54). Humanity needed to have confidence in its own interpretations of events and a recognition that knowledge was not divine and or removed.

Pre-Enlightenment humanity lacked the courage of its convictions and even though some people had the courage to stand by their own understanding or interpretation others did not. People are lazy and even when freed from guidance remain 'immature for life' (Kant, 1995a). Revolution can change an autocratic regime into one that is democratic. However, a revolution is unable to bring about changes in the way people think as similar ideas to the previous regime will take the place of those that controlled the unthinking masses, such as happened in the English, French and Russian revolutions. True enlightenment of this kind requires freedom, the freedom to question and 'make public use of one's reason in all matters' (Kant, 1995a: 55). Truth is found through humanity learning to think for itself 'to look within oneself ... for the supreme touchstone of truth; and the maxim of thinking for oneself at all times is Enlightenment' (Kant, 1995a: 249). If people fail to do this they will not warrant such freedoms, they will be unworthy of liberty and will surely lose it. Indeed, those who do not use the freedom available will undermine those who attempted to use their freedom correctly; that is, those who did have the best interests of humanity at heart (Kant, 1995a).

According to Kant, philosophy became critical through Enlightenment and critique; through Enlightenment philosophy came of age. However, when Kant spoke of critical thinking he did not simply mean critique of books or systems but of the very faculty of human reason of thought itself. Hegel argued that by its nature philosophy needed to be prepared and made palatable for common people; it was the opposite of common sense 'by which we understand the local and temporary limitations of generations; in its relation to this common sense, the world of philosophy as such is a world turned upside down ... (because) the beginning of philosophy must be a lifting of oneself above the truth given by common consciousness, the premonition of a higher truth' (cited in Adredt, 1982: 35). For Marx, the link between theory and practice was critique. For Kant the interactive element between theory and practice was judgement. He was thinking of the doctor or lawyer who initially learns theory then practices medicine or law. Applying general rules to specific cases. Kant's moral teaching relies on the 'ethical', because ethics is based on a thought process; act so that the maxim of your action can be a general law, a law that you too would have to obey. It is, again, the same general rule; do not contradict yourself (your thinking ego) or the entity that determines both thinking and acting. 'Critical thinking according to Kant and ... Socrates exposes itself to the test of free and open examination' and this means that the more people who participate in it the better (Adredt, 1982: 39). Political freedom is required and this is clearly defined throughout Kant's works as 'to make public use of one's reason at every point' by which he meant the 'public use of one's reason . . . as a scholar before the reading public' (Adredt, 1982: 39). The scholar is not the same thing as citizen; the scholar is a member of the society of world citizens and in this context should lay difficulties and problems before the public and give them the opportunity to afford judgement. Fundamentally, freedom of thought and speech provide the right for an individual to indicate opinions and persuade others to think. The Kantian perspective opens the way toward social science and especially critical theory perspectives regarding individual and social existence. Through critical approaches to social existence the way we assess and analyse existence has become wider and with the application of methodologies beyond positivism, we have extended the means by which we are able to comprehend self and community.

Critique and understanding presupposes some rationality both in self and the community at large. Kant (1952) argued that critical thinking and even the act of thinking itself 'depended on its public use; without the the test of free and open examination' no thinking and no opinion formation are possible. Reason is not made 'to isolate itself but to get into community with others' (cited in Adredt,

1982: 40). It is agreed that thinking is a solitary business; dialogue between selves. However unless this thought can be communicated either in speech or writing anything discovered in solitude will wither on the vine. As noted, knowledge accumulation and transfer moves beyond self; knowledge, understanding and truth are determined and verified through discussion in communities where it involves both self and other recognition. Kant proposed that it was humanity's natural vocation 'to communicate and speak one's mind, especially in all matters concerning man' (Kant, 1995b: 85–6). Humans are social entities that need to interact through communication, without discussion and debate, critical thinking would be impossible and the realisation of freedom unassailable. Without others we would not be able to think nor test our thinking in a public realm. For antiquity there was little point in having great insights then remaining silent. In this context, individual philosophers were held responsible for what they thought and taught which allowed the transformation of philosophy into the means by which truth and knowledge may be pursued. Initially, this transformation was initiated by the sophists who have been considered the representatives of the Greek Enlightenment, it was then nurtured and sharpened by Socrates 'this is the origin of critical thought whose greatest representation in the modern age . . . was Kant who was entirely conscious of its implications' (Adredt, 1982: 42). Fundamentally, we witness the very foundation of thought within social science, one that involved critique from objective and subjective perspectives; knowledge does not reside in some higher echelon, it is a social and practical phenomenon. Knowledge is not simply bound up with common sense, but social grounding does provide a level of understanding and is consequently an element incorporated in knowledge accumulation.

Thinking critically does not simply apply to received doctrines and systems but to one's own thought and the prejudices and traditions one inherits. By taking a critical stance in relation to one's own thought one develops the art of critical thought. To obtain a non-bias position or objectivity one must take the thoughts of others into account. Kant (1952) argued that objectivity was not some higher standpoint but the very fact of understanding the social and subjective nature of others. Objects need to be viewed from different perspectives and so expand ones point of view 'from a microscopic to a general outlook that it adopts in turn to every conceivable standpoint, verifying the observations of each by means of the other' (cited in Adredt, 1982: 42). Research involves the relationship between the individual undertaking the investigation and the environment being researched as well as previous research and the thoughts and analysis of others.

Individual thought is enhanced by taking into account the thoughts of others. We compare and contrast the possible judgements of others by putting ourselves in their place through imagination and empathy (we analyse and critique). Critical thinking is only possible when the judgements of others are brought into the equation; when the standpoints of each and all are open to inspection. Consequently, although critical thinking is done alone it does not cut one off from all we are within the world and social entities and have knowledge of wider perspectives.

Through imagination others are brought into the equation and the space for analysis becomes totally public and the forum for Kant's world citizen or the investigator of issues and problems (the researcher). Through the research process in terms of critique and analysis the researcher learns to 'think with an enlarged mentality (and) train's one's imagination to go visiting' (Adredt, 1982: 43). That is to go beyond one's locality through generalisation and theoretical thinking.

Critical thinking does not allow one to understand what goes on in the minds of others, it means to think for oneself and through analysis achieve liberation from prejudice. This does not mean a completely objective stance but one that recognises attempts at non-bias but subjective analysis; what Kant labels 'enlarged thought'. By enlarged thought Kant meant abstraction from the limitations we attach to judgement, which can involve self-interests and our ability to think critically. The more adept the individual at moving from perspective to perspective the more generalised his/her thinking will be. Not in terms of the generality of concept, for example, dog but one that is closely connected with particulars 'with the particular conditions one has to go through in order to arrive at one's own general standpoint' (Adredt, 1982: 43–4). The general perspective has been considered objective or impartial as it is a point from which to watch and judge; to reflect on human affairs. One is not told how to act nor apply wisdom found through occupying the general perspective to the particulars of political life. Kant informs us about 'how to take others into account; he does not tell us how to combine with them in order to act' (Adredt, 1982: 44). So is the general perspective simply the perspective of the spectator? Obviously, a relationship exists between the spectator or the researcher and the entity or individual under investigation; objectivity is important but within the analysis a level of subjective assessment is required, Kant is unclear about the combinations between subjectivity and objectivity. That said, this issue is contestable today and points toward different ontological and epistemological positions.

Conclusion

This chapter outlined issues and difficulties for individual researchers, projects and programmes; regarding what is the relationship between the world, thought, the researcher, the researched and the issue under investigation? To what extent can an external reality exist and what are the implications for the researcher, truth and knowledge accumulation? Does common sense or practical world have any place in the development of knowledge? Schopenhaur (1966) perceived representation and the objective world as encompassing two extremes. 'The one extreme is the knowing subject without forms of knowing and the other crude form without quality. Both are absolutely unknowable; the subject because it is that which knows; matter, because without form and quality it cannot be perceived' (Schopenhaur, 1966: 15). Intellect and matter are different sides of the same coin and 'the one exists only for the other, both stand and fall together; the one is only the others reflex; They are in fact really one and the same thing, considered from two opposite points view' (Schopenhaur, 1966: 15–16). Concepts should relate to the empirical world it does not matter how abstract notions become 'the proper function of these is to make such concepts … suitable for use in the experiential world' (Kant, 1995a: 237). In any research project such a perspective requires some consideration; some reflection regarding the relationship between mind and the external world is necessary.

One may argue that for both Schopenhaur and Kant there exists two concepts of truth, reality, knowledge and theory developed to reflect and explain these phenomenon. The first involves an intense commitment to truthfulness, that is, a wish to see through the counterfeit to see reality and have (to an extent) a level of theoretical certainty and predictability; in this context, knowledge is attainable. The second perceives the difficulty of attaining such lofty outcomes and that a subjective or relativist position is the best we may accomplish. For example, Heidegger argued that truth was 'a word for what man wants and seeks in the ground of his essence, a word therefore for something ultimate and primary' (1962: 9). Truth is ground in human Desein or becoming and derived from 'a primordial experience of world and self' (Heidegger, 1962: 9). What is sought already exists in the very essence of being and understanding; every study is consequentially subjective in nature.

Heidegger indicates that the search for truth is embedded within us and the world and as Hamlet identified 'the truth will always out'. Consequently, we briefly outline four positions that relate to truth, reality, knowledge and theory: correspondence; coherence; pragmatism and consensus/constructivist positions. Each of these positions is underpinned by ontological and epistemological assumptions that are discussed in more detail in the following chapters but for now we will outline the basics before we go on to discuss the relationships between theories, paradigms of inquiry and methodology.

The first position considers that there exists a correspondence between truth and reality; notions of truth and knowledge correspond with something that actually exists and there is a relationship between statements thoughts and things. This is a traditional model of knowledge and truth which is gauged by how entities relate to an objective reality. Truth and knowledge are universal and absolute (absolute knowledge exists, which is true at all times). In the same way theory should accurately reflect objective reality through thoughts, words and symbols. There are difficulties with this in terms of apprehending objective reality and using language in a precise manner. For example, in many instances meaning is unclear and transient.

The second position requires that truth, knowledge and theory fit with a coherent system; that truth and knowledge through theory are the properties of a system of propositions and may be applied to specifics only in accordance with the general system. However, there is discussion regarding whether there is one absolute true knowledge system or many possible systems. For Hegel, truth and knowledge involved the whole or completeness, which must by its very nature, then be present in each of its moments. If a single material fact cannot be reconciled then the proposition or entity is not true knowledge and the theoretical framework regarding this notion is disproved. Both the correspondence and coherent positions link closely or are underpinned by aspects of positivism, the former incorporating a naïve realist position and the latter (especially the idea of multiple true systems) a more critical realist perspective. In a critical realist context, pragmatism considers that truth, knowledge and theory need to be verified through experience and practical application. For William Pierce, truth, knowledge and theory were fallible and always incomplete partial approximations. John Dewey argued that truth was incomplete and found through experience but always self-corrective through being tested by the community. Truth is confirmed through application to concepts and practice (as with Kant, theory and practice were necessary components). Indeed, such an approach moves toward a historical realism and the development of reality through historical and social formulations. However, each necessitates metaphysical objectivism where truth exists independently of beliefs.

In a similar vein, the consensus position argued that there are many ideas of truth, knowledge and reality because each is socially constructed in cultural and historical terms and shaped by power struggles in the community. In contrast with correspondence, coherence and to an extent pragmatist positions, constructivists considered that no external objective reality or system exists. Knowledge, truth, reality and theory are considered contingent and based on human perception and experience. *Verum ipso factum* (truth in itself is constructed) (Vico, 1999). Truth, theoretical reflection or the basis of reality and knowledge are agreed through democratic processes and discussion. The dilemma regarding the constitution of knowledge, truth, reality and theory relates to broad perspectives of ontology and epistemology outlined by positivism and phenomenology. The former considers that a truth is consistent; that it is observable, understandable and exists in an external context (of course the post-positivist would consider a truth as such until it was displaced and question whether humanity is able to fully understand truth). The latter, to varying degrees considers that because interpretations of reality, knowledge and truth are intrinsically tied to the subject externality is difficult to establish, consequently truth and knowledge and the theories that reflect these are transitory and flexible.

Rorty and Engel (2007) debated the concept of truth; Richard Rorty considered that truth involved limited explanatory use and that some sort of metaphysical entity or substance labelled truth did not exist. The idea of truth fails to correspond with some independent entity that existed within the world; that is a certain reality. No correspondence between statements, propositions or judgements and reality existed (attempts to engineer correspondence was meaningless). Statements should be justified and no differentiation between justification and truth existed. Indeed, justifications are agreed by groups, communities and societies so no final agreed truth is possible. Therefore the search for ultimate

Table 1.2 Truth and reality

Correspondence theory	Clear relationships exist between truth and reality. Reality is clearly and accurately reflected through words and numbers (positivism and post-positivism).
Coherence theory	Truth and knowledge should fit with coherent systems. Coherency exists between specifics and the general (positivism and post-positivism).
Pragmatism	Truth and knowledge are verified through experience and practice (critical theory).
Consensual/constructivist theory	Truth is developed through consensus within communities and between groups (constructivist and participatory).

truth cannot direct nor be the objective of science and philosophy. However, even though the idea of truth has been rendered mythical it does not follow that we can say nothing about the world and humanity. Values worth defending and championing remained, for example, liberty, democracy, tolerance and community. Rorty argued that truth involved no more than the endorsement of a statement; we can believe x is true but this does not mean such is the case. In other words, just because we assert that x is true this does not mean that it is so, we simply provide the assertion with the compliment of truth. No distinction exists between truth and justification; truth involves the justification held by a given community. Truth becomes a device that is used when human beings make statements and involves the objective of scientific inquiry. However, the validity of truth as such an objective loses credibility when we argue that truth is an impossible thing to realise; it is an unrealistic endeavour. Indeed, if truth is impossible to achieve then how can it incorporate an ultimate goal? Truth is unable to determine and regulate inquiry because it is impossible to know. In response to this perspective of truth, Pascal Engel argued that truth involved more than a simplistic mechanism for assertion or a means of affirmation through stating that x is true; truth incorporates more than an assertion regarding a statement and corresponding belief. Indeed, an assertion statement and belief may only be identified as correct if it is true. Basically a belief can only be correct if it is true. Consequently, belief is the aim and basis of truth. If an individual does not believe a proposition for any other reason than the fact that it is true, he/she would be acting irrationally or does not truly believe the proposition identified. There exists triangulation relating assertion, belief and truth which involves a normative element which identifies truth as a correct belief and ultimately what we conceive as knowledge. An individual may assert that they do not simply represent themselves in believing that x is true but that they represent themselves in terms of knowing x so that a wider audience may ask how x is known. Consequently the idea of knowledge as encompassing a correct belief becomes normative.

Through synthesising ontological positions, theoretical perspectives and methodological approaches, this text identifies interpretations of truth as theory and assesses the extent that this may be observable in relation to human action. Chapter 2 intends to develop these considerations with an emphasis of the role of theory in the research process and the relationships this may have with ontology, epistemology and methodology.

Further Reading

Arendt, H. (1982) *Lectures on Kant's Political Philosophy*. Chicago, IL: University of Chicago.

Critchley, S. and Schroeder, W.R. (1999) *A Companion to Continental Philosophy*. Oxford and Massachusetts: Blackwell Publishers.

Denzin, N.K. and Lincoln, Y. (1994) *Handbook of Qualitative Research*, 1st edn. Thousand Oaks, CA: SAGE Publications.

Denzin, N.K. and Lincoln, Y. (2000) *Handbook of Qualitative Research*, 2nd edn. Thousand Oaks, CA: SAGE Publications.

Denzin, N.K. and Lincoln, Y. (2005) *Handbook of Qualitative Research*, 3rd edn. Thousand Oaks, CA: SAGE Publications.

Gjertsen, D. (1992) *Science and Philosophy: Past and Present*. London: Penguin Books.

Honderich, T. (1995) *The Oxford Companion to Philosophy*. Oxford: University Press.

Kant, I. (1995) *Political Writings*, ed. H. Reiss, trans. H.B. Nisbet. Cambridge Texts in the History of Political Thought. Cambridge: Cambridge University Press.

Rorty, R. and Engel, P (2007) *What's the Use of Truth?* New York: Columbia University Press.

Williams, B. (2004) *Truth and Truthfulness*. Princeton, NJ: Princeton University Press.

TWO

Explaining and Understanding Theory

Introduction

Chapter 2 further examines the relationships between theory, truth, knowledge and reality. Indeed, it concentrates on the notion of theory and considers how this underpins and/or relates to research in social science. This chapter also considers the links between ontological and theoretical perspectives in relation to theory and paradigms of inquiry. The etymology of theory is found in antiquity and derives from the term *theoria*, which means to behold or view. Indeed theory has the same root as theatre, which provides reflections on society and the world. Consequently, one may argue that theory involves a way of viewing or reflecting on the world and in this way it is different from knowledge of how the world is (reality or truth). Conversely, one may also consider that theories do actually identify knowledge of how the world is through providing means of looking at it; that there is no difference between knowledge or truth and the theories that reflect these.

   The 20th century witnessed an exponential growth in the social sciences; they have overtaken the arts and depending on one's comprehension of what they should achieve they now confront or mimic natural sciences. Indeed, it is this distinction within the social sciences that underpin and facilitate how social sciences are perceived and applied. This distinction involves debate regarding the very nature of knowledge (ontology), the relationship between humanity and knowledge (epistemology) and issues regarding the rigour required when developing or testing knowledge (methodology). What social science entails and why it is important for humanity is intrinsically linked with philosophical debates regarding empiricism, rationalism and phenomenology in relation to emergent paradigms of inquiry that provide the basic beliefs of individuals when using methodological approaches in the development of distinct research programmes within the social sciences. Winch (1991) pointed out that a certain fallacy existed regarding social sciences and their slow development in relation to the natural sciences. Indeed, the social sciences had developed gradually because they were slow to fully mirror natural science procedures; they had failed to fully emancipate themselves from philosophy. Winch (1991) accepts the idea that social science may not have found a Newton but does not consider that if social science is to evolve it should adhere to natural science premises rather than philosophical perspectives. This text acknowledges this position and explains different perceptions of the social sciences and theoretical frameworks employed in relation to scientific or positivistic positions and the relationships with philosophical premises regarding phenomenology. Overall the distinctions provide backdrops for what different schools consider social science theory is capable of achieving.

Social science is by its nature theoretically informed. Consequently, theory discovery, development or meta-theorising should be encouraged as it is a necessary component for rigorous social science research. Theorising involves the systematic study of social activity through explicating, interpreting, understanding and predicting small- or large-scale human action. Social science research incorporates a search for reliable theoretical frameworks. Theory generates pluralism, produces choice, creates alternative scenarios, formulates debate and communication, increases awareness and develops understanding.

Definition Box

Reasons for Theory

Theory is usually seen as being pointless; people usually considering it to be all well in theory but that it will not work in practice. Theory is seen as something beyond everyday existence and unimportant for people's daily lives. However, theory provides a means by which individuals may consider the difficulties they face on a day to day basis or may understand other individual, social or political problems. Theory allows generalisation and through synthesising the theoretical and the practical, understanding is enhanced. Fundamentally everyone thinks in a theoretical manner, the problem is we do not realise we are doing so and undertake this thinking in an unsystematic way. When effected by situations or policies they cannot control individuals theorise; I am unemployed because of EU membership and incomers from other Member States or I am unemployed because of austerity cuts and recession. Each is an example of theorising about one's specific situation in relation to a general rationale. Overall, theory can explain our everyday close experiences by relating these to something more distant and abstract. Indeed, theory can inform us about that which we have no experience; theory can inform an individual about the world. This is closely related to the Kantian idea of going visiting.

Rather than pursue proof, social science theory can be defined by its ability to provide understanding of situations at precise moments in time. Take positivism and post positivism, the former theory involves the pursuit of laws and the latter approximations derived from experimentation in idealised situations, which allows explanation of phenomenon through what has been labelled thin-data. For critical theory, constructivism and participatory paradigms of inquiry theory is about providing frameworks for understanding situations and phenomenon through thick-data (for further on paradigms of inquiry see below). Theory and practice are two sides of the same coin; good practice is informed by accurate theoretical frameworks and accurate theory through sound understanding of practical situations. The relationship between theory and practice has been discussed for centuries with some incisive considerations being determined during Enlightenment. Indeed, as noted in Chapter 1 we discussed how Immanuel Kant undertook a consideration of the relationship between theory and practice during the late 18th century and argued that theory and practice were inseparable and should be assessed together in all analyses and studies.

Theories entail different understandings or explanations of truth, reality, knowledge development as well as acquisition, application evaluation and critique. The paradigms of inquiry discussed in this chapter render explicit the linkages between theory ontology and methodology. Furthermore, different types of theory in terms of theory development, ideational formulation, normativism and levels of theory in terms of grand, meso and substantive theory are explored. This chapter also draws on the abstract philosophy discussed in Chapter 1 and assesses how this underpins theoretical perspectives and ultimately identifies a means of theoretical synthesis in relation to paradigms of inquiry and methodological approaches. Theory incorporates a 'set of well-developed concepts related through statements of relationship, which together constitute an integrated framework that can be used to explain or predict phenomena' (Strauss and Corbin, 1998: 15). Social science is theoretically informed and that ontological perspectives determine one's interpretation of truth, reality and/or theory. Consequently, theorising, theory discovery, theory building or development should be encouraged. Theorising involves the systematic study of social activity through explicating, interpreting, understanding and if possible predicting small- or large-scale action. Furthermore, this chapter discusses what theory is and its role in relation to practice and contends that theories enable pluralism and choice; provide communication and open debate, encourage sensitivity toward data and open deliberation as well as enhances awareness of dogmatism and greater understanding of alternative perspectives.

What Is Theory?

Do theories reflect reality, knowledge or truth? Or are they an aspect of the knowledge, truth and overall reality that is being expressed? In examining these questions or different perspectives of theory it may be worth assessing how theories have been used in the past. Take the theories of the heavens: antiquity considered that celestial bodies were different from earthly counterparts and this differentiation is what made things with earthly elements fall and entities such as the stars and comets to remain in the heavens. With Newton's theory of gravity the lenses for observing the world (theory) changed so knowledge transformed in relation to this. The distinction between earthly and heavenly matter dissipated and gravity in relation to planet orbits and the speed matter fell to earth became the means of explaining why some things fall and others do not. The universal theory of gravity sufficed for many centuries but was surpassed during the early 20th century when challenged by relativity and quantum theories. Consequently, if Newton's theory of gravity was seen to fully correspond with reality it encompassed truth and knowledge of reality until around 1900 when it was, in post-positivist terms, falsified. Or based on Kuhnian (see below for further) paradigm shifts in a critical theory, constructivist or participatory context the theory continued to infinitely develop as a form of insight into reality; that is, there is no end-game where an absolute truth exists in relation to a theoretical perspective. There exists a continual dialectical process involving parts of the older theory in relation to the present theory out of which a future theory will emerge. Knowledge is shaped by our theoretical lenses; knowledge of planetary movement shifted from Ptolemaic epicycles to gravitational forces, then relativity and quantum theory. In a similar fashion the idea of fixed species in biology gave way to the theory of evolution. Fundamentally, theory provides the means by which we are able to organise factual evidence that determines knowledge. The way we think provides the means by which we organise or categorise data; our conceptualisations of space, time, causality, relativity, universality, and so on, provide general forms of categories that inform or constitute the basis of theoretical insight.

Clear perception requires a general awareness of how experience is shaped by theories that implicitly or explicitly inform the way we think. In this way, experience and knowledge incorporate the same space and involve the same process, they are not separate but synthesised entities; knowledge and experience are located in the same space. Theories are ever changing and continually shaping and forming our experience and knowledge. Indeed, theorising in relation to nature is similar to theorising in relation to humanity. If one approaches a person as an enemy then the reaction of the individual concerned will confirm this apparition; the theoretical position will be self-fulfilling. If one approaches nature from a specific theoretical perspective then it is likely that this position will be self-fulfilling. If we believe in a positivistic sense that that theory gives immutable laws relating to truth or knowledge then it verifies what already exists and underlines the fact that such will always exist. This leads toward a blinkered comprehension of society, nature and the individual; can we ever have ultimate knowledge or know reality as it really is? Can a reality totally independent of our thought and theoretical perspectives exist? If so then we may approach the object with fixed concepts and theories and continue to confirm the limitations of these theories and thoughts in relation to experience. Every theoretical perspective involves a distinct mode of thinking, for example, antiquity heavenly and earthly matter or Newtonian centrifugal forces. These differences can be seen as separate ways of observing rather than denoting what really exists; in this way, they do not imply the separate existence of matter from thought. Conversely, theories may be considered as precise descriptions of reality. However, when historical changes to theory are considered this seems unrealistic. We should be aware of how we think through theoretical frameworks and see these as modes of observing rather than providing a true likeness of reality as it actually exists. In this context, theory may be seen as a particular way of viewing an object that provides an appearance of the said entity. Fundamentally the observer and observed become the same through the theoretical perspective used by the observer specifically determining the outcome or interpretation of the observed. Reality is indivisible and involves a close if not symbiotic relationship between theory and practice. In this context, there is wholeness to the world and the way it is analysed and researched. Theory provides a kind of adhesive that brings together the subject and the object which allows the observer to look closely and learn from the whole process of thought and discover activity relevant to understanding the world in a holistic context.

In contrast with practice or action, theory incorporates contemplation about what is viewed. In the natural sciences and positivistic studies, theory involves the relationship between cause and effect through the study of observable phenomenon whereas the social sciences and humanities deal with ideas and activity which are not so easy to observe or interpret. Theory is closely related to the idea of truth and consists of a set of statements that give a true understanding (knowledge) regarding certain phenomenon. That said, truth is always relative to a given theory and may be true in one context but not in another; consequently, interpretation becomes a central element regarding relationships between truth, knowledge and theory. In sum, through truthful statements theory reflects and explains reality and provides knowledge of phenomenon under analysis. The authority of theory and the academics that expound them 'must be rooted in their truthfulness'; through accuracy and sincerity true beliefs and knowledge are formulated (Williams, 2004: 11). Theoretical frameworks rely on metaphysical subjectivism in that truth depends on beliefs and is relativist to situations and across cultures.

Kantian Ideas on Theory and Practice

Kant (1995b) argued that a collection of rules even when they are practical are identified as a *theory* when the rules are general and abstractions from the practical. In constrast, all practical activities are labelled practice. Rules with a particular purpose incorporating 'conceived principles of procedure' are considered *practical* (Kant, 1995b: 61). From such a position Kant deduced that no matter how complete a theory (to provide a link with practice) the middle ground between theory and practical application must be realised. A theory contains a general rule that needs to be judged when the practitioner determines the extent the theory fits with it in practice and when it does not (see Toumlin below for a similar explanation). However, rules that direct judgement cannot be provided on every occasion with judgements 'subsuming each instance under the previous rule (for this would involve an infinite regress' (Kant, 1995b: 61). Indeed, because of such many theoreticians can be found that lack judgement so may never be practical; Kant considered that a number of lawyers or doctors who even though well educated were unable to provide practical advice. Conversely, even though someone may have good judgement, theory will be always be incomplete and may only be continually improved (or for Kant perfected) through further and future experimentation and experience from which the theoretician draws new rules that informed and finally completed the theory. Consequently, it is not surprising that in numerous contexts the theory may be wanting but this is not necessarily the fault of the theory. The problem is that not enough theory exists; we need to learn from experience and develop further theories. Kant argued that 'no one can pretend to be practically versed in a branch of knowledge and yet treat theory with scorn, without exposing the fact the he is an ignoramus in his subject' (1995b: 62). That said the ignoramus that ignores theory in practice is easier to excuse than the theoretician who denies the use of theory in the practical world.

The individual that is immersed in theory then denies the relevance for practice may be seen as to create 'philosopher's dreams' or 'empty ideals' with no 'practical validity' (Kant, 1995b: 62). This would mean that mechanics or electrics would have no relevance for engineers and medical theory no relevance to general practitioners (GPs) or medical consultants. However, a theory which deals with more abstract phenomenon in terms of perception or philosophy may consist of reason and have limited practical application. In this context the distinction between theory and practice may be more explicit. Overall, for the social sciences there is a relationship between theory and practice because theory explains and assesses knowledge or truth which is derived from reality or practical, empirical situations and contexts.

Paradigms of Inquiry and the Impact on Theory

Theory is concerned with building substantive understanding, normativism and ideational simplification. Substantive theories are built on the basis of the data collected and normativism determines theoretical frameworks that have an ethical or moral dimension (there is an 'ought' aspect to the theory). Ideational theory involves simplification of confounding variables and is closely linked to the positivist and post-positivist paradigms of inquiry. Theories entail different understandings of knowledge and truth, knowledge development as well as acquisition, application evaluation and critique.

There are a number of understandings of theory that clearly relate to distinct paradigms of inquiry (further discussions regarding philosophical positions and paradigms of inquiry are undertaken below). In general, theory can be positivistic or law orientated, in the natural sciences universal laws are pursued whereas in the social sciences law-like regularities are developed (the distinction between positivism and post-positivism is discussed in more detail in Chapter 3). Both natural and social scientific laws should enable prediction. Overall, this theoretical perspective is a universal law-oriented understanding of theory relating to a positivist paradigm of inquiry and methodology in the pursuit of regularities and prediction. Theory in this context is concerned with immutable laws and prediction.

A positivistic perspective of theory involves an idealised or simplified understanding of reality or truth. It is impossible to understand all variables and those that confound should be removed with focus on conditions that provide ideal situations. Perfect knowledge cannot be wholly realised but it is assumed in the shape of a model; prediction is sought in an ideal situation. Theory in this context incorporates falsification and prediction in an idealised or model world. Consequently, perfect knowledge at a given moment in time is assumed to hold; but for post-positivism only until such is challenged and usurped.

Both positivism and post-positivism perceive theory as an indication or statement of relationships between abstracted ideas covering a number of empirical observations. This is an empiricist view of theory development, which through observation identifies hypotheses or nulls hypotheses that are tested through reliable (replicable) scientific methods. The goal for positivist theory is parsimonious explanation and prediction; generalisation and deterministic relationships between cause and effect are imperative.

Critical theory, constructivist and participatory paradigms involve interpretive perspectives of theory which emphasise understanding and the relationship between interpretation and the phenomenon under investigation. Emphasis is placed on the interconnection between patterns rather than the identification of cause and effect. Theory involves interpretation through wide-ranging imaginative analysis and allows for multiple meanings, realities and uncertainty. Values and facts are intrinsically linked and knowledge or truth is dialectical or changeable and provisional. As social life evolves into different things/epochs so too does the theory that reflects or provides an understanding of this transformation. As the phenomenological approach has challenged positivism, interpretive theory has continued to become more prevalent in social science research. Theory and practice are closely related and praxis is developed. Aristotle considered that free human beings were engaged in three fundamental activities: *Theoria* for which the objective was truth; *Poeisis* where the objective is production; *Praxis* where the end goal or telos was action. Praxis eventually comes to mean the process by which the relationship between reflection and practice or theory and practice can transform society and individuals within it. Fundamentally, theories are situated in specific contexts and the experiences and perspectives of people and institutions within these locations. Interpretive theories deal with the abstraction of phenomenon and clearly illustrate the depth and relevance of the theories to the phenomenon under investigation. Subjectivity involves a central position because it is not possible to remove the researcher and the bias involved from the investigation. Theories allow sense-making and are the means for making ideas fit with phenomenon; relationships between phenomena are made explicit. This process involves theorising that incorporates engagement with those being researched while at the same time bringing abstract conceptualisations to bear upon the investigation. It also stimulates imagination and provides further lenses and perspectives for comprehending the empirical data. Indeed, there are numerous methodologies that provide the means for interpretive theory construction including, grounded theory, ethnography, hermeneutical and action research (each of these will be discussed in greater detail below). Furthermore, interpretive theories are based on ontological and epistemological positions that are relativist and subjective.

A critical theory perspective asserts that influential groups define what theories entail; they are developed in relation to historical change and incorporate ethical challenges to the existing state of affairs. There are close linkages between theoretical development and ethical reflection. Habermas (1971) related social science to human interaction based on ethical considerations. Changes in society have brought about human emancipation and social science should not be defined in terms of its accumulated stock of knowledge but its commitment to ethical principles. Society is in a state of flux so theories cannot be determined through correspondence to a present state of affairs because social mobilisation may prove the existing state of affairs unjust. Furthermore, because social scientists participate in the research process their judgements are part of interpretations underpinning knowledge and/or theoretical frameworks. Indeed, Habermas edges toward a constructivist perspective where theory is no different from everyday life and ground in communities. In this context, theory takes the form of axiomatic models and ongoing theory development. Social science theory is defined in terms of its ability to provide validity and understanding rather than its ability to enable measurement, proof or prediction. Constructivism can mean that individuals actively engage with and create their worlds; that is people perceive reality differently and create their own understanding of phenomenon. Or that phenomenon exists in its own right and involves a fundamental meaning that enables a predictable and true interpretation of reality. The latter perspective involves some form of externality that impacts on the individual in a uniform context and leans toward critical theory and positivist ontologies and the former a 'radical constructivism' that considers reality is different for each individual and adheres to a participatory ontology. These distinctions can also be explained in terms of the distinctions between constructivism and constructionism; that is, the extent to which the individual has control of constructions and how far these constructions are socially determined through institutions and/or interaction between agents and society. However, there is core agreement between constructivism and constructionism and certain authors have attempted a synthesis of these approaches (these are discussed in more detail in Chapter 6).

The participatory inquiry paradigm advocates a philosophy in which the researcher and those being researched are treated interdependently and responsive to one another in the research process. Torbert argued that 'a participatory ontology treats the role of subjective experience in research as essential, and looks to the research process as a means of healing the split that so often exists among knowledge, experience, and action' (2001: 3). Furthermore, 'a true social science will integrate subjective (first-person), intersubjective (second-person), and objective (third-person) inquiry in ongoing real-time, for the sake of developing all humans' capacities for inquiring more and more of our time how to act in a timely fashion' (Torbert, 2001: 3).

Positivism is extreme in its interpretation of ontology and epistemology and is difficult to deal with in the social sciences, which causes a number of problems when attempting to synthesise positivist interpretations of theory with other paradigms. For instance if there is one totally understandable reality that may be discovered through immutable laws this contradicts the ontological positions of each of the other paradigms. With the change in ontology and epistemology between positivism and post-positivism we observe the recognition of human fallibility and theory replacement through critical analysis. This accepts that theory changes through falsification, which in itself is part of a historical process; critical theory through challenging the status quo, renders this same point explicit. Consequently, although ontologies, epistemologies and methodological approaches initially seem exclusive, when we examine them in more detail they may be considered inclusive and provide the opportunity for mixing theoretical perspectives to attain explanation and understanding of phenomenon. Furthermore, these gradients of theory identify levels of normativism; for instance positivism would try and deny normative perspectives whereas constructivism and participatory paradigms would embrace them.

In the following discussions, for the sake of clarity the above paradigms will be labelled in a general sense, as positivist and phenomenology, the former includes and primarily incorporates the above definition of post-positivism, the latter includes critical theory, constructivism and participatory paradigms (discussed in more detail in the following chapters). This text understands the former as leaning toward modernism and the latter postmodernism. In the former, theory has to be objective, identify cause and effect, provide generalisation or prediction and ensure reliability. The latter however, is more concerned with frameworks for providing insight, understanding and validity in historical and specific circumstances.

Table 2.1 Types of theory

Personal theorising	Reflection regarding individual experience in relation to wider notions or rationales.
Substantive theory	Derived from data analysis, rich conceptualisations of specific situations.
Models	Simplified perspectives of phenomenon.
Meso theory	Middle-range theories that draw on substantiated substantive theories and models.
Grand theory and philosophical positions	Sweeping abstract explanations of phenomenon and existence.

Definition Box

Theory Typology

- Philosophy
- Grand theory

(Continued)

- Meso or middle-range theory
- Substantive theory or models
- Individual.

Individuals theorise in relation to experience through considering empirical phenomenon in relation to non-empirical phenomenon. Substantive theory is more systematic than this but draws on experience either through a combination of selves or the individual researcher interpretation collation and synthesis between theory and practice occurs. Grand theory involves combinations of meso theory and meso theory combinations of substantive theories. Philosophy involves total abstraction and limited relationships with practice. Grand theory and meso theory can collectively be known as formal theory.

To enable a more detailed comprehension of theory in relation to the distinct philosophical positions, this chapter now concentrates on positivism from a social science perspective so mainly consists of post-positivist perspectives and phenomenology (which included the idea of a general critical theory, constructivism and participatory paradigms). Given these philosophical positions the text arrived at distinctions in theoretical perspectives, and differences in the way theory can be used in explaining and/or understanding phenomenon. The work provides different levels of theory, on the one hand, and different intensities of normative expectation, on the other hand. As noted above, for positivism, theory is the pursuit of laws and for post-positivism approximations in idealised situations and explanations of phenomenon through thin data. For phenomenology theory is about providing frameworks for understanding situations and phenomenon through thick data.

This text constructs a typology in relation to levels of theory. Broad philosophical perspectives and grand theory are not able to fit well with the positivist interpretation of theory even though grand theory would correspond more easily with post-positivism. On the other hand, although meso theory could also correspond with elements of phenomenology it does provide a means by which post-positivist stipulations regarding theory could be realised. Substantive theory is derived from one specific area or part of the research and can be identified by breaking down theory into constituent parts. Philosophical frameworks, grand and meso theories are incrementally more abstract and consequently conceptually advanced.

The more simplified the theory, the easier it is to identify cause and effect or dependent and independent variables. However, the greater this simplification the more difficult it is to provide a full understanding and explanation. Consequently there exists a distinction between simplified models and more in-depth substantive theories. Substantive theory is developed through inductive more constructivist procedures whereas models are normally positivistic simplifications. Synthesis of substantive, meso and grand theories provides insight and understanding with some identification of cause and effect. However, grand theory and philosophical

Table 2.2 Paradigms of inquiry

Item	Positivism	Post-positivism	Critical theory	Constructivist and participatory
Ontology The form of reality. What can be known about reality?	Reality can be totally understood. Reality exists and it can be discovered.	Reality may only be understood imperfectly and probabilistically. Reality exists but humanity unable to totally understand it.	Reality shaped by history. Formed by values that are crystallised over time.	Reality is locally constructed. Based on experience although shared by many. Dependent on person/group changeable.
	(Naïve Realism)	(Critical Realism)	(Historical Realism) Breakdown of a clear distinction between ontology and epistemology.	Participatory: co-created through mind and world. (Relative Realism) Breakdown of a clear distinction between ontology and epistemology.
Epistemology The relationship between the investigator and what can be discovered.	The investigator and the investigation are totally separate. Values are overcome through scientific procedure. Truth is a possibility.	Abandonment of total separation of investigator and investigation. Objectivity still pursued.	The investigator and the investigated linked. Accepted that historical values influence the inquiry. Results subjective.	As critical theory. However, the findings are created as the investigation proceeds. Participatory: paradigm findings are developed between the researcher and cosmos.
Methodology How does the investigator go about finding out what he/she believes can be discovered.	Scientific experiments based on hypothesis, these are usually quantitative. Conditions that confound are manipulated.	Multiple modified scientific experiment. Pursues falsification of hypotheses; may include qualitative methods.	Needs dialogue between investigator and the subject of investigation. Structures may be changeable. Actions effect change.	Create a consensus through individual constructions including the construction of the investigator. Participatory: similar methodologies can be employed (primarily action research).

Source: Adapted from Lincoln and Guba (2000) and Heron and Reason (1997).

frameworks allow understanding in a generic context but is unable to produce prediction or historical determinism (even though it may seek to accomplish these objectives). Because of this deficiency and the fact that they were difficult to verify in a positivist context in the 1960s and 1970 grand theory came under an onslaught of criticism. This led to a re-assessment of what social science theory could actually achieve. Positivist notions of prediction were challenged and through a synthesis of post-positivist and phenomenology meso and substantive theory emerged and gave more incisive theoretical explanations for social science.

Philosophy, grand, meso and substantive theory are closely interrelated because (as noted by Kant above) reality, truth/knowledge and theory develop through interactions between historical environments, institutions and individuals (practical situations). Consequently, we may argue that social actors in a changing historical and social context construct reality truth/knowledge and theory. Researchers are not objective impassive analysts; they themselves are part of the construction process and as social values change theory is re-assessed in relation to these changes (George, 1976). Prediction in the social sciences is difficult if not impossible to formulate, consequently grand theory should be seen as a means of 'organising concepts', 'selecting relevant facts' and determining how the 'narrative should be constructed' (George, 1976). That said, social research is about a mix of ontological and epistemological positions through a synthesis of methodological approaches and methods of data collection.

Conclusion

Overall, these deliberations have continued to have resonance for philosophers during the 20th century and researchers today identify these distinctions in terms of paradigms of inquiry in relation to different methodological approaches used in diverse research programmes. To comprehend the relationship between subjective and objective stances in research programmes in terms of specific paradigms of inquiry and methodological approaches, this chapter has assessed the differentiations between positivism, post-positivism and three distinct phenomenological positions. Positivism and post-positivism are linked with the modernist tradition and phenomenological positions can be seen to incorporate differentiated levels of postmodern approaches. However, these distinctions vary and can become opaque when closer inspection is undertaken. For instance, 'falsification' and the distaste for grand theory apparent in post-positivism in certain contexts render it postmodernist. Furthermore, distinctions between epistemological and ontological positions are identified when one assesses differences between the philosophical positions of the main phenomenological thinkers. Differences are apparent between Husserl's 'transcendental phenomenology', Heidegger's 'hermeneutical phenomenology' and Merleau-Ponty's world of 'inalienable presence'. Phenomenology is not a single unified body of ideas and the tradition encompasses diverse interpretations and philosophical positions (Giddens, 1977). In this text, the distinctions between these philosophical positions are explored in an attempt to clarify some of the issues relating to ontology, epistemology and methodology for distinct paradigms of inquiry.

In general, the critical theory paradigm included theoretical perspectives that challenged the status quo, for example, neo-Marxism, feminism, determinism, and provided a specific understanding of reality in that it is shaped by 'social, political, cultural, economic and gender values crystalised over time' (Denzin and Lincoln, 1994: 105) (critical theory is outlined further in chapter 5).

Overall, this chapter outlines the relationship between a number of different paradigms of inquiry identified by Denzin and Lincoln (1994, 2000, 2005). These involve: positivism, post-positivism, critical theory, constructivism and participatory. In general terms the former two can come under the heading of positivism whereas the latter three may be perceived as displaying elements of phenomenology. Each paradigm of inquiry identifies specific methodological approaches and theoretical perspectives and indicates how these fit together when underpinning research projects and programmes.

Further Reading

Denzin, N. and Lincoln, Y. (1994) *The Handbook of Qualitative Research,* 1st edn. Thousand Oaks, CA: SAGE Publications.

Denzin, N. and Lincoln, Y. (2000) *The Handbook of Qualitative Research,* 2nd edn. Thousand Oaks, CA: SAGE Publications.

Denzin, N. and Lincoln, Y. (2005) *The Handbook of Qualitative Research,* 3rd edn. Thousand Oaks, CA: SAGE Publications.

Honderich, T. (1995) *The Oxford Companion to Philosophy*. Oxford: Oxford University Press.

Howell, K.E. (2004) *Europeanization, European Integration and Financial Services: Developing Theoretical Frameworks and Synthesising Methodological Approaches*. Basingstoke: Palgrave MacMillan.

Kant, I (1995) 'On the common saying: this may be true in theory but it does not apply in practice', in H. Reiss (ed.), *Political Writings*. Cambridge: Cambridge University Press.

Kuhn, T.S. (1970) *The Structure of Scientific Revolution*. Chicago, IL: University of Chicago Press.

Winch, P. (1991) *The Idea of a Social Science and its Relation to Philosophy*. London: Routledge.

THREE

Empiricism, Positivism and Post-positivism

Introduction

Research involves understanding the relationship between theory, philosophy (ontology and epistemology), methodology and methods. Any research project whether this be a dissertation, thesis or research paper requires some understanding and explanation of the relationships between these areas. This text explains these relationships through a discussion of rationalist arguments in Chapter 1, theory in Chapter 2 and empiricist, positivist and phenomenological positions in this and the following chapter. It is useful to have some knowledge of these positions when undertaking research projects because the paradigms of inquiry and subsequent methodological approaches and methods of data collection extend what may be considered valid knowledge generation or accumulation actually entails. Based in empiricism, positivism provided an important and relevant addition to our conceptualisation of how knowledge may be measured, defined and accumulated.

In a bid to fully explain the relationship between methodology and the philosophical and scientific underpinnings of specific paradigms of inquiry, this chapter analyses the differentiations between empiricism, positivism and post-positivism each of which, it may be argued, exemplifies a certain modernist approach to knowledge generation. However, this demarcation can become problematic when a close analysis is undertaken. For instance, as noted above, the falsification process and the distaste for grand theory apparent in post-positivism in some contexts render it postmodernist.

The modernist/postmodernist debate picks up on a number of issues identified in Chapters 1 and 2 in terms of ongoing debates regarding the nature of reality, truth, knowledge and theory. That is, whether or not the world has a real existence beyond human thought? Positivists consider an external reality exists that can be understood completely whereas post-positivists argue that even though such a reality can be discerned it may only be understood probabilistically. Empiricists consider that scientific truth and reality are based on experience and observation and that 'human consciousness which is subjective is not accessible to science, and thus not truly knowable' (Polkinghorne, 1989: 23).

This chapter considers that positivism is based on aspects of empiricism and identifies how this involves an adherence to natural science perspectives of reality and methodology. In addition, the chapter goes on to identify how this adherence to empiricism provided a number of problems for positivism when it attempted to understand social existence. Indeed, initially through the work of Popper (1969, 1994, 2002, 2002a) positivism was challenged by post-positivism and a more amenable and less entrenched methodological approach developed. However, post-positivism still adhered to the idea of an external reality and dualist objectivity, which was questioned by phenomenologist philosophers in terms of the level of interaction between self and the world and solipsistic positions.

Chapter 3 deals with these issues in more detail and covers an assessment of empiricism and a short discussion of thinkers in the empiricist tradition. Positivism is analysed in relation to how it uses ideas initially devised for empiricism and how these were challenged through post-positivism. Overall, this chapter identifies the distinction between positivism and post-positivism and considers the implications this has for knowledge generation and research in general.

Reflection Box

Solipsism

Solipsism comes from the Latin for *solus* (alone) and *ipse* (self) and involves the idea that only the individual mind certainly exists; all else could be a figment of one's imagination. The world beyond the individual mind cannot be known and there is a chance that it as well as other people may not exist. Furthermore, even if an independent reality does exist how may an individual know this reality in an objective fashion? Knowledge is the content of the individual mind and no necessary link exists between experience and thought. Methodological solipsism argues that mind and thought is independent of environment or facts regarding this environment; mind content is determined by facts about the thinking object.

Consider the following statements in relation to the requirements for your research project and the notion that objective knowledge can be attained and accumulated.

- Nothing can exist.
- If something does exist nothing can be known about it.
- Even if something does exist and we are able to know something of it communication of this knowledge is impossible.

Empiricism: Bacon, Hobbes, Locke and Hume

Empiricism considers that knowledge is dependent on the five senses and that through experience knowledge can be derived and accumulated. Empiricism is based on the belief that we can only know what the world tells us; through objective or neutral observation true knowledge may be realised and understood. The human mind is a blank sheet on which sense-based information is transmitted. Sense data is provided or 'given' pre-interpretation, then the mind becomes active and manipulates sense data in numerous ways; that is, through abstraction and synthesised interpretations of sense-data which give understanding and knowledge as well as building relationships between ideas and providing the basis for further observation. The search for immutable laws since has been accepted as the norm for scientific inquiry from the 17th to the 21st centuries. Science carries out controlled experiments and makes measured observations at a designated point between the known and the unknown. Findings are recorded and published then further reliable data accumulated. Eventually general elements emerge and hypotheses are formulated (law-like statements which fit with the accumulated reliable data and portray causality). Hypotheses are then tested with the intention of proving these correct. Verification or proof formulates a scientific law and is used to excavate new information and enhance the stock of human knowledge. Through procedures labelled induction (data accumulation) and deduction (hypothesis testing), human ignorance is gradually eliminated. Knowledge accumulation is progressive and benefits humanity. Natural science justified its view of knowledge on the basis of observation and experiment, that is, an empiricist view of knowledge. Empiricist philosophers return the compliment and considered that natural science embodied the highest form of genuine knowledge. For example Ayer (1946) was keen to draw a distinction between genuine knowledge (science) and belief systems like religion, metaphysics and Marxism. In fact, he labelled these belief systems pseudo-sciences that had little if any claim to knowledge embodiment. However, the difficulty here was that the reasons for excluding Marxism or psychoanalysis in many instances ruled out a great deal of established natural science. Overall, the empiricist view of science can be characterised on the basis of the following doctrine (see Definition Box).

| Definition Box |

Empiricism

Empiricism incorporates the idea that genuine knowledge can be tested by experience and that claims of knowledge must be observable. Scientific laws involve statements of recurring patterns of experience and a scientific explanation is an instance of a scientific law. Prediction is achievable and science is objective as it separates testable factual statements from value judgements (Benton and Craib, 2001).

This doctrine incorporated the underpinnings of positivism and is based on the assertion that human science should be treated as natural science and anything that failed to adhere to such a presupposition and process was not knowledge.

Francis Bacon

In *Novum Organum* (1620), Francis Bacon (1561–1626) outlined his belief in the accumulative creation of knowledge, which could be derived through divine revelation or sensory experience. Bacon said little about divine revelation and most knowledge, it would seem, is formulated through the senses. Sensory interaction with the world allows the development of knowledge, which Bacon divided into three types: knowledge of humanity; God; and nature. However, Bacon was unhappy with the state of knowledge and considered that most treatises and texts were repetitions and entailed the same arguments, they may vary in method, which provides a mirage of plenty, but on closer examination proves to be illusory.

Francis Bacon may be considered as outlining an embryonic interpretation of inductive scientific method because he argued that inductive procedure rather than deductive reasoning should incorporate the basis of knowledge generation. He argued that on the basis of observation and experience, logical statements could be uttered and scientific generalisations made based on the logical ordering of empirical observations and experiences. However, nowhere does Bacon use the term scientific method but his ideas may be considered as the basis or starting point for such a perspective of scientific procedure.

Bacon argued that the human mind was prone to weaknesses (idols of the mind) and these required attention before inductive reasoning could proceed. Indeed, these idols of the mind distorted the truth, so needed to be eradicated. Idols of the mind included; those of the tribe, mental weaknesses held by humanity in general and idols of the den or cave that involved a preponderance to assess everything from a subjective standpoint or through the prioritisation of one's own interest or perspective. The idols of the market incorporate the misuse and meaninglessness of language and idols of the theatre the misuse of power. The idols formed a falsity and impinged human capability for seeing things as they truly are; humanity is capable of perceiving truth but only once these vagaries (idols) were negated. Human potential for knowledge generation and understanding was beyond question, however, through laziness, avarice or over-confidence in our abilities, our capabilities and capacities have largely been misused. Through the scientific method humanity may be liberated from its erroneous ways and mistake free truth or an approximation of true knowledge realised. In his utopian state called New Atlantis, knowledge is uncovered and nature interpreted in the House of Solomon. Humanity benefits from the continued development and practical application of science and knowledge; through inductive reasoning knowledge is developed and the human condition improved. Bacon identified objectivity and the non-biased accumulation of knowledge; the very basis of all rigorous research.

Thomas Hobbes

In *Objections* (1641), Thomas Hobbes (1588–1679) reiterated that philosophy and knowledge accumulation had remained stunted and advocated that people should ignore pointless attempts at philosophy and concentrate on daily experience and common sense. For Hobbes, philosophy was more than the knowledge of cause and effect and sensory experience and was rather the product of rationalisation. Philosophy is different from knowledge by sense because sensory knowledge is formed through 'motions' or events that are associated and ordered in the mind. Experience and history provide foresight and prudence; they lead to the formation of expected outcomes. However, this does not incorporate philosophical knowledge or true science; sense and memory are common to all living creatures and are a form of knowledge but because they are simply given and not formed through rationalisation they are not philosophy. For Hobbes knowledge began with sense-perception, consequently the initial step for developing understanding was to comprehend what sense-perception actually entailed. Sense-perception involved motions in matter;

Table 3.1 Empirical knowledge

Francis Bacon	Unimpressed with the stock of human knowledge and considered the mind and human thought to be weak and limited.
Thomas Hobbes	Knowledge is based in sense-perception. Causation involves matter in motion which sees knowledge as either effects developed through understanding, general causes or causes determined through general effects.
John Locke	If all things came from experience then how can we deal with generalisation when we may not experience every occurrence? Understanding not given by experience alone because all wholes or totalities in relation to generalisation cannot be accounted for by experience alone.
David Hume	Perceptions of the mind appear twice (as reflections of each other, on the one hand as an impression and on the other as a corresponding idea of sensation. Consequently, any idea must be associated with some experienced impression.

sensory ideas were motions in matter. Indeed, everything involved matter in motion. The pressure of objects, for example, sounds, shapes, colours, are not part of the object but caused by sensations; they are the qualities that emerge through interaction between thing or the observed and sensations of the mind (they are in motion).

Hobbes identified the concept of causes and effects or appearances of things that incorporated their ordinary observable qualities and causes are broken down into two types; efficient causes which bring about effects and entire causes which involved a combination of causes and effects. Causation involves matter in motion which sees knowledge as either effects developed through understanding general causes or causes determined through general effects. However, philosophical knowledge is not simply based on cause and effect but the idea of ratiocination (a process of logical thinking and knowledge of phenomenon through understanding what generated it). Consequently, knowledge is not simply derived through sense but by sensory images (referred to as external phenomenon) that when repeated through motion become imprinted on our minds. Indeed, sequence recollection identifies and orders our experiences. History incorporates a general or social sequence recollection which enables prediction, foresight and prudence. However, because history depends on sense, and memory is dependent on wide experience and not reached through ratiocination, it does not encompass philosophy. Knowledge derived through ratiocination is different from experiential knowledge but both begin with history and this is essential for philosophy. History informed philosophy but long epic historical accounts were not a necessity for total ratiocination as they can inform the initiation of the methodology but can be quickly peripherised once one begins to excavate the area studied.

Ratiocination is a form of methodology that understands complexity through simplification or breaking matter down into constituent parts and determining how these parts fit with each other. Subsequently, causes or the observable variables are initially made distinguishable (made known), then through synthesis of these variables the original effect can be identified. Effects are directly known through nature and in any study we must begin with effects when we investigate concealed causation. However, even though we initially experience effects, they actually come second to the concealed causes. Indeed, in Hobbes we have the basis of discovering theory and incorporated inductive procedures whereas a methodological approach that begins with identifying causation and consequent effects is more deductive and based in proving hypotheses. Hobbes labels causation to effect composition or synthesis and effect to causation resolution or analysis.

John Locke

Both Bacon and Hobbes were empiricists in that they recognised the primacy of sensory experience but it is also evident they saw the need for rational thought and the mind in the formulation of knowledge. Conversely, in *An Essay Concerning Human Understanding* (1690), John Locke (1632–1704) questioned how the mind is given ideas and knowledge. Indeed, he resoundingly answers through experience! For Locke the mind was a blank sheet and all knowledge derived through sensory experience. If all things came from experience then how do we know that a whole is equal to its parts? How do we deal with generalisation when we may not experience every occurrence? Locke realised that such is not given by experience alone because all wholes or totalities in relation to generalisation cannot be accounted for by experience alone. However, he rejects the very basis of this argument and considered that no dichotomy between experiential and innate knowledge existed. Indeed, he considered that all knowledge is found through experience or the senses but it did not necessarily follow that all emanated from this. Experience provided the materials of knowledge or ideas but once these have been determined we are able to make generalisations and recognise that wholes are equal to the sum of their parts. Through observation and experience the senses provide the building blocks of knowledge (ideas). Experience is divided into sensation and reflection which involves the latter taking into consideration how the mind operates, that is how it thinks, constructs beliefs or perceives when dealing with sensation. Locke claimed that pre-experience the mind was a blank sheet and all ideas emanated from this source; experience involves a dual source of ideas 'void of all characters without any ideas; how comes it to be furnished? … To this I answer in one word from experience: in that all knowledge is founded and from that it ultimately derives itself' (*Essay Concerning Human Understanding, Book II, Chap I, Sec 2*). Some ideas emerge through interaction with the external world or sensation while others develop through reflection or perception (activity or operation of the mind). The mind reflects on ideas reached through experience; however, no matter how abstract or removed from experience this reflection becomes the source exists in interaction with the world. Ideas for Locke involved mind-dependent entities and can involve internal sensations as well as external perceptions. Bottom-line, ideas can be simple or complex; that is ideas clearly derived from experience incorporate simple ideas and even though complex ideas need not be derived from experience but constructed through component parts experienced directly. That is not to say that complex ideas cannot be experienced directly, for example, time, space and infinity, may be experienced directly and these are not simple ideas. Locke uses the distinction between simple and complex ideas to underpin his claim that all ideas are found in experience. However, Locke failed to deal with the dichotomy between empiricism and rationalism. Indeed a solution to the problem between knowledge derived from experience or externality and the relationship with mind or thought continues to exist as a difficulty today.

David Hume

In *An Inquiry Concerning Human Understanding* (1748), David Hume (1711–1776) reasserts the hypothesis that all ideas are derived from experience but considers there to be a relationship between perceptions and ideas. He argued that perceptions of the mind appear twice or are reflections of each other; on the one hand as an impression and on the other hand as a corresponding idea of sensation. So any idea must be associated with some experienced impression. However, unlike Locke, for Hume reflection involves secondary impressions which are determined through pleasure and pain and involve feelings such as anxiety and expectations.

David Hume concerned himself with extending the realm of science beyond the natural world and developed a human science or an embryonic social science. He argued that the bedrock of understanding involved a comprehension of humanity and society; knowledge regarding human nature was a necessary premise for a clear perception of science in general. The relationship between human nature and science is clearer when dealing with issues relating to morality, logic or politics than it is when investigating the natural world. However, even though the natural world is not about humanity, it is studied by it, that is, it is studied by individuals who display a specific human nature. Indeed in Hume's writing we witness the very basis of social science and the idea that understanding human nature is central to our comprehension of anything else; he argued that through explaining human nature we develop the foundations of all human endeavours. He built on the work of Francis Bacon and proposed that as natural science had been based on experimentation and observation such should also be the foundation for human science. His text *An Enquiry Concerning Human Understanding* was sub-titled *An Attempt to Introduce the Experimental Method of Reasoning into Moral Subjects* where he argued for the use of experimental philosophy for developing understanding of human beings.

Experience and observation were considered the basis of understanding but Hume did not consider that observations should simply be accumulated and knowledge derived from this, rather he proposed that because appearances were deceptive hypotheses should be constructed and experimentation undertaken. Hume develops his argument through perceptions that he breaks down into impressions and ideas; ideas involve faint images of more vibrant impressions. Impressions involve the feeling of pain or happiness whereas the idea involves a recollection of these emotions; the difference between the two is one of intensity or degree rather than kind. In such a way all ideas are derived through experience; they are the faint image of something experienced. However, certain ideas exist that do not have impressions, for example, a different life form on another planet or a fourth dimension in which life could be very different. Hume subsequently distinguishes between the 'complex' and 'simple' where he accepts that one may have ideas about entities that have not been experienced completely but these are based in relevant partial experiences. For example, it is easier to imagine a different planet and life form than to conjure up exactly what a fourth dimension would encompass. Our existence on this planet and images of others in our solar system gives experiences that can be extrapolated to other unseen planets and our ideas of aliens are usually based in life-form seen here on Earth, for example, insects or reptilian. However, a fourth dimension is difficult because no experience exists outside of the three dimensions we exist within. Consequently, the correspondence between impressions and ideas is limited to simple cases; overall to have meaning an idea must be associated with something experienced. Hume argued that the correspondence between ideas and impressions formed the basis of human nature and that such would be useful in further investigating matters relating to human existence.

QUESTION

EMPIRICISM

Provide an assessment of the empiricists identified above and compare and contrast their distinct perspectives. Which thinker's understanding or philosophical position most clearly describes empiricism?

Positivism: Auguste Comtè

Positivism was initially identified during the mid-19th century and was closely linked with certain perspectives of empiricism and fitted well with the idea of progress that typified this period. In *A General View of Positivism* (1844/1856), Auguste Comtè (1798–1857) developed a hierarchy of knowledge which put human science at the apex and emphasised the science of humanity or sociology. He argued, that human thought evolved through three distinct stages; the religious, metaphysical and scientific. The scientific stage was the most important but both the religious and metaphysical stages had their value and were not to be discarded as primitive or useless.

Comtè considered it possible to build social science based on the same principles as those in natural sciences, for example, physics or chemistry. He further argued that if we used the same methods as the natural sciences a 'positive science of society' could be achieved. Consequently, based on empiricism this attempt to mimic the principles outlined for the natural sciences within the social sciences was coined as positivism. Through empirical observations immutable laws would illustrate that that humanity was governed by cause and effect. Based on Hume's empirical position in terms of the theory of regularity, he argued that the only content of causal laws involved the set of events that have been or will be observed. Events are identified by their temporal proximity to later occurrences and the probability that events precede specific types of occurrences. Agency activity or other mechanisms are irrelevant; to indicate causality is simply to say that an event of a certain type regularly precedes an occurrence of a certain kind.

Through studying case numbers positivism assesses the correlations and confidence levels that events precede occurrences. Such negates complications involved in the study of individual and collective action regarding internal processes of institutions. Through causality laws would be as immutable as those displayed by the natural sciences. In such a way, Comtè believed that the behaviour of humanity could be measured in exactly the same way as matter; that human behaviour could be objectively quantified. It was becoming clear that people (at least as masses) were suitable phenomenon for scientific study, a realisation that led to humanity being studied through positivist methodologies in developing institutions.

Following Comtè there was less emphasis on the categorisation of human development; the emphasis on the centrality and all embracing perspective of science remained but metaphysics and religion were denied. Positivism was both descriptive and normative; it described how human thought had evolved and prescribed norms for how it should develop. It had an axiological perspective, which argued that human duty was to further the process that existed, though positivism was more concerned with methodological approaches than prescribing ethical norms. However, there was an emphasis on furthering the inevitable, a trait which it shared with Marxism in terms of dialectics and economic determinism.

Positivism became a critical approach to what social science actually was and what it could achieve. Social science should be based on observation alone, and no appeal should be made to the abstract or invisible. There should be no recourse to metaphysical debate, all should be simplified and prediction pursued. Consequently, positivism emphasised observation of human behaviour and argued that things that could not be observed such as feelings or emotions were unimportant and may undermine or mislead the study. Emphasis on observation relates to a belief that through causality human behaviour can be explained in the same way as the behaviour of matter. As with the natural sciences there was little reason to investigate the meanings and purposes of matter; matter reacts to external stimuli and so did human beings. The task of the scientist whether social or natural was to observe, measure and explain.

Positivism 'has been based upon the principle that only reliable knowledge of any field of phenomena reduces to knowledge of particular instances of patterns of sensation' (Harre, 1987: 3). Indeed, as noted in Chapter 2, for positivism such patterns are immutable laws, which enabled prediction of future events. Theoretical frameworks are logically structured amalgamations of laws and used to enable prediction.

Ontologically, positivism considered that an external reality existed, which could be discovered and totally understood; a comprehension of reality that is sometimes labelled 'naïve realism'. The positivist epistemological position is one where the investigator and the external world (or what could be discovered) are totally separate and objectivity sought through scientific procedure; truth can be found. Methodologically, this could be achieved by attempts to prove hypotheses through scientific experiments and the manipulation of confounding conditions. For positivism, theory provides sets of immutable laws, which enable prediction. However, immutable laws and prediction are difficult enough in the natural sciences, but in the social sciences, in most instances, almost impossible. This was one of the major criticisms levelled at positivism by post-positivists who argued that reality or truth existed, however it could only be understood imperfectly or probabilistically.

Identify the difficulties for social science when dealing with:

- immutable laws;
- prediction;
- objectivity.

Inductive Procedure and Deductive Inference

Popper (1994) asserted that developing knowledge through inductive proce-dure is questionable because the validity of induction and science assumes and accepts clockwork regularity in nature. Only if we assume the future will be like the past can we accept that natural laws exist. However, how can the future be verified through observation? Such is impossible as is verification through deduction and rational argument because we cannot truly establish that future futures will continue to mirror past pasts. David Hume dealt with this dilemma by accepting that inductive validity is difficult to verify but may be accepted psychologically; we see them work in practice so accept the logic of induction. However, scientific laws or truth cannot be verified through induction or deduc-tion so have no secure rational foundations. 'Deductive inference may be said to be valid if and only if it invariably transmits truth from premises to the conclu-sion; that is to say, if and only if all inferences of the same logical form transmit truth. One can also explain this by saying: a deductive inference is valid if and only if and no counterexample exists' (Popper, 1992: 143). Popper argued that deductive inference is absolute and objective; it is a truth. That said there was a caveat here and even though we cannot always identify the objectivity or valid-ity of deductive inference there are number we can prove to be true. However, 'we cannot have a general criterion of truth' (Popper, 1992: 144). Such would necessitate omniscience, which is presently beyond human endeavour.

Popper (1992) further argued that he is not a 'belief philosopher'; just because some statement or inference has strong support and is believed in does not mean it is valid. For deduction or a theory of truth, beliefs are meaningless; truth is not about belief but about fact, argument and critical debate. However, we may question this position and ask whether Popper is here propagating a belief? Induction bases general statements about the world or theoretical frame-works on accumulated observation. For many years inductive procedure in both natural and human science (social science) indicated true scientific endeav-our. Observation and experimentation provided scientific statements based on fact that encompassed truth, knowledge or reality. However, David Hume raised some disturbing questions regarding this status quo when he argued that accumulated singular observations can never provide a general statement or prove a theory. Just because one event follows another on one occasion it does not automatically follow that such will occur again. Indeed, such would be the case if there had been 10,000 observations; we might expect the same occurrence but this is not certitude.

☐ Reflection Box ☐

Recurring Observations

A regularly used example of the uncertainty of recurring observations involves laws of physics and the rising sun; that is, based on the laws of physics we can predict the sun will rise tomorrow morning. Hume argued that this prediction may be disputed through two arguments. First, simply because the laws of physics have in the past been immutable this does not mean this will be the case tomorrow. Second, as noted the laws of physics are general statements, which cannot be proved by observations (no matter how many times an activity occurs).

Consider recurring observations and the implications for natural and social science.

This text recognises the difficulty in giving precise definitions of induction and deduction and the point where the former begins and the latter ends (and vice versa) and acknowledges the grey area between the two. Alfred Marshall argued that '(y)ou make all your contrasts rather too sharply for me. You talk of the inductive & deductive methods: whereas I contend that each involves the other & that historians are always deducing, & that even the most deductive writers are always implicitly at least basing themselves on observed facts' (Marshall, cited in Coase, 1995: 169). Ultimately, Marshall wished to emphasise the mutual dependency of induction and deduction; this text recognises the difference and necessary interdependency. Indeed, this is a good point to develop when dealing with a research project that involves either theory development or theory testing. In general the former would be considered more deductive whereas the latter inductive; the reality is that no one is able to enter the field with no pre-conceptions and hypotheses are generated through some understanding of the subject consequently a continuum exists with variable levels of a synthesis between deductive and inductive approaches utilised in research projects.

Differentiating Post-positivist Approaches

Positivists argued that social science should establish laws and as with the natural sciences such laws should be beyond challenge. Such an approach to knowledge generation and the realisation of truth undermined the critical aspect of positivism and in many instances became a barrier to scientific discovery. If laws could not be challenged then progress was restrained; positivism omitted and alienated many approaches to generating theoretical frameworks that reflected understanding and knowledge and was eventually challenged by post-positivism. Indeed, the relationships between positivism, post-positivism and critical theory exist on a sliding scale and there is more of a continuum between them rather than hard and fast demarcations. That said, even though much criticism of positivism from positions more closely linked with critical theory emerged between the 1950s and 1970s, one of the first to deliver a broadside was Karl Popper. Later post-positivists include: Toulmin, Lakatos, Feyerabend, Kuhn and Bhaskar (each of these researchers is covered in greater detail below).

Falsification and Karl Popper

Popper (1994) considered that immutable laws led to the stagnation of theory and that theory development should be open to criticism. Through falsification 'we can get rid of a badly fitting theory' before it overrides investigation and undermines objectivity (Popper, 1994: 4). In Popper (2002a, 2002b) falsification offers a solution to the problem of immutable laws and rational foundations. He argued that no matter how many times a white swan is observed we can never universally state that 'all swans are white'. However, one observation of a black swan allows the statement 'not all swans are white'. In such a way even though generalisations are not verifiable they are falsifiable. Consequently, scientific laws can be tested because even though they cannot be proved they can be falsified. The methodology for the post-positivist position is about falsifying standing scientific laws and the ontology concerned with criticising existing reality. If a single case exists that refutes a given law then as long as the case is reported correctly a scientific law is refuted. However, the reported case may have been reported incorrectly so we can always doubt the evidence; for instance the black swan may not have been a swan or because it is black we may decide not to label it a swan. In such a way all falsifiable evidence could be rejected.

Popper suggested that 'progress in science ... based on a revolutionary use of trial and the elimination of error by criticism which includes severe examinations or tests – that is, attempts to probe into the possible weaknesses of theories, attempts to refute them' (2002: 7). Popper (2002a) argued that because of varied and divergent human behaviour if we looked for confirmation then verification was easier to realise in the social sciences. Every test of a theory should be an attempt to falsify it, 'testability is falsifiability: but there are degrees of testability: some theories are more testable, more exposed to refutation than others they take, as it were, greater risks' (Popper, 2002a: 48). However, Popper indicated that complete or conclusive falsification was also difficult if not impossible to achieve. 'If you insist on strict proof (or disproof) in the empirical sciences, you will never benefit from experience and never learn from it how wrong you are' (2002b: 28).

| Definition Box |

Theory Falsification

- If confirmation or verification of theory is pursued then the confirmation or verification of the said theory is simplistic and straightforward.
- Sound theory prohibits certain events and occurrences; the more entities forbidden then the sounder the theory.
- Scientific theory is refutable; non-refutability is a vice not a virtue.
- Falsification is the only genuine test or refutation of theories.
- Theories display levels of falsifiability or refutation; some theories are more testable than others.
- Confirmation of theory should only be accepted if it has been subject to an attempt to be falsified and continued to retain validity.
- When theory is refuted falsification needs to be accepted. Reinterpretation and auxiliary assumptions should be avoided.

Falsification uncovers new arguments, perspectives and experiences which should be taken into consideration even if they bring into question the most relied upon or recent theoretical explanations. Because conclusive falsification is difficult at the methodological level, refutation should not be evaded through re-interpretation. Outcomes of refutation require acceptance and uncomfortable outcomes integrated with our understanding. However, scientific laws should not be given up lightly and defended stoutly in the face of competing theoretical frameworks.

A certain level of dogmatism is required for progress to occur. If old theories are not defended and do not struggle for survival, the newer theories cannot be robustly tested for levels of truth and explanatory power; an evolutionary survival of the fittest environment should exist. Intolerant dogmatism, however, is one of the main obstacles to science. Indeed, 'we should not only keep alternative theories alive through discussing them, but we should systematically look for new alternatives. And we should be worried when there are no alternatives – whenever a dominant theory becomes too exclusive. The danger to progress in science is much increased if the theory in question obtains something like monopoly' (Popper, 1994: 16).

However, Popper (1969) indicated that certain theories were still upheld even when they were found to be false. Through manipulating confounding variables or re-interpretation theory may be rescued from refutation, but only at the price of losing its credibility as a bona fide scientific theory. By making interpretations of the theory vague anything that may refute the theory can be explained away: if prediction is vague and unclear it becomes irrefutable. For instance, the 'Marxist theory of history, in spite of serious efforts of some of its founders and followers, ultimately adopted this soothsaying practice' (Popper, 1969: 49). Popper (2002a) argued that Marx historical materialism or dialectics of history that predicted the dictatorship of the proletariat. Popper (1969) thought highly of Marx idealism but considers him a false prophet. 'He was a prophet of the course of history and his prophecies did not come true; but this is not the main accusation. It is much more important that he misled scores of intelligent people into believing that historical prophecy is the scientific way of approaching social problems' (Popper, 1969: 82). Even though Marx historicism had been refuted by data or events, Marxists re-interpreted the theory and empirical data in order to deal with the refutation. 'In this way they rescued the theory from refutation ... (but) destroyed its much advertised claim to scientific status' (Popper, 2002a: 49).

| **Definition Box** |

Situational Analysis

Situational analysis involves:

- physical entities with elements of properties and states;
- certain social institutions and their properties;
- certain aims;
- certain elements of knowledge.

Positivistic immutable laws hold up scientific inquiry and provide false prophets. Post-positivism challenges positivism and through Popper identified a critical method of falsification and refutation. Russell (1980) identified the link between this philosophical position and methodology when he considered that one begins with a body of knowledge or data which is complex, vague and confusing. 'By analysis we reduce them to propositions which are as nearly as possible simple and precise ... These initial propositions are premises (which) are ... quite different from data – they are simpler, more precise, and less infected with logical redundancy (Russell, 1980: 214).

Popper (1994) argued that because falsification is extremely difficult to achieve, explanations in the social sciences required the analysis of social situations. This he labelled 'situational logic', which based on 'situational analysis' incorporated information or knowledge that was relevant to the situation. Indeed, 'situational analysis' turned the entity under analysis into a generalised anyone or anything that shared the relevant situation. It reduced individual aims of personal knowledge to a typical/situational model that in principle is able to explain a number of structurally similar events. In such a way we are able to comprehend a social event which is animated through replacing individual consciousness and situation with abstraction and an assumption that the agent will act, appropriately or adequately, in accordance with the situation (rational agent).

The situation should attempt to involve all relevant aims, complete relevant knowledge regarding these aims and the agent should act appropriately or rationally in relation to the situation. This is sometimes referred to as the 'rationality principle', which states that once the model is constructed it is assumed that agents act within the terms and realms of the model. Furthermore, because all variables are not involved in the understanding of motivations, the situations and agents are explained in ideal terms. Through 'situational analysis' it is possible to discuss, criticise and in some situations test models and if the test fails then learn from the flaws in the models and comprehend how they are over simplifications. The 'rationality principle' does not assume that human beings will always adopt a rational attitude. However, it is a methodological device which conjures a minimum principle 'which animates all our explanatory situational models, and which, although we know that it is not true, we have some reason to regard as a good approximation of the truth' (Popper, 1994: 181).

Kuhnian Paradigm Shifts

Kuhn (1970) argued that falsification did not actually occur in the research process. Indeed, two types of research existed; normal research which involved the on-going research within a given paradigm and research that is brought about through paradigm shifts. Normal science involves 'the activity in which most scientists inevitably spend almost all of their time (and) is predicated on the assumption that scientists know what the world is like' (Kuhn, 1970: 5). To ensure successful outcomes it is possible that normal science stifles innovation and remains within the realm of tried and tested techniques.

Normal sciences are based on observation and experiment in different fields, for example, physics, biology, chemistry, which is identified as a paradigm because they encompass a group of followers or individual adherents and leave numerous difficulties for following generations of practitioners to deal with (Kuhn, 1970). That is

Table 3.2 Falsification and paradigm shifts

Falsification	If a case exists that refutes a given law then as long as the case is reported correctly the said scientific law is refuted. However, the reported case may have been reported incorrectly so we can always doubt the evidence; for instance in the case of the black swan, it may not have been a swan or because it is black we may decide not to label it a swan. In such a way all falsifiable evidence could be rejected.
Paradigm shift	Scientific theory does not evolve through the accumulation of facts but through historical process. Change happens through the emergence of different intellectual circumstance and possibilities (different paradigm). This involves a range of ideas available at a given time and the discourse and terminology for a given epoch.

accepted practice in terms of laws, theories and applications provide the basis of scientific research (a certain belief system about how research should be conducted and what knowledge entails). Indeed, required paradigm norms are learned by students in specific scientific areas where they will eventually become a practitioner and join those who also learned the same required norms prior to full membership. Consequently, practice within the community seldom invokes dissent with given fundamentals; scientists with similar backgrounds and rule orientations are unlikely to challenge the paradigm or normal science practice and procedures.

Adherence to the paradigm norms ensures the continuation of normal science procedures and the research tradition related to this. However, a moment occurs when tried and tested techniques do not provide the expected results and the normal way of doing things is challenged and a paradigm shift occurs. 'Led by a new paradigm scientists adopt new instruments and look in new places. Even more important during revolutions they see new and different things when looking with familiar instruments in places they have looked before' (Kuhn, 1970: 111). Kuhn (1970) argued that scientific theory did not evolve through the accumulation of facts but through historical process. Change occurred through the emergence of different intellectual circumstance and possibility. Such involved the range of ideas available at a given time and the discourse or terminology for a given epoch.

Analysis of the history of electricity provides an example of the way science develops. In the early 18th century there existed many conceptual perspectives regarding electricity but all 'were partially derived from one or another version of the mechanic-corpuscular philosophy that guided all scientific research of the day' (Kuhn, 1970: 13–14). Furthermore, each theoretical perspective was considered scientific because it had been derived through scientific method in terms of observation and experimentation (Kuhn, 1970). However, even though researchers in this area would have read each other's results and all experimentation was electrical the theoretical perspectives that emerged only accorded slight resemblance. It was not until the work of Franklin and his successors that some unity could be formed that provided 'a subsequent generation of "electricians" with a common paradigm for ... research' (Kuhn, 1970: 15). Kuhn (1970) argued that similar long term disagreements and discourse occurred before a paradigm and 'somewhat arbitrary' name emerged in terms of Aristotle and motion, Newton and gravity, Boyle and chemistry or Hutton and geology. Given this one can see that the formation of a research paradigm is a long-term and difficult route. Indeed, for example aspects of biology paradigms, such as heredity, are quite recent and so 'it remains an open question what parts of social science have yet acquired such paradigms at all' (Kuhn, 1970: 15).

Khun thought that paradigms incorporated a specific mode of thinking, provided a certain perspective regarding the history of science and what these modes of thinking entailed. For example, the existing positivistic paradigm as the main mode of scientific discovery provided the dominant paradigm or normal science for many years until it was challenged and usurped by post-positivism.

Indeed post-positivism did not completely fulfil the requirements for social science research and analysis and was consequently challenged through critical theory and constructivism. Indeed, paradigm shifts can take place in relation to ontology and epistemology as well as theoretical perspectives. Such then determines a new basis for our comprehension of knowledge truth and theory as a generic concept. For its continuation a certain consensus within the research community regarding the core normal science is essential. It is the consensus regarding the core theories or methodological approaches of normal science that break down and brings about a paradigm shift. However, what would maintain such a consensus and what would this entail? Khun argued that on the one hand a paradigm incorporates a universal perspective or 'shared commitments' of a scientific community whereas on the other hand it identifies a particular sub-set of the community with a specific particular commitment within the more generic community. The initial community is broad and entails a broader conceptualisation of the theory employed in the philosophy of science. Indeed, in explaining the more generic idea of the paradigm, Kuhn uses the term 'disciplinary matrix' 'disciplinary because it refers to the common possession of the practitioners of a particular discipline; matrix because it is composed of ordered elements of various sorts, each requiring further specification' (1996: 182). The key elements of a disciplinary matrix incorporate: symbolic generalisations which involve 'expressions deployed without question or dissent by group members … they are formal or the ready formalised components of the disciplinary matrix' (Kuhn, 1996: 182), for example, general laws of nature and their underpinning definitions. A second part of the disciplinary matrix involves 'the shared commitment' to metaphysical beliefs in specific models that would include a more heuristic type of model. A heuristic model consists of experiential techniques which enable discovery and learning, and which provide generic comprehension and rapid means of problem solving, for example, intuition, common sense, trial and error. Fundamentally, models exist on an ontological/heuristic continuum and the commitment to these models vary; models provide accepted community discourse and identify acceptable puzzle solutions and the pecking order of puzzles that require solutions in the designated area of research. Linked closely to the models and discourse developed in defining problems and solutions is the idea of values. Though values are apparent at all times their importance becomes explicit when members of a community are involved in disputed discourse, fissure and eventually incompatibility within the discipline. Even though commitment to models exist within communities and values are widely and deeply shared by members, values can be subjective and 'affected by the features of individual personality and biography that differentiate the members of the group' (Kuhn, 1996: 185). So shared values determine group behaviour even though all members do not hold the values with the same voracity or consistency and this differentiation identifies distinctions and challenges norms within a community. A further aspect of a paradigm involves the basic education that students of scientific communities require before full membership is granted; this Kuhn argued involved the dissemination of exemplars through accepted textbooks, examinations and other forms of assessment, for example, dissertations and doctoral studies. Indeed, by undertaking a higher degree one is learning the norms identified in the specific discipline; such will consequently be applied in a practitioner and theoretical context and the disciplinary matrix reinforced. Modes of normal science are reinforced until challenged and a paradigm shift realised.

Through 'research programmes' Lakatos (1970) attempted to resolve the discrepancy between Popper and Kuhn. Lakatos argued that theory may be considered as a number of theories strung together in a succession T1, T2, T3, each of which share some central common idea that he labelled 'hard core' and such a succession of theories may be considered a 'research programme'. Indeed, through 'research programmes', the theoretical core of the theories may be protected or shielded from falsification by a 'protective belt' of 'auxiliary hypotheses', that is the scientist may manipulate hypotheses so the core of the theories is not challenged. The main point propagated by Lakatos involved a judgement regarding the quality of the theory; what was important was whether one theory was more applicable than another not whether or not it was true or false.

Toulmin (1953), who pre-dated both Kuhn and Lakatos, argued that rather than tested, theories should be considered in relation to their usability. Theories can be compared with sets of rules; that a general limited set of rules may be identified in the context of a domain and entities toward which the rules apply clarified. Instances that do not relate to the rules are determined. Consequently, the rules do not need to stand or reflect every context or in all cases but outline an area where the rules apply (area of application). Normally society would respect individual liberty but incarcerate someone who had committed a crime. Usually it is wrong to take a life but this action is accepted when in the name of the state when fighting in a war. Theory relates to reality through a set of rules some of which correspond and others which do not; the analysis involves determining which rules apply in a given domain or situation and which are redundant. Overall, on different levels each of these thinkers existed on an ontological continuum between critical realism and historical realism in terms of falsification on the one hand and a historical transformation of knowledge and how this is reflected through theoretical transformation on the other hand. Indeed such a synthesis of ontology may be perceived in the less naive and more in-depth understanding of critical realism developed by Roy Bhaskar.

Critical Realism: Roy Bhaskar

A post-positivist ontology perceives reality as external to humanity but considers our intellectual capabilities unable to fully understand opaque and confounding truth. On an ontological level this has been identified as 'critical realism' (Bhaskar, 1975; Denzin and Lincoln, 1994, 2000, 2005). Critical realism involves a distinction between the production of knowledge by human beings (as a social product) which can change in the same way that any human product may and knowledge that is of things (that is ground within them). The latter knowledge is not produced by humanity but discovered (it is knowledge that does not depend on human activity), for example, gravity, light propagation. If humanity ceased to exist, light would continue to travel and the moon would circle the Earth in exactly the same way; even though there would be no one to know this.

Bhaskar labels the latter 'the intransitive objects of knowledge' and the former the 'transitive objects of knowledge', which include facts, theories, paradigms and models. In terms of Darwin's theory of evolution the transitive objects involved 'facts of natural variation, the theory of natural selection and Malthus' theory of population' (1975: 21). Indeed he used these to discover and illuminate what had been occurring for eons. If we imagine a world without humanity but containing similar intransitive objects (in such a situation there would be no science to explain phenomenon so things would not be explained but still exist). Natural events and processes would continue to occur whether or not someone was able to understand and or explain them (osmosis would continue and atoms would still amalgamate). Consequently events are not 'dependent on our knowledge nor perception they are the intransitive, science dependent, objects of scientific discovery and investigation' (Bhaskar, 1975: 22).

For social science or the social world the situation is a little more problematic. The social world is a social construction that does not exist completely independent of human theory and discourse so does not clearly illustrate an intransitive dimension of knowledge. However, this knowledge is likely to be historical or understandings ground in the past rather than that posed by present day researchers.

Social science could reject the critical realist position and argue that no independent or intransitive knowledge exists in this domain. Since social science includes theories that are transitive and these have an impact on practice, the social world is unable to reflect an intransitive dimension: fundamentally, an independent knowledge of the social sciences cannot exist. However, if one is to contend that the critical realist position does exist in the social science some form of distinction between transitive and intransitive knowledge is required. In addition, with more researchers employing reflexivity this recognition of subject influence makes it increasingly difficult to test social theory against independent social reality. Reality becomes multi-faceted with different facets reflecting on each other and confronting themselves in different forms and ways. Indeed, as with a hall of mirrors they reflect upon themselves and the clear distinction between subject and object diminishes (ontology becomes epistemology).

| Reflection Box |

Intransitive and Transitive Knowledge

Intransitive knowledge incorporates the objects of study or science in terms of physical processes or social phenomenon. Transitive knowledge involves the human dimension in terms of theories and discourses (however, as elements of the social world they may be seen as intransitive). Rival theories and discourses are competing transitive perspectives whereas intransitive perspectives are continuous.

Consider the possibility of intransitive knowledge for the social sciences.

| Reflection Box |

Reality

A tree falls in the middle of the desert but no one is there to witness this; does it make a noise when it hits the ground?

Conversely, one could consider reflexivity as a useful if not necessary element of critical theory in the social sciences because it provides critical examination of different standpoints and perspectives. Indeed, reflexivity may guard against levels of projection and selection that could misrepresent the objective reality. Realists are always in a position that relates to the objective reality; reflexivity enables a critical comprehension of this position and the extent to which this affects the study. Self exists in relation to history and social existence; contemporary theory can be considered transitive and historical theory and interpretation intransitive. Fundamentally, knowledge is always gathered or derived though a selection process and reflexivity uncovers the mirage of total separation of researcher and researched. Social science involves multi-faceted reflections where theories both direct and confront perspectives. (For further on Reflexivity see the Methods chapter.)

QUESTION

- Explain the differences between transitive and intransitive knowledge.
- Identify the difficulties this distinction may have for social science.

Conclusion

Empiricism is an idealised term coined in the 19th century to illustrate distinctions between those thinkers who considered experience as the route to knowledge and those who considered the mind as the starting point, that is, rationalists.

As noted in Chapter 1, philosophers, such as Kant and Schopenhaur, outlined the relationship between internal and external worlds and how understanding, truth, reality, theory and knowledge involved a synthesis of the two. In this chapter we identified a number of empiricists and outlined how each dealt with the difficult relationship between experience of the external world and thought or rationalisation. However, the main point for Bacon, Hobbes, Locke and Hume was that experience and observation was the starting point. This is the premise positivism embraced and provided the basis for social science knowledge accumulation throughout the 19th century.

The objective of both positivism and post-positivism is explanation, control and prediction; positivism looked for the verification of hypotheses, facts and laws whereas post-positivism pursued falsification. Consequently theory, knowledge or truth for the former involves verified laws and the latter non-falsified laws that were probably true. In this way knowledge is accumulated through law, building and adding to the stock of knowledge through cause and effect and generalisation. Indeed, knowledge is intrinsically valuable and an end in itself. Any action relating to the research is minimised; it is limited and highly controlled as involvement is perceived as subjective and a threat to objectivity and validity. The quality or criteria of knowledge is measured through internal and external validity, reliability and objectivity; value is denied and scientists are removed from the research. However, there is a distinction here as the positivist acts as advisor for policymakers and change agents whereas the post-positivist is involved in policymaking and is a change agent through activism and advocacy. Both use technical qualitative and quantitative techniques, develop substantive theories, formulaic text and the researcher is the main voice. That said, for post-positivist critical theory, reflexivity, may be utilised but for positivists this technique or method impinges on objectivity.

Positivism mimicked methodologies set out for the natural world and wished to form immutable laws that enabled prediction. If new theory did not adhere to the given immutable laws it was usually discarded. This had implications for scientific progress and the development of new knowledge. Indeed, it provided an authoritarian modernist approach to knowledge creation and dissemination. Post-positivist epistemology abandons the ideal of complete separation between the investigated and investigator, however objectivity and distance are still pursued. This leads to a methodology that deals with multiple modified scientific experimentation and hypothesis falsification. Theory is not about the discovery of immutable laws but approximations of truth. A new theory may deal with some difficulties but will invariably open many new problems. If the theory provides significant progress then 'the new problems will differ from the old problems: the new problems will be on a radically different level of depth' (Popper, 1994: 4). Theory development is open to criticism. Consequently, through falsification 'we can get rid of a badly fitting theory' before it overrides investigation and undermines objectivity (Popper, 1994: 4).

Post-positivism gave greater scope for human endeavour. Popper noted that the 'future is open. It is not pre-determined and thus cannot be predicted … the possibilities that lie in the future are infinite' (1994: xiii). However, the future depends on humanity, we are responsible for our future. 'It is our duty to remain optimists, this includes not only the openness of the future but also that which all of us contribute to it by everything we do: we are all responsible for what the future holds in store. Thus it is our duty, not to prophesy evil but, rather, to fight for a better world' (Popper, 1994: xiii). However, the very nature of post-positivism throws up new problems for research and phenomenology forms criticisms of both positivism and post-positivism. Indeed, even though phenomenology was defined by Hegel (1977) and more specifically for our purposes by Husserl in the 19th century, it is not until Heidegger, Sartre and Merleau-Ponty in the 20th century that the phenomenological approach began to challenge the (by then) dominant position of post-positivism. Chapter 4 explores these different phenomenological perspectives and outlines the main distinctions between the influential thinkers in this area.

Further Reading

Bhaskar, R. (1975) *A Realist Theory of Science*. London: Version.

Blackburn, S. (1994) *The Oxford Dictionary of Philosophy*. Oxford: Oxford University Press.

Denzin, N. and Lincoln, Y. (1994) *The Handbook of Qualitative Research,* 1st edn. Thousand Oaks, CA: SAGE Publications.

Denzin, N. and Lincoln, Y. (2000) *The Handbook of Qualitative Research,* 2nd edn. Thousand Oaks, CA: SAGE Publications.

Denzin, N. and Lincoln, Y. (2005) *The Handbook of Qualitative Research,* 3rd edn. Thousand Oaks, CA: SAGE Publications.

Honderich, T. (1995) *The Oxford Companion to Philosophy*. Oxford: Oxford University Press.

Kuhn, T.S. (1970) *The Structure of Scientific Revolution*. Chicago, IL: University of Chicago Press.

Popper, K. (2002) *The Logic of Scientific Discovery*. London: Routledge.

FOUR
Aspects of Phenomenology

Introduction

This chapter does not incorporate a full and comprehensive analysis of phenomenology, and further nuances and distinctions between the different thinkers could be explained in more detail. However, the objective of this text is to identify and illustrate how phenomenology underpins the research process and the extent to which it challenged the pre-conceptions of positivism and post-positivism outlined in Chapter 3.

Phenomenology provides us with interpretations regarding the distinctions between the internal and external world as well as levels of objectivity and subjectivity. This said, for phenomenology there is a general comprehension that there is a relationship between mind and world. This chapter attempts to identify and explain different positions regarding the relationship between these phenomena in terms of objectivity and subjectivity. Georg Wilhelm Friedrich Hegel (1770–1831) argued that phenomenology dealt with the way things seemed for consciousness or with forms of consciousness. Fundamentally, the starting point was the naïve mind's emergent comprehension of reality that was external to it. Mind becomes aware of itself. Self-consciousness is neither exclusively subjective nor objective. Subjective awareness of self is not enough to enable self-consciousness. It cannot tell us what we are like in the world. We need a complimentary objective stance. This means an objective recognition of its own consciousness which will provide an understanding of its own reality. Only another being can do this, through reflecting for that consciousness a sense of its own external being. Objective truth lies in mutuality of recognition. Others define self and self defines self in relation to the definition forwarded by others. Community defines the self and self defines community. In this way recognition of self and other are different in different situations. Consequently, the recognition of other things is different in separate situations. Understandings of consciousness must acknowledge the objective (community or world) as well as the subjective (self), both are intrinsic parts of interpretation and contemplation. Through historical and philosophical process, humanity, knowledge and understanding are in a state of becoming Hegel (1977). The emphasis on the subjective as the defining factor of the world in relation to the external has, however, for different phenomenologists incorporated different weightings.

In a bid to comprehend the philosophical and scientific underpinnings of specific paradigms of inquiry and methodology, this chapter assesses certain differentiations between phenomenological thinkers. These differences range from Husserl's eventual reliance on 'transcendental phenomenology', Heidegger's 'hermeneutical phenomenology' or 'Dasein' and 'Being-in-the-world' as well as Merleau-Ponty's world of 'inalienable presence'. Husserl identified the distinction between the intentionality of consciousness (*noesis*) and that toward which consciousness is directed (*noemta*). The former incorporates the act of believing or desiring something whereas the latter involves that which is believed or desired. Transcendental phenomenology concentrates on noematic aspects of consciousness or what is believed or desired and the relationships between these rather than the act of consciousness. Hermeneutic phenomenology concentrates on the lifeworld, and uncovering, clarifying and illustrating the importance for understanding and meaning what may be considered as trivial elements of human existence. Consciousness and world are not separate entities but a holistic construction of lived experience. Understanding is not about how we know the world but our very essence; our understanding of the world is who we are. Through our personal histories, culture, language and environment, individuals are provided with an understanding of the world through which reality is identified. For Merleau-Ponty this is directly there so it exists and we are within this before any research, understanding or reflection begins, the world has an 'inalienable presence' which provides 'a direct and primitive contact with the world and endowing that contact with philosophical status' (Merleau-Ponty, 1999: vii). This contact and pursuit of philosophy provides the basis of rigorous science and offers descriptions of time, space and the world in which we exist. Indeed, this chapter investigates these distinctions in more detail and attempts to clarify some issues relating to ontology, epistemology and methodology. These issues are then looked at in more detail in the following chapters.

Husserl and Transcendental Phenomenology

Edmund Husserl (1859–1938) argued that phenomenology necessitated consciousness experienced from personal perspectives and was practised whenever we considered what we heard, saw or felt. Such consideration involves why we thought or think something and why we undertake certain tasks. Experience is attended to as we answer in the first person and describe or give meaning to the components of the experience. Meaning and conscious experienced are central to phenomenology; through meaning we are presented with a structured world which includes ourselves (Husserl, 1969). His ideas were developed over a number of decades and were published in numerous texts (Husserl, 1969, 1992, 1997, 1998a, 1998b). Phenomenology should be pre-suppositional, not use pre-existing theoretical frameworks and steer clear of deductive procedures; for example in Cartesian Meditations he indicated that the investigator or enquirer must discover everything 'including ... philosophical terms' (Moran, 2008: 126). That said, even though he considers we should avoid philosophical and theoretical pre-conceptions we should use experiences and everyday language in the study. Indeed, 'nothing must be taken for granted or assumed external to the lived experiences themselves as they are lived' (Moran, 2008: 126). Phenomenology entailed the 'essence of consciousness' in that all acts of consciousness are experienced by the subject; acts or experiences of consciousness happen in relation to an object, that is, something is understood, perceived or, judged. Phenomenology involves first-person descriptors in terms of 'I see the farm', 'I hear the cows mooing' or 'I imagine visiting the moon', such terms are known as phenomenological descriptions. Each descriptor indicates the subject's point of view regarding a particular act of consciousness which captures experiential essence (essence of consciousness) (Husserl, 1969).

An Explanation of Intentionality

Husserl identifies intentionality as the essence of consciousness as it involves the relationship between an act and the object of consciousness (intentional relation). 'We understood under Intentionality the unique peculiarity of experiences to be the consciousness of something' (Husserl, 1969: 242). There is a relationship between the subject and the object through intentionality because 'acting concerns action, doing concerns the deed, loving the beloved' (Husserl, 1969: 243). It is the capability of the mind to direct itself on things or entities; intentionality involves mental states including beliefs, hopes, thoughts, which are directed at something. An individual must believe or desire something and consequently undertake an intentional act. 'Husserl's phenomenology is the science of the intentional correlation of acts of consciousness with their objects and that it studies the ways in which different kinds of objects involve different kinds of correlation with different kinds of acts' (Bernet, 1999: 198). Intentionality concerns interaction between subject and object in relation to background, content, act and horizon.

Definition Box

Intentionality

- Background
- Subject
- Content

(Continued)

(Continued)

- Act
- Object
- Horizon

Intentionality involves turning one's attention to a given entity; it becomes a part of or an element of a perceptual perspective.

So as to deal with intentionality let us imagine a game of football and a corner kick; the background involves the game and more precisely the corner kick and the subject is a player in the penalty area. The football (object) that is crossed into the penalty area incorporates the content (perception) and the act of consciousness is the relationship between Subject 1 (S1) and the object (the trajectory, speed and flight of the ball). The horizon identifies the possibilities for S1 given the object. Of course, a number of subjects (S1, S2, S3, S0) will be in the penalty area each with his/her own act of consciousness in relation to the object.

The act of consciousness is an experience and it is with this that we are mainly concerned and involves a visual experience or a perception. The experience is abstracted from the background environment in which the game is played; the park, the rain; the rules of the game and the football pitch. The act is a mental process and completely different from the object (the football) toward which the act is directed. The object is the ball floating into the penalty area according to the laws of gravity or physics; the ball exists so it is not a solipsistic entity. The subject is the individual that has the experience (the 'I' or ego). The content involves what is seen, thought, imagined or perceived; a description of what is seen as 'I' perceives it. In this context, 'this is football'. Content identifies the object of perception; it represents the object in a specific way S1, S2, S3, perceive the trajectory, spin, speed and height of a ball in a specific way and expects it to behave in relation to certain scientific laws. The subject involved in the corner kick will require some knowledge regarding footballs and how to head them or kick them, the rules of the game (in this situation, specifically the corner kick), strategies of the game as well as physical capability (height, ability to jump, speed, position of others). The horizon of possibilities involves those open to the object; the football cannot simply stop dead and fall to the ground, neither can it levitate, as this is unrealistic and ludicrous given the background of the content act. Content prescribes the object and if there is an object that satisfies the content, then this incorporates the object of consciousness; the intended object is the act of consciousness. 'To intend' means that consciousness is aimed or directed at something. Intentionality is an act of consciousness undertaken by a subject and directed through content toward an appropriate object that is identified through the subject's horizon of meaning about such objects. The content of an experience is sense (Sinn) or its meaning. 'Intentionality is the title which stands for the only actual and genuine way of explaining, making intelligible' (Husserl, 1969: 168). Returning to 'the unities of the formation of meaning is to proceed toward a comprehension ... would leave no meaningful question unanswered' (Husserl, 1969: 168).

Reflection Box

Intentionality

Through an experience of your own, identify an example of intentionality. Consider sports you may play, or a routine experience at college or work.

Things: Essence and Existence

Husserl also distinguished between 'the world of natural experience' and 'the world of scientific theory' (1997: 219). The natural world is all around us and experienced directly; a world that existed in the past, the present and extends into the future. We stand before the world as points of reference consequently the world is spatial and temporal. Objects are entities in themselves with changing properties and relations but they do this in relation to humans that inhabit spatial, socio and temporal positions. Conversely, the world of scientific theory involves bodies with mass, for example, mechanics, physics, chemicals.

Definition Box

Thing

A thing incorporates three elements:

- the entity in itself;
- its essence (types, qualities and relations);
- as well as sensible qualities (some visible others not).

Appearances or adumbrations (faint outline or foreshadow) of a sensible thing

---

An entity has an essence and existence apart from that being observed, the magpie has properties including a distinct shape and black and white feathers. The feathers are different when the sun shines on them or the wind blows them in different directions (when the sun stops shining or wind stops blowing these changes disappear) and further difference emerges. If one was observing a fish in the water the same situation occurs as we know the shape of the fish but it is distorted through the water. This complexity is labelled the 'constitution' of the object as given in my experience.

To start 'phenomenological analysis there is appearance of the thing' and the appearance of the magpie is already constituted as a spatial entity as a black and white thing in my perceptive range (Woodruff Smith, 2007: 220–1). However, the magpie changes through its temporality as it lands in the tree and pecks the branches then flies toward a lamppost. It is temporal as well as spatial. Husserl does not reduce the magpie to its appearances, he points out that these appearances are adumbrations of qualities. The magpie is distinct from properties which may change over time (size, weight, flight). Furthermore, the sensible qualities of the properties (shape, colour, attitude) are distinct from their appearances. Indeed, the colour of the magpie or shape may be very different from another perspective or another given time; it's 'appearance changes over time as it flies in and lands on the fence, as it shifts its head around ... the shape appearance changes over this time period' (Woodruff Smith, 2007: 221). Consequently, the constitution of the magpie begins with an assortment of experience not in a simple sensory context but in terms of numerous distinct 'properties' and 'sensible qualities'. For example, when a single magpie is initially perceived, individuals consider this unlucky (one for sorrow) and we respond with 'morning Mr Magpie'; the bird already involves meanings bound in a cultural context. Furthermore, if more than one magpie is apparent then the way these are perceived will be different than if a single bird appears. Overall, 'intentionality of consciousness may be defined as a relation which all, or at least certain, acts bear to an object' (Gurwitsch, 1967: 118). To experience an act 'the subject is aware of an object, so that it may be characterised ... as consciousness of an object' (Gurwitsch, 1967: 119).

The constitution of the thing or entity as experienced begins with 'a manifold of appearances of its visible qualities'. However, what is seen is 'not simply sensory appearance but ... various properties including sensible properties that exhibit such appearances as I see the bird from various sides, in various lighting and so on' (Gurwitsch, 1967: 119). The bird is an object that involves many 'further properties including its biological species and geological relations ... is past activities ... and so on' (Gurwitsch, 1967: 119).

The magpie is a member of a species (carrion), it is related to other species of birds and has a past and future and exist beyond my intentionality. They transcend what is known of them at the moment they are observed; there is always more to the object than is intended by the subject. When an object is perceived we only see certain parts of this object we 'only see it from one side in a certain kind of light from a certain angle and so on' (Moran, 2008: 116). Whether the observer or the observed is the moving object we get 'glimpses of the same object from different perspectives' (Moran, 2008: 116). Husserl argued that what we actually see is the carrion not a 'set of visual sensations' we do not hear 'a bare sound but ... a door closing' (Moran, 2008: 116). Whether listening to something in close proximity or from a distance, no matter how different this makes the broadcast, we are certain that we listen to the same programme. Fundamentally for the listener it is the same object (Moran, 2008: 116). Overall, Husserl considers that mental processes are usually 'object-directed acts. When directed at a material object, the act is always only a partial view of the object; nevertheless, it has the sense of grasping the object as it is' (Moran, 2008: 118). This grasping the object enables the development of the non-intentional experience (the act of interpretation or interpreting sense); a sense which is consequently acknowledged by the quality or substance of the act whether this be 'a judgement, a wish, and so on' (Moran, 2008: 118).

Epoche: Suspension and Judgement

In his phenomenology, Husserl (1998a, 1998b) formulated the concept of epoche; through epoche one suspends judgements regarding whether objects of consciousness exist. We must not assume that external objects exist (that an objective reality exists), which then causally engages with human sensitivity (hearing, sight, touch), this means suspending or bracketing our natural attitude to the world. Bracketing involves seeing things as they really are; through dealing with presuppositions relating to phenomenon we get to the core and perceive it as it truly is. Bracketing requires three steps: identification of phenomenon and the retention of this in thought; the imagination of numerous experiential variations of the phenomenon; the integration of variations through the synthesis of experiences. Such a process leads to understanding and description of the essential structures of the phenomenon.

Husserl based his work on the Cartesian 'I think' but considered that Descartes moved too quickly from 'I think' toward I am a thinking entity. He considered that the conceptualisation of I as a thinking entity needed to be bracketed. I who am a thinking entity is both conscious of and in this sense distinct from experiences (Husserl, 1992). He considered this similar to Kant's 'I think' or transcendental ego. 'A transcendental principle is one through which we represent a priori the condition under which alone things can become Objects of our cognition generally' (Kant, 1952: 20).

Definition Box

Transcendental

Transcendental refers to entities that overarch or exist beyond other objects; they are abstract. The transcendental ego (individual) understands that even though a real world exists it can only exist through transcendental subjectivity (so a form of objectivity exists). Language could be seen as existing beyond individuals yet it is also used by the ego so the transcendental part of language and the using subject co-exist.

On the one hand, Husserl infers that reality can only exist if it is constituted through consciousness so conversely could not exist without it. Whereas on the other he also considered that nothing could be conceived without being an object of consciousness. The basis of the distinction involved the difference between intentional and real objects. When conceptualising something one makes this an object of consciousness. The former perspective denies the existence of an external world whereas the latter accepts that such exists but could not be realised without intentionality and consciousness. However, this does not automatically make the thing a real object. One can think of a fantasy world as the object of thought but one is not able to think of this as an object of one's thought and suppose oneself one of its inhabitants. In this way, Husserl attempted to explain how solipsism can be denied in his phenomenology, by indicating that transcendental egos experience each other on a par and together distinguish between intentional and real objects. Indeed, this was similar to the Hegelian master/slave dialectic and the rationale for subjective and objective recognition.

Husserl identified the necessity of transcendental phenomenology or philosophy which meant inquiring into the ultimate source of all the formations of knowledge and the knower reflecting on self and life. Through this process Husserl turns his attention to the essence of history itself; with the essential historicity of consciousness and the preconditions that history demands. To further explain his position, Husserl developed the idea of the lifeworld which involved the inter-subjective world of our pre-theoretical experiences and activities. He considered that our theoretical attitude developed against the background of the lifeworld which itself still persists even with the formation of the theoretical 'spirit'. The lifeworld is prior to theory and the emergence of theory from the lifeworld owes something to the eidectic reduction (a reduction to essence) and epoche (suspended judgement) by suspending our practical engagement with the world as well as our scientific propositions. However, in his later work Husserl does move some considerable way from his early position and closer to the ontological and epistemological positions of Heidegger. This becomes clearer in Husserl (1992) in which he attempted to investigate what positivist science meant for humanity and human existence and examine the extent that 'the total worldview of modern man in the second half of the 19th century, let itself be determined by the positivist sciences and be blinded by the "prosperity" they produced'. Which he considered detracted from 'questions which are decisive for a genuine humanity' (Husserl, 1992: 5–6).

Husserl argued that the basis of knowledge involved the lived experience in the lifeworld. That is we are inserted into a world not of our making; we are spatio-temporal prisoners in an uncertain world. People are nodes in a net of meanings which provides the very basis of their worlds. We pursue understanding through intentionality and wish to develop this in practical rather than theoretical contexts; this then provides the very basis for realising the possibilities of our existence. We are beings that do not simply exist but act in the world; consequently we are not entities to be researched but actively engage in the research process. Understanding is made up of pre-understanding as well as emotion and empathy.

Intentionality involves a pre-understanding of the situation under analysis so the positivist notion of subject and object is undermined as the notion of emergence takes precedence; emergence of an understanding that already exists. This emergence allows people to understand the practical world in which they exist and furthers their comprehension of self; it provides self understanding.

LIFEWORLD

How does the idea of lifeworld or being-in-the-world affect the relationship between the researcher and researched?

> ## ⌐ Reflection Box ⌐
>
> ### Lifeworld
>
> Identify times when you think you have been in a situation that you wished to understand. Provide examples of when you consider you have not been in the world but an abstraction looking from without. Is this possible?

Language was considered the means by which lifeworlds and horizons were transmitted; language mediated meanings and traditions. Indeed, in order to synthesis horizons we enter other horizons, which include texts with our own horizon and pre-conceptions; we move between the familiar and unfamiliar. Historicity is an important element within this process as each interpretation involves pre-conceptions derived from history that are applied in the present to develop the future through expectations and strategies. Each interpretation involves a dialectical process consisting of past, present and future, the mediation of which comes through language and discourse. Given this, even truth or knowledge is historically conditioned, which means it is relative to the culture of a given moment; different aspects of truth and knowledge are revealed through different cultures at different historical moments.

In his early work Husserl would have had excepted a level of externality when it came to the research project or phenomenon under analysis. In his later works he recognised the deficiencies of a purely positivistic stance and that different forms of analysis were required if humanity was to be fully understood; his later works further acknowledge being-in-world and related closer to ideas propagated further by Heidegger and Merleau-Ponty. For example, Husserl argued that when it comes to understanding others we may consider that every other or other's world gives a horizon of meaning. Horizon (may be considered the outlook of the individual at any given time (the outlook here and now); it is also flexible and can change from one moment or situation to another. Individuals move into one another's horizons through empathy. However, each person is entangled in his/her horizon with all the pre-conceptions that this involves. Consequently one is never free from the perceptions and pre-understandings inherited from past experience and pre-conceptions are a barrier to fully understanding. This begins to relate with phenomenological hermeneutics which recommends an interactive and iterative process between entering another world and referencing back to one's own position.

HUSSERL

Define, discuss and give examples of:

- inclusivity;
- epoche;
- bracketing;
- transcendental phenomenology.

Heidegger: Hermeneutical Phenomenology

Martin Heidegger's (1889–1976) work is deeply rooted in *Being and Time* (1962/2004) in which he considered that interpretation was necessary when studying social beings. Heidegger argued that 'every inquiry is seeking [suchen]. Every seeking gets guided before hand by what is sought. Inquiry is a cognizant for an entity both with regard to the fact that it is and with regard to its Being as it is ... Inquiry itself is the behaviour of a questioner, and therefore of an entity, and as such has its own character of being' (1962/2004: 24). The meaning of being is already within us because 'seeking must be guided beforehand by what is sought ... we always conduct our activities in an understanding of Being' (1962/2004: 25). He questioned the very meaning of Being and like Hegel perceived a process of becoming. Indeed, the investigation of Being starts with an entity whose very existence involves raising such a question. Heidegger wished to penetrate presuppositions, which shape our understanding rather than revert to a position of no inherited presuppositions as in Husserl's pre-suppositionless phenomenology. Distinct from Husserl's 'transcendental phenomenology', Heidegger identified 'hermeneutic phenomenology' which rendered explicit the 'implicit clues that organise understanding, identifying the horizon of Being that allows entities to appear as they are and then explicates the implicit clue around which that horizon is organised and by which it is nourished, which is the meaning of the Being of those entities' (Caputo, 1999: 225).

| Definition Box |

Hermeneutical Phenomenology

Hermeneutical phenomenology argues that meaning is linked directly with time. Being is historical and systematic; it is temporal. Heidegger demonstrates the 'temporal structure of every historical understanding of Being (as) a structure that needs to be forced out since the temporal clues operating in these historical texts are hidden' (Caputo, 1999: 225).

Heidegger considered that we were in the world and there was no differentiation between subject and object because Being-in-the-world rendered this distinction obsolete. As human beings, the world and the individual are continually at one with one another; we are in the world before we think or reflect so we are both subject and object and at one with the world. This calls into question the idea of empathy between subject and object identified in objectivist hermeneutics. Indeed phenomenological hermeneutics wishes to comprehend facticity (the facts of being) which may only be found in the lifeworld or the practical pre-abstract pre-theory existence. What is important is our existence within the world and how we belong to our environment. As Heidegger noted, we are thrown into an existence and world that we did not construct and in this strange perplexing world we have to find our way. Phenomenological hermeneutics is not about abstract supra-individuals or transcendental egos, rather it involves understanding actual people in actual situations.

The idea of care plays a central part in our survival and understanding of concrete selves and situations. As human beings we are linked with past, present and future; our decisions are based on past experience and resources as we attempt to understand and second-guess future possibilities. That said we become the vessel of possibility; humanity's and the individual's free choice and responsibility are possible in reality. However, on what criteria should responsible free choice be founded? There is no abstract so any criteria will be of our own design; value can and will only emanate from us. In a way we are condemned to freedom as we must make decisions in a world of adversity we cannot surrender to the world and no choice is still a choice. It is 'not possible not to choose. I can always choose but I must know that if I do not choose, that is still a choice ... when I confront a real situation – for example that I am a sexual being able to have relations with a being of the other sex and able to have children – I am obliged to choose my attitude to it, and in every respect I bear the responsibility of the choice, which in committing myself commits the whole of humanity' (Sartre, 1973: 48). Embedded in a concrete situation of which he or she is part, the individual choices involve choice for all; the individual must choose whether he or she remains single or marries, but either choice underpins a moral stance regarding social institutional and ethical behaviour. The individual is in the world and through choice constructs the world.

To surrender renders us 'inauthentic' which is opposite to an 'authentic action' is based on the realisation that we are free, autonomous, responsible individuals. This is what renders us human; we are in the world and have free choice. However, we continually fall into the world of every day triviality but the cry of consciousness calls us back to the authentic life; this is an abrupt ear-piercing cry that deafens our every day existence it asks what are you doing are you throwing your life away on triviality? (Heidegger, 2004). Indeed, such questions can clarify or as Heidegger indicated provide 'uncanny clear-sightedness' which can change our lives forever. From clear-sightedness emanates anxiety, which gives true understanding of the everyday world within which we reside; not triviality but the essence of our everyday existence. Free from toil when walking back down the hill, Sysphus is able to see clearly and assess his situation. We are able to capture the authenticity of the world in which we live and so capture its emptiness and our own insignificance within it. In such a way we rediscover ourselves and become responsible entities that make non-trivial decisions (see Heidegger, 2004; Sartre, 1973). The upshot of this position is clarity in relation to self, as we understand our strengths and weaknesses in a composed and thoughtful manner; we neither overestimate nor underestimate ourselves. Thus everyday life continually brings in the trivial because it is inundated with the mundane that continually limits our degrees of freedom. Furthermore everyday life omits the idea of death; it denies death so we are infinite beings, which affects our decision-making in relation to our notion of the future (Heidegger, 2004: 278). Death denotes an end that if embraced may enrich understandings of life, if finitude is taken on board then the likelihood of wasting life may be negated. Such finitude may be seen in other aspects of life, for example, retirement from work, redundancy and the time span of projects. If these finitude issues are taken into consideration the individual starts to truly comprehend self.

For Heidegger the idea and pursuit of truth had continually been in decline since antiquity and Plato. Truth already exists but is hidden by the very procedures meant to uncover it. Truth will not be uncovered through expressing propositions then comparing this to reality; truth or knowledge will emerge through insight and intuition. Husserl considered that intuition should be used to explore the basic structure of phenomena through imagination or thought-play. The phenomenon is isolated from other phenomena as well as historical and spatial contexts. For Heidegger this went against the very core of phenomenology because the idea was to analyse in relation to historical context and identify distortions that are the upshot of this. Historicity is a key part of phenomenological hermeneutics as it concentrates on the process of becoming and the meaning of being. The later works by Husserl (1992) took up this point and recognised the importance of history in the phenomenological process.

Dasein: Becoming

Heidegger posited an 'existential analytic' that dealt with what we are in terms of 'Dasein'; which is to be of the world where it is manifested or made explicit. Dasein is the event of world manifestation and as soon as a being such as Dasein exists, then a world exists. 'Dasein is an entity which in its very being comports itself understandingly toward that being' (Heidegger, 2004: 78).

Dasein

Dasein is existence; its essence is an entity that is becoming through fashioning its own existence. Fundamentally, 'we are ourselves the entities to be analysed. The Being of any such entity is in each case mine. These entities, in their being comport themselves toward their Being ... Being is that which is an issue for every such entity' (Heidegger, 2004: 67).

All research and analyses are driven by an attempt to understand self in relation to humanity as elements of becoming. For Heidegger 'an understanding of being is already included in conceiving anything which one apprehends as an entity' (2004: 22). Dasein actualises its own authentic possibility or fails in the attempt. However, as a being that fails Dasein tends to cover up its own being as existence. Indeed, the 'existential analytic' counters Dasein's fall into the world of mediocrity and the daily trudge through seeking the obtuse and founding structures of Dasein's primordial authenticity. The everyday world of Dasein is passed over and being in the world is sought. This raises problems regarding what the world entails. For Heidegger the world is a continual linkage of instruments leading to and from Dasein 'to which Dasein belongs more primordially than it can say, with which Dasein is always already pragmatically involved so that the epistemological problem of existence of this world makes no sense' (Heidigger, 2004: 226). The world is already shared with others and far from a solipsistic ego, Dasein like Hegelian recognition necessitates others. These are not entities 'who are other than the I but among those whom the I is also, by whom Dasein is in fact dominated like an anonymous they (das 'man') and from whom it must learn to differentiate itself into an authentic self' (Heidegger, 2004).

Definition Box

Aspects of Dasein

- Dasein involves a threefold phenomenon in terms of care: projection toward possibilities: to be self.
- Throwness toward these possibilities: Dasein although free finds itself in situations not of its making.
- Fallenness among worldly possibilities which negates true possibility or the possibility to be self.

This threefold unity is explicated through anxiety or the sense by which Dasein finds there is nothing other than Dasein's own freedom to sustain projection from which it continually takes flight (its falling). Heidegger considered that through freedom from immortality, Dasein is brought back out of its fall by taking over its projectedness into death rather than taking flight from it. Dasein does not have temporality as a defining feature because it is temporality. It is the unity of three temporal ecstasies upon which the threefold structure of care is based. Temporality is the meaning of care and so of Being or Dasein.

Dasein is futural and stands before indefinite possibilities which are always coming toward Dasein and drawing it out of itself. In this way Dasein comes back to itself, to the possibility that it has always been and continually moves toward. Finally, Dasein encapsulates the moment and what it has always been in relation to this. It catches a glimpse of and seizes the possibility to be self. 'The tripartite ecstatic structure of temporality provides the basis for an analogous theory of historicality in which an entire generation can repeat or seize upon historical possibility (or destiny) which is sent to it as a collective unity from its own deepest historical having been (Heidegger, 2004: 227). Dasein incorporating individual, community, society or species.

Husserl argued that human science failed because it did not take into consideration intentionality or the way the individual mind is directed at objects and provided pre-understanding or the mental content that represented them. Indeed, he considered that human consciousness involved self-contained meanings or intentional content. That is, you approach something with preconceptions and pre-understanding that gives intelligibility to everything people encounter. Heidegger provided a slightly different form of intentionality and argued that mental content actually directed self-sufficient individuals at the world and that everyday skills incorporated or indicated the basis of intelligibility. Indeed, the work of both Husserl and Heidegger is further explained through the phenomenology of Merleau-Ponty, who considered that they identified different ways of looking at the world and the means by which we undertake and approach research and knowledge generation.

QUESTION

DASEIN

- What is Dasein?
- How does Dasein affect a research project?
- How would you include Dasein in your research project?

Merleau-Ponty: Essence of Consciousness

Maurice Merleau-Ponty (1907–1961) investigated whether science was capable of providing humanity with a complete picture of the world; he did not wish to limit scientific knowledge but identify whether it is entitled to rule out forms inquiry that do not begin with 'measurements and comparisons and, by connecting particular causes with particular consequences, end up with laws such as in classical physics' (Merleau-Ponty, 2004: 43). He indicated that in the 20th century positivism had already accepted that its laws and theories did not provide a clear picture of the world and continual simplification was required; 'in other words, these laws and theories constitute knowledge by approximation. Science subjects the data of our experience to a form of analysis that we can never expect will be completed since there are no intrinsic limits to the process of observation' (Merleau-Ponty, 2004: 43–4). Through Husserlian methods, Merleau-Ponty looked to uncover the 'roots of rationality', which involved the 're-awakening of an understanding of the original acts whereby humans come to awareness in the world' (Moran, 2008: 400). Phenomenology and philosophy were identical and they each wished to teach humanity to relearn how to perceive the world and reveal and illuminate the 'birth of being … disclosure of the world' and 'the mystery of the world of reason' (Merleau-Ponty, 2004: 154, xx-xxi, xvi).

Inalienable Presence

Merleau-Ponty (1999) understood phenomenology as the study of essences and that all problems amount to finding definitions of essences, that is, essence of consciousness or perception. His is a philosophy, which brings essences back into existence and one that does not expect to arrive at an understanding of humanity through facticity. It is a philosophy that identifies a world that already exists prior to reflection 'as an inalienable presence'. It aims to directly re-achieve contact with the world and through this give it a philosophical status. In a similar way Heidegger saw any inquiry as being guided by what is sought. So the meaning of an entity must already be known to the inquirer prior to the investigation and must already be available to us in some way. Merleau-Ponty emphasised 'the inseparability of self and world' and that people should be seen as 'integrated into the natural order, as fundamentally belonging to the world, though not merely as objects in the world as their presence generates the social world of culture' (Moran, 2008: 403).

Phenomenology is only accessible through its method. Consequently, let us bring together the strands that have 'grown spontaneously together in life' (Merleau-Ponty, 1999: viii). From the start phenomenology is a rejection of science. One is unable to understand oneself as more than a bit of the world. One is a sociological, biological entity that cannot shut out the world and exist in the realm of science. 'All my knowledge of the world even my scientific knowledge is gained from my own particular point of view, or from experience of the world without which the symbols of science would be meaningless' (Merleau-Ponty, 1999: viii). Science is a second order expression of the world. Consequently, if we are to rigorously scrutinise science we must begin with this and understand it as built on the world as it is directly experienced. Science will never be the same as the world because it is an explanation of the world. 'I am not what science defines me as, I am the source, 'my existence does not stem from my antecedents, from my physical and social environments; instead it moves out towards them and sustains them, I alone bring into being for myself' an existence that can be understood (Merleau-Ponty, 1999: viii). A scientific point of view that considers that existence is a moment of the world is not only naïve but dishonest. Positivists and post-positivists take for granted consciousness through which a world forms itself around me and begins to exist for me. When we return to things themselves we return to a world that precedes knowledge, a world, that knowledge speaks of which all scientific schemes are an abstract sign-language as geography (a map) is in relation to the countryside (terrain), that is, we have already learnt what a river or field is, then find this in abstract form denoted on the map. 'Phenomenology can be practised and identified as a manner or style of thinking, that it existed as a movement before arriving at complete awareness of itself as a philosophy' (Merleau-Ponty, 1999: vii).

| **Definition Box** |

Pre-Understanding

Inquiry is guided by what is sought. Consequently, the meaning of an entity must already be known to the inquirer prior to the investigation and must already be available to us in some way. Humans are sociological, biological entities that cannot shut out the world and exist in the realm of science. The world is 'there' before human analysis and this analysis should move toward the inner view of the phenomenologist and away from the outer stance taken by the positivist perspective.

Return to Consciousness

A phenomenological return to consciousness is distinct from the idealist return to consciousness, which denies analytical reflection and scientific explanation. Both Descartes and Kant detached the subject or consciousness by illustrating that nothing could be apprehended as existing until it was apprehended through the act of it being apprehended. For Kant unity of consciousness is achieved simultaneously with the world. Phenomenological '(a)nalytical reflection starts from our experience of the world and goes back to the subject as to a condition of possibility distinct from that experience, revealing the all embracing synthesis as that without which there would be no world' (Merleau-Ponty, 1999: ix). Indeed, this moves away from positivist ontological/and epistemological perspectives as it recognises the necessary interaction between the cosmos and consciousness in that the very fact of consciousness identifies our subjective perspective of the world and that reality is a human construction.

In general, for Meleau-Ponty, phenomenology sees the world as being there before any human analysis and 'it would be artificial to make it the outcome of a series of syntheses which link, in the first place sensations, then aspects of the object corresponding to different perspectives, when both are nothing but products of analysis, with no sort of prior reality' (Merleau-Ponty, 1999: ix). However, he argued that analysis should move toward the inner view of the phenomenologist and away from the outer view stance taken by the positivist perspective. Analytical reflection believes that it can arrive at the inner being and that through a constituting act it can trace back the course and arrive at a constituting power that is synonymous with the inner self. Consequently, reflection is 'carried away and transplanted in an impregnable subjectivity, as yet untouched by being and time' (Merleau-Ponty, 1999: ix). However, this loses sight of its own beginning. When one begins to reflect, reflection bears upon an unreflected experience and cannot be unaware of itself as an event, so it appears to itself.

QUESTION

PRE-UNDERSTANDING

Explain pre-understanding and consider the implications for issues regarding subjectivity and objectivity. Identify how pre-understanding would be incorporated in a research project.

'We see things themselves the world is what we see ... a faith common to the natural man and philosopher ... the strange thing about this faith ... is if we ask ourselves what is this we, what seeing is and what thing or world is we enter into a labyrinth of difficulties and contradictions' (Merleau-Ponty, 1968: 3). No distinction exists between perception or the perceiver and what is perceived there is no differentiation between the act of perceiving and that toward which it is directed. 'Any contention that the perception is indubitable whereas the thing perceived is not must be ruled out ... To see something is to see something. To see red is to see red actively in existence' (Merleau-Ponty, 1999: 374). Through his phenomenology Merleau-Ponty attempted to provide direct descriptions of experience through the perspective of the first person (that is describing the experiences being experienced in the situation perceived). Merleau-Ponty takes umbrage with Husserlian ideas regarding a return to things in themselves, because to return to something is to indicate that at some point the situation was vacated; to return to a world that existed prior to knowledge. Phenomenology incorporated the attempt to find the spirit of a civilisation 'not a law of the physico-mathematical type, discoverable by objective thought, but the formula which sums up some unique manner of behaviour towards others ... nature, time and death: a certain way of patterning the world which the historian should be capable of ... making his own' (Merleau-Ponty, 1999: xviii). Fundamentally, no distinction exists between the researcher and the world under investigation; the researcher is and will always remain intrinsically linked with that which is observed or more specifically seen.

Conclusion

Phenomenology distinguishes between perceptual properties and abstract properties. Take two, red snooker balls identified as A and B. The red colour of A, which can be seen by the eye is said to be located in the space where A is. Likewise the red of B is said to be located where B is. In addition, it is considered that the red of A is not identical with the red of B because they are located in different places. According to phenomenology an abstract colour shade or a universal red exists and humans are able to perceive not only instances of red but also a universal red. This perception is called 'eidectic intuition' through which we have knowledge of the essential essences of the world. This implies a universal or Platonic red that can never be known completely, which to an extent fits with the critical realism of post-positivism. It is accepted by post-positivists that an external reality, in this case a universal red, cannot be completely understood or perceived by human beings.

Conversely, the ontological and epistemological positions of phenomenology indicate a reality that is formulated by the human mind. Not a solipsistic reality but one that necessitates interaction between the world and human or mind in terms of being or becoming in the world. This incorporates the idea that human beings are essential ingredients in defining and determining each perceptively different reality. Different reds existing in relation to a universal incorporates differentiated situations that can be studied in isolation in relation to a general concept. This can allow generalisation from one like situation to other similar situations and challenges positivist and post-positivist ontological, epistemological and methodological perspectives.

The phenomenological approach is made explicit when knowledge of things are divided into two aspects; direct and indirect knowledge. Essences are known directly but perceptual objects are only known indirectly. There are also mental things and self or selves. How are these known? Consciousness like essence is known directly but external objects are not. There is a difference between the subjective and objective worlds, unlike the former, the latter are never given wholly. But the self, the entity from which all mental acts transpire, is only presented to us like a perceptual object; that is, indirectly. The realm of individual things or subjectivity is divided into an imminent part (consciousness) and two transcendent parts (perceptual objects and the self). Consciousness is special because what we directly and truly know is only consciousness. This accepts subjectivity as an important part of the research process and leans toward historical and relativist ontological perspectives. Indeed, the distinction is explicit when we speak of humanity being-in-the-world and the differences between inanimate objects, most animals and Dasein. Inanimate objects cannot relate themselves with their own Being and can be researched from positivist and post-positivist perspectives; human beings can bring together what they are and who they are within the world and this is a far more difficult entity to research and understand. In other

Table 4.1 Types of phenomenology

Husserl (transcendental phenomenology)	Transcendental phenomenology concentrates on what is believed or desired and the relationships between these rather than the act of consciousness.
Heidegger (hermeneutic phenomenology)	Hermeneutic phenomenology concentrates on the lifeworld and uncovering, clarifying and illustrating the importance for understanding what may be considered as trivial elements of human existence. Consciousness and world are not separate entities but a holistic construction of lived experience.
Merleau-Ponty (inalienable presence)	The world is directly there, it exists and we are within this before any research, understanding or reflection begins, the world has an 'inalienable presence'.

words because 'Dasein is in each case its own possibility, it can in its very being choose itself; it can also lose itself and win itself; or only seem to do so' (Heidegger, 1962: 68). Given the simplification process, identified by positivism and post-positivism, how are we to understand this process if it is not through phenomenological procedures and a comprehension of essence? Phenomenology comprehends the becoming entity in an uncertain changing world with numerous, varied, unclear variables to ensure an in-depth understanding. To emphasis validity of situation, rather than reliability or experiment repetition, we need to use paradigms of inquiry based on phenomenological approaches that identify the links between subjectivity and objectivity in an explanation of human behaviour.

In the main, this chapter overviewed ideas that have been taken up as criticisms of the positivist tradition that include the phenomenological perspectives of Husserl, Heidegger and Merleau-Ponty. Positivism considers that an external reality exists, which may be perceived in an objective manner, whereas phenomenology argues that 'reality was not an objective entity the mind duplicates within itself; it is the result of that something and the mind's percipient activity ... There is therefore, no objectivity. Or if there is, it can only reside in the knowledge of the possible forms of perception, of all their relations and interdependencies, which may be reducible to a certain formulae and might represent in sum, the knowledge of the perceiving subject as a whole; of a transcendental knower, in and by which (or whom) all our perceiving takes place' (Mairet, 1973: 13). Indeed, that an explanation of humanity has to begin from the subjective (Sartre, 1973). Furthermore, positivism takes up external positions whereas phenomenology attempts to understand and construct an inner view. However, even though at first sight these paradigms are very different, when we start to investigate and analyse the nuances in phenomenology and post-positivism, similarities begin to emerge and linkages and differences between ontological, epistemological and methodological perspectives become clear. For example, in his early work Husserl does not expect to provide an understanding of humanity and the cosmos from any starting point other than facticity. On the one hand, this involves a transcendental philosophy, while on the other hand, the world is always already in existence before reflection begins. In this way, the dualist perspective leans toward the post-positivist perspective while at the same time the transcendental involves greater relativism and the solipsistic ego. Phenomenology pursues a philosophy that is a rigorous science, which provides an understanding of space, time and the world in which we live. Chapter 5 will investigate the critical theory paradigm of inquiry and render explicit a number of the distinctions and similarities raised here.

Further Reading

Critchley, S. and Schroeder, W.R. (1999) *A Companion to Continental Philosophy*. Oxford: Blackwell.

Honderich, T. (1995) *The Oxford Companion to Philosophy*. Oxford: Oxford University Press.

Kearney, R. and Rainwater, M. (eds) (1998) *The Continental Philosophy Reader*. London: Routledge.

Moran, D. (2008) *Introduction to Phenomenology*. London: Routledge.

Sartre, J.P. (1973) *Existentialism and Humanism*, trans. and intro. P. Mairet. London: Methuen.

FIVE
Critical Theory

Introduction

On the basis of a mixture of both positivist and phenomenological perspectives, in Chapter 5 attention is turned toward critical theory and identifies the problems post-positivism left for those social sciences that sought to identify and challenge what was taking place in institutions from historical and mainly qualitative perspectives. Critical theory was initiated by the Institute of Social Research (ISF) at the University of Frankfurt in the late 1920s; consequently, most commentators argue that the critical theory position was developed by members of the Frankfurt School. Nevertheless, when we examine the works of members of the Frankfurt School, none claimed to have formulated a unified approach to social investigation and criticism.

Critical theory stems from a critique of German social thought and philosophy, particularly the ideas Karl Marx (1818–1883), Max Weber (1864–1920), Theodor Adorno (1903–1969), Erich Fromm (1900–1980), Max Horkheimer (1895–1973) and Herbert Marcuse (1898–1979). Marxism is a type of critical theory because it critiques capitalism and illustrates problems with existing institutions, as is the Weberian theory of rationalisation and the limiting effect on the human spirit; indeed through such a critical theory perspective the ideas of Marx and Weber may be combined. In general, Adorno, Fromm, Horkheimer and Marcuse argued that modern society involved totalitarian regimes that negated individual liberty. In early work this was seen as the outcome of Marxist understandings of capitalist modes of production, whereas later thinking stressed technology and instrumental reason (these ideas and thinkers are dealt with in more detail below). Instrumental reason argues that rationality may only be concerned with choosing effective means for attaining arbitrary ends. Indeed, in contradiction with Weber's objective causality the Frankfurt School was based on neo-Marxist dialectical reasoning and subjective tendencies. There existed two generations related to the Frankfurt School: the first included Adorno, Horkheimer, Fromm and Marcuse and the second a number of thinkers of whom Jurgen Habermas was the most distinguished. The main tenet of critical theory involved a necessary re-interpretation of modernist positions in the aftermath of the First World

War (1914–1918) and the depression, unemployment and hyperinflation that followed during the 1920s and 1930s. It was recognised that capitalism was changing, consequently Ardorno, Fromm, Horkheimer and Marcuse assessed and analysed changes in power and domination that was related to this.

When the National Socialists took power, the main players from the Frankfurt School left Germany for the USA and took up residence on the West coast. These critical theorists were shocked by the positivistic nature of research in the USA and how this form of inquiry was taken for granted in the social sciences. Indeed, critical theory was viewed as a means of temporarily freeing researchers from the bonds of positivism in particular and post-enlightenment thought in general. Following the Kantian tradition Fromm considered that even though:

> Enlightenment taught man that he could trust his own reason as a guide to establishing valid ethical norms and that he could rely on himself. The growing doubt of human autonomy and reason created a state of moral confusion where man is left without the guidance of either revelation or reason. (Fromm, 1997: 3)

Enlightenment had removed both spiritual and rational guidance and rendered nature an objective entity external to human existence. 'Men pay for the increase of their power with alienation from that which they exercise their power' (Adorno and Horkheimer, 1997: 9).

Within the critical theory approach there emerged the 'discourse of possibility', which was intrinsically linked with the dialectical transformations within the social sciences and the broader social changes these could bring about. In contrast to Enlightenment, thinkers such as Hegel and Marx and their dialectical immutable laws of spirit, history and the idea that (at least to a certain extent) human beings determined their own destinies and existence gave an impetus to social research. Indeed, critical theory was perceived as a generalised perspective where through education different strands of the tradition or schools of thought provided values, understanding and knowledge that engendered empowered critical beings who questioned the status quo. The main idea for critical theory was the formulation of social theory based on philosophical positions and empirical studies. Horkheimer (1972) considered that research programmes should absolve the opposition between the individual and social structures and the relationship between objectivity and subjectivity should be embraced.

What Is Critical Theory?

So what exactly is critical theory? In general, one may argue that critical theory is 'characterised by an interpretive approach combined with a pronounced interest in critically disputing actual social realities … The aim … is to serve the emancipatory project, but without making critical interpretations from rigid frames of reference' (Alvesson and Skoldberg, 2008 144). Unfortunately, for a number of reasons this is a difficult question to answer. As one would imagine because of its very nature there is much room for disagreement about what critical theory entails and a definitive perspective negate the very premise of critical theory. In such a way a number of different critical theories exist that renders it a continually evolving dialectical set of ideas. However, certain similarities between the strands of critical theory exist in terms of criticism of occidental complacency and that ruling elites and ideologies should be challenged as well as greater equality and liberty sought. Furthermore, most critical theorists consider that individual assumptions are influenced by social and historical forces and that historical realism provides a unifying ontological position.

Given these similarities it becomes possible to synthesise points of agreement and determine the basis for a paradigm of inquiry with a specific ontology, epistemology and appropriate methodological approaches. Such a synthesis exposes positions of power between institutions, groups and individuals as well as the role of agency in social affairs. In addition, this synthesis identifies the rules regulations and norms that prevent people from taking control of their own lives; the means by which they are eliminated from decision making and consequently controlled. Through making clear the relationships between power and control, agency may be extended and humanity emancipated. Of course, individuals are never completely free from the social and historical structures that they both construct and from which they emanate. Through shaping consciousness, power dominates human beings in social settings. Individual critical theorists disagree but one may argue, that power constitutes the foundation of social existence in that it constructs social and economic relations; that is, power is the basis of all political, social and organisational relationships.

Initial perspectives of critical theory espoused by Horkheimer considered that the paradigm of inquiry was about connecting critical theory with everyday life in the interest of abolishing social injustice. One of the main concerns for critical theory, as Adorno and Horkheimer argued was investigating the ultimate source or foundation of social domination, For Adorno and Horkheimer (1997) state intervention in the economy abolished the capitalist tension between the 'relations of production' and 'material productive forces of society', which according to traditional critical theory, constituted the primary contradiction within capitalism. The market (as an unconscious mechanism for the distribution of goods) and private property had been replaced by centralised planning and socialised ownership of the means of production. However, contrary to Marx's prediction, this did not lead to revolution but fascism and totalitarianism. As such, critical theory was bankrupt and left without anything to which it might appeal when the forces of production synthesise with the relations of production. For Adorno and Horkheimer, this posed the problem of how to account for the apparent persistence of domination in the absence of the contradiction that, according to traditional critical theory, was the very source of domination. Horkheimer, Adorno, Marcuse and Fromm rejected positivism and attempted to build 'social theories that were philosophically informed and (involved) practical political significance' (Alvesson and Skoldberg, 2008: 145).

The idea of the objective observer was challenged and 'specific methodological rules for acquiring knowledge' disputed (Alvesson and Skoldberg, 2008: 145). Knowledge recognises the opaqueness of common sense perceptions because as with the platonic cave what we see does not correspond with reality. Most individuals are 'half awake or dreaming'; to know means to 'penetrate through the surface in order to arrive at the roots, and ... knowing means to see reality in its nakedness ... to penetrate the surface and to strive critically and actively in order to approach truth ever more closely' (Fromm, 1997: 33).

In the 1960s, Habermas raised the epistemological discussion to a new level when he identified critical knowledge as based on principles that differentiated it either from the natural sciences or the humanities through orientations toward self-reflection and emancipation. Adorno and Horkeimer considered that the modern era illustrated a shift from the liberation of Enlightenment toward enslavement. Indeed the Enlightenment equates with positivism, because for 'the Enlightenment that which does not reduce to numbers, and ultimately to the one, becomes illusion; modern positivism rights it off as literature' (1997: 7). 'Under the leveling domination of abstraction (which makes everything in nature repeatable) and of industry (for which abstraction ordains repetition) the free themselves finally came to form that "herd", which Hegel has declared to be the result of Enlightenment' (Adorno and Horkeimer, 1997: 13).

Hegemony and Ideology

Hegemony (see Definition Box) is an important factor for critical theorists and exists when power is exercised through consent rather than force. People consent to their own domination through accepting notions propagated by cultural institutions, for example, the media, family, school and so forth. Even those researchers that comprehend hegemony are affected by it; this is because understandings of the world and knowledge fields are structured by different and competing definitions of society. Certain social relations are legitimised and considered the natural order of things; we give our hegemonic consent. However, this is never total because different groups in society have different perspectives and compete for hegemony. Critical theorists note these distinctions and utilise them in their research programmes. This given, it is difficult to divorce the idea of hegemony from that of ideology. Hegemony indicates the means by which powerful institutions formulate subordinate acceptance of domination through ideology. Ideology incorporates the meanings, norms, values and rituals that facilitate the acceptance of the social situations and the place of the individual within this. Hegemonic ideology allows critical theorists to understand the complex nature of domination and move beyond the idea that power is simply about coercion. Individuals are manipulated through media, education and politics to accept oppression as normal and the only situation that could exist; change is unthinkable and utopian.

Critical theorists comprehend hegemonic ideology as a means by which ideology and discourse construct our ontological positions or notion of reality. Consequently, different ideological positions exist at different points in time and provide the basis for a historical reality and that this reality changes through dialectical transformation. Indeed, the epistemological position places the researcher in the world that is constructed through people manipulated by power. Such identifies on-going struggles between and among individuals, groups and classes within society. Through their understanding of hegemonic ideology critical theorists investigate the relationships between classes and groups and the different values, agendas and visions they portray and adhere too. Furthermore, discourse is seen as historical and not a clear reflection of society but an unstable practice with meanings that shift in relation to the context within which it is used. Discourse does not provide a neutral objective description of an external world but incorporates the very building blocks we use to construct it.

The concentration on hegemonic ideology has implications for economic determinism and Enlightenment thinking some commentators consider was displayed by Karl Marx and Freidrich Engels in the *Communist Manifesto* (1849). Certain thinkers interpreted Marx and Engels as concentrating solely on the economic base rather than the social and political dynamisms of dialectical change. For Marx, economic base determined superstructure or economic factors determine all other elements of social life. Following the death of Marx, Engels did deny this but in works such as the *Communist Manifesto* and *Das Kapital,* this does seem to be the case. Engels stated that historical materialism involved the production and reproduction of reality and that neither, he nor Marx had ever inferred more than this. Indeed Engels indicated that economic determinism was senseless and that numerous variables relating to superstructure (ideology, politics, culture) were also part of the dialectical process. Neo-Marxists, such as Antonio Gramsci, accepted this position and further argued that through hegemony and ideology there existed interaction between base (economics) and superstructure. Indeed, based on neo-Marxist thought, the Frankfurt School accepted that many forms of power existed, for example, racial, gender, class.

Definition Box

Hegemony

This involves the means by which ruling elites obtain consent to dominate subordinates within their dominion. The worldviews of the rulers is diffused throughout society so as these become common sense; to question such norms appears to be nonsensical. The

(Continued)

exercise of hegemonic subordination involves a combination of 'force and consent which balance each other reciprocally without force predominating excessively over consent' (Gramsci, 2005: 80). Attempts are made to ensure that force is supported or consented by the majority and this is expressed through the 'so-called organs of public opinion – newspapers and association – which therefore in certain situations are artificially multiplied' (Gramsci, 2005: 80). Hegemony illustrates how ruling elites perpetuate their rule and domination through consent rather than coercion. Contending groups in any society must aim to control ideas in civil society; 'a social group must, already exercise leadership before winning governmental power' (Gramsci, 2005: 57). Leadership is a precondition of winning power and the consequent exercise of power; domination can only be legitimised and continued through hegemonic consent.

Critical Theory as a Critique of Instrumental Rationality and Positivism

As noted above, critical theorists also question the idea of instrumental rationality that is closely linked with Enlightenment thought. Such an understanding of rationality concentrates on a positivistic methodology and simplification. Research is limited to questions regarding 'how' or 'how to' rather than 'why' or 'why should'. Critical theorists argue that such a positivistic approach directs the researcher toward procedure and method rather than the more humanistic elements of the research process. Instrumental rationality is mainly concerned with objectivity and separates values and facts, which loses the interactive and iterative nature between values and facts in interpretation and understanding.

Critical theory accepts certain assumptions, these include:

- social and historical constituted power relations affect and mediate all ideas and thinking;
- values and facts can never be separated;
- facts always contain an ideological dimension;
- ideas and objects are mediated through social relations;
- relationships between signifier and signified are continually in flux;
- relations of capitalist production and consumption affect relationships between individuals and society;
- subjectivity is determined by discourse;
- privilege and oppression characterises social relations;
- oppression is more endemic when subordinates accept the hegemonic inevitability of their position in society;
- oppression is multi-faceted;
- positivistic research is elitist and unwittingly reproduces existing social power relations.

Critical theory involves ideas relating to empowerment of the people; it should challenge injustice in social relations and social existence. Whereas, for more traditional research approaches the objectives involve attempts at description, understanding and explanation, for critical theory transformational conscious emancipation is central and involves initial moves toward political activity. Research is not about the accumulation of knowledge but political activity and social transformation.

Reflexivity is a central mechanism for critical theory; or self conscious criticism. Underlying ideological perspectives are made explicit in relation to self-conscious subjectivity, inter-subjectivity, normative morality and epistemological precepts. Subjective pre-conceptions in terms of epistemological and political positions are incorporated with the research process. These are reflected upon and analysed in relation to the research and may change as this process progresses (for further on reflexivity see Chapter 13).

Reflection Box
Reconnecting Meaning

Bullying in the workplace may not be interpreted as isolated action pursued by socially pathological individuals but narratives of transgression and resistance identified by unconscious political perspectives underlying everyday interactions and related to power relations in terms of race, class and gender oppression.

Consider how bullying may be identified as a social phenomenon and assess its relationship with power.

Change in assumptions may emanate from a realisation of emancipator actions, which are revealed through interaction between the researcher and researched and the realisation that the dominant culture is not a natural state of affairs. This involves understanding both 'self' and society or 'other' in greater detail so inequality, exploitation and injustice are rendered explicit. Critical theory requires reconstruction of worldviews in ways that challenge and undermine what appears normal or natural. Research needs re-location toward transformative practice that pursues the alleviation of oppression and autocracy (see Reflection Box above). Questions regarding how things have become are paramount and link closely with the phenomenological position. Critical theorists challenge positivistic positions and traditions and questions whose interests are served by institutional arrangements. Correspondence theory is challenged and it is argued that facts are constructed in relation to values and meaning. Engagement in critical research involves formulating a critical world in relation to a faint idealised world conditioned by equality, liberty and justice; critical theory is about hope in a cynical world.

Critical theory involved a critique of the dominant position of positivism. Positivism had provided the basis for scientific study and knowledge accumulation during the rise of capitalism but by the 20th century incorporated endorsement of the status quo. In his essay 'Traditional and critical theory' Horkheimer asks 'what is theory?' He considered that for most individual researchers 'theory ... is the sum total of propositions about a subject, the propositions being so linked with each other that a few are basis and the rest derive from these' (1972: 188). In social research, basis propositions can be arrived at either inductively or deductively, then the researcher attempts a 'laborious ascent from the description of social phenomena to detailed comparisons and only then to the formation of general concepts' (Horkheimer, 1972: 192). How the primary principles were arrived at is secondary as the important element is that division exists between conceptual knowledge and the facts from which this was derived; or those facts to be subsumed under this framework. Indeed for traditional theory the 'genesis of particular objective facts, the practical application of the conceptual systems by which it grasps the facts and the role of such systems in action, are all taken to be external to the theoretical thinking itself' (Horkheimer, 1972: 208). Conversely, critical theory argued that such were false separations or alienation and the researcher was always part of the object under study so that object and subject were inextricably linked. The researcher is neither embedded in society nor abstraction from it; values, action, knowledge and theory generation were inseparable. Critical theory pursued change and liberation whereas traditional theory thought the 'individual as a rule must simply accept the basic conditions his existence as given and strive to fulfil them' (Horkheimer, 1972: 207).

Adorno and Horkheimer (1997) considered this issue further and examined two types of reason:

- pursuit of liberation from external constraints and compulsion;
- instrumental reason and technical control.

The former was linked to critical theory and the latter related to Enlightenment thought and during the early 20th century became the basis of totalitarianism, fascism and National Socialism. Positivism equated with Enlightenment as for each 'whatever does not conform to the rule of computation and utility is suspect' (Adorno and Horkheimer, 1997: 6). Indeed, like Aldous Huxley in his novel *Brave New World*, they argue that the culmination of Enlightenment involves non-thinking pleasure and limited analytic capability. 'Pleasure always means not to think about anything, to forget suffering even when it is shown. It is flight: not as is asserted flight from wretched reality, but the last remaining thought of resistance. The liberation that amusement promises is freedom from thought and negation' (Ardono and Horkheimer, 1997: 144). 'The power to respond to reason and truth exists in all of us.' However so too does the 'tendency to ... unreason and falsehood – particularly ... where the falsehood evokes some enjoyable emotion (and) primitive sub human depths of our being' (Huxley, 1994: 47). Critical theory perspectives accept our ability to reason and truth challenges negation and promotes resistance. Furthermore, Marcuse (2004) identifies how marketing and mass media achieves control and standardisation of expectations and needs. Marketing and mass media enables social control and develops individuals into malleable and predictable people who without critical analysis accept social situations and consumerism. He argued that in contemporary society under the rule of repression freedom and liberation could be used as a 'powerful instrument of domination' (2004: 9). The choices available do not determine the 'degree of human freedom, but what can be chosen and what is chosen by the individual. Free elections of masters does not abolish masters or slaves' (Marcuse, 2004: 9–10). Overall, critical theory challenged acceptance and wished to develop individual antipathy.

Critical Theory and Habermas

Habermas argued that control and understanding should be subordinate to emancipation and liberation. That social science should initially comprehend the 'ideologically distorted subjective situation of some individual or group … explore the forces that have caused that situation and … show that these forces can be overcome through awareness of them on the part of the oppressed individual or group in question' (Dryzeck, 1995: 99). The shift is one that challenges post-positivism through an interpretive, phenomenological approach to social science. Verification, in this context, is not achieved through experimentation but the action of those involved in the research process, who on reflection decide on a perspective based on their suffering and means of relief. In this way, post-positivism itself could be seen as a dominant form of reasoning which distorted reality in relation to liberal ideals and progress. Critical theory should initially 'understand the ideologically distorted subjective situation of some individual or group, second … explore the forces that have caused that situation and third to show that the forces that have caused this situation can be overcome' through making these forces clear to those groups or individuals that exist within these situations (Dryzeck, 1995: 99). Consequently, critical theory involves reflective action, specifically the reflective action of those individuals and groups involved in the research programme.

Critical theory illuminated the very basis and 'truth content' of liberal ideals such as freedom truth and justice and used them in its pursuit of an improved existence for humanity. In introducing his critical theory, Habermas (2004) identified the need for a fundamental paradigm shift. Understandings of theory needed to be moved from intellectual situations in which the ends justify the means or instrumentalism to one where communicative rationality took centre stage. Post-positivist pursuits of objectivity that ignored the worldviews, values and norms through which the world is structured failed to fully comprehend social phenomenon.

'Habermas was able to draw on developments in the phenomenological, ethno-methodological and linguistic traditions and thus ... anticipate the decline of positivism and rise of interpretivism' (McCarthy, 1999: 400). However, he argued that it would not be helpful to reduce social research to the interpretation of meaning because such meaning may conceal or distort as well as reveal and express human conditions. Habermas attempted to identify the main difficulties with positivism through a historical analysis of its early proponents and its links with Enlightenment.

> In place of controlled observation ... there arises participatory relation of the understanding subject to the subject confronting him. The paradigm is no longer the observation but the dialogue-thus, a communication in which the understanding subject must invest part of his subjectivity. (Habermas, 2004: 10–11)

Based on Pierce's reflections on natural science, Dilthy's historical and cultural inquiry and Freud's self-reflection, Habermas uncovered different types of knowledge and argued for an 'internal connection between structures of knowledge and anthropologically deep-seated human interests' (McCarthy, 1999: 401). He distinguished between technical interest in terms of positivistic prediction, control and objectified processes and the practical interest of mutual understanding and emancipatory interest of free flow undistorted communication between individual subjects (McCarthy, 1999: 401). Habermas attempted to 'reconstruct the formative process of the human species phenomenological self reflection was meant to expand the practical self understanding of social groups. Critical of ideology, it analysed the development of the forms of the manifestation of consciousness in relation to constellations of power and from the standpoint of an ideal social arrangement based on undistorted public communication' (McCarthy, 1999: 401). Critical theory 'resorts to interpretation based on hermeneutic disciplines, that is, we employ hermeneutics instead of a measurement procedure, which hermeneutics is not' (Habermas, 2004: 11).

'Critical of ideology (critical research) asks what lies behind the consensus, presented as a fact, and does so with a view to the relations surreptitiously incorporated in the symbolic structures of the systems of speech and action' (Habermas, 2004: 11–12, author's brackets). This may be achieved through communicative competence, which by uttering sentences, draws together subjectivity and objectivity through placing 'sentences in relation to the "external world" of objects and events, the "internal world" of a speaker's own experience, and a "social world" of shared normative expectation (McCarthy, 1999: 401–2). This recognises the existence of many truths and claims to truth regarding the external world and actions in relation to 'the shared social world' (McCarthy, 1999: 402). Social systems are different from machines or systems and reflect learning and subjective tendencies 'and are organised within the framework of ... communication' (Habermas, 2004: 12). Consequently, a systems theory for the social sciences 'must be developed in relation to a theory of ordinary language communication which also takes into consideration the relationship of intersubjectivity and the relation between ego and group identity' (Habermas, 2004: 13).

Conclusion

A general perspective of critical theory ontology involves an understanding that reality is shaped through social and historical processes and may be defined as 'historical realism'. The epistemological aspect of the critical theory paradigm considers that findings and theoretical perspectives are discovered because the investigator and investigated are intrinsically linked through historical values, which must influence the inquiry. This leads toward a specific methodology, which identifies a dialogic and dialectical approach. Dialogue is needed between the researcher and the researched and between past and present. In this methodology structures are changeable and actions affect change. In this context, theory is changeable in relation to historical circumstance. Theory is developed by human beings in historical and cultural circumstances as the interaction between researcher and researched and historical values influence the analysis.

Definition Box

Historical Realism

An example of this would be the nation-state in terms of its changing role within international relations and the issues this raised for ideas such as sovereignty and democratic accountability. As the role of the nation-state changes, so does our understanding of it, which has implications for our interpretation of reality in terms of the role of the state, the nation and sovereignty. Indeed, the EU and international institutions have implications for changes regarding these issues and provide the impetus for theoretical change as well as empirical outcomes (Howell, 2004).

Definition Box

Theory

Theory is not defined from a positivist perspective where immutable laws predict either forever or until they are displaced, but developed in a historical context: theory is developed by subjective humans in a historical context.

Aspects of the critical theory paradigm are based on phenomenology and include theoretical perspectives that challenged the status quo, for example, neo-Marxism, feminism, determinism and so forth, and provided a specific understanding of reality in that it is shaped by 'social, political, cultural, economic and gender values crystalised over time' (Guba and Lincoln, 1994: 105). Indeed, in his search for the essence of truth Heidegger begins with the question of what is truth which leads to historical reflection and that the pursuit of truth is to understand it in a historical context and as a reflection of the past. Humanity

> alone can be historical i.e., can stand and does stand in that open region of goals, standards, drives, and powers by withstanding this region and existing in the mode of forming, directing, acting carrying out, and tolerating. Only man is historical – as that being which, exposed to all beings as a whole, and in commerce with these beings, sets himself free in the midst of necessity. (Heidegger, 1994: 34)

This incorporates historical ontology, a process of temporality and being in the world. An example of this would be the nation-state in terms of its changing role within international relations and the issues this raised for ideas such as sovereignty and democratic accountability. As the role of the nation-state changes, so does our understanding of it, which has implications for our interpretation of reality in terms of the role of the state, the nation and sovereignty (Howell, 2004). Indeed, these changes having implications for Being and interpretations of the world in relation to Being which provide the impetus for theoretical change as well as empirical outcomes.

Phenomenology is also displayed in the epistemological aspect of the critical theory paradigm, which considered that findings and theoretical perspectives are discovered because the investigator and investigated are intrinsically linked through historical values, which must influence the inquiry. However, in this context the distinction between ontology and epistemology begins to break down. For example, 'Heidegger breaks with Husserl and Cartesian tradition by substituting for epistemological questions … ontological questions' (Dreyfus, 1991: 3). Substituting questions relating to the relationship between the investigator and the researched, for questions regarding what can be known and how humanity is bound with the intelligibility of the world (Dreyfus, 1991). The means by which we can know the world was re-assessed and 'by attending to the enigmatic of the everyday – exposing the unnoticed metaphysical presuppositions by means of which we understand the everyday and behind which the everyday is concealed' a clearer understanding and explanation of being and the world may be realised (Faulconer, 2000: 3).

Further Reading

Adorno, T.W. and Horkheimer, M. (1997) *Dialectic of Enlightenment*. London: Verso.
Critchley, S. and Schroeder, W.R. (1999) *A Companion to Continental Philosophy*. Oxford: Blackwell.

Denzin, N. and Lincoln, Y. (1994) *The Handbook of Qualitative Research,* 1st edn. Thousand Oaks, CA: SAGE Publications.

Denzin, N. and Lincoln, Y. (2000) *The Handbook of Qualitative Research,* 2nd edn. Thousand Oaks, CA: SAGE Publications.

Denzin, N. and Lincoln, Y. (2005) *The Handbook of Qualitative Research,* 3rd edn. Thousand Oaks, CA: SAGE Publications.

Fromm, E.T. (1997) *To Have or To Be?* New York: Continuum.

Fromm, E.T. (2004) *The Fear of Freedom.* London: Routledge.

Honderich, T. (1995) *The Oxford Companion to Philosophy.* Oxford: Oxford University Press.

Kearney, R. and Rainwater, M. (eds) (1998) *The Continental Philosophy Reader.* London: Routledge.

SIX

Constructivist and Participatory Paradigms of Inquiry: Introducing Action Research

Introduction

This chapter provides two further examples of paradigms of inquiry (constructivism and participatory) that relate to phenomenological ontological perspectives in terms of 'being-in the-world' and having 'inalienable presence'. Constructivism understands reality as being locally constructed and based on shared experiences and, because groups/individuals are changeable, identifies it as 'relativist realism' or 'relative ontology'. Epistemologically, constructivism is similar to critical theory, however research results are created through consensus and individual constructions, including the constructions of the investigator. Theory in this paradigm is relative and changeable, reliability and prediction almost impossible and cause and effect difficult to identify. Navon argued that 'for a rationalist, the mind *unveils* reality; for post-modernists, the mind *invents* reality whereas for constructivists the mind *creates* reality and claims that facts are produced by human consciousness' (Navon, 2001: 624).

The participatory paradigm involves a co-created reality through the interaction between mind and world; in other words both subjective and objective elements exist and a participative process develops reality. For the participatory paradigm, experience underpins the epistemology; critical subjectivity or reflexivity interacts with the practical world and the common sense knowledge related to this. Consequently, the methodological position involves collaboration and action with everyday existence and language or discourse involving a primary aspect of the research process. Both paradigms of inquiry construct and develop reality through interaction between mind and world. However, the participatory paradigm relies heavily on action research, consequently this chapter explains this specific methodological approach and its close relationship with this paradigm. Action research considers that research incorporated undertaking experiments in the field (Lewin, 1946). Lewin (1946) argued that an action research experiment must express theory in such a way that the results of the experiment can be fed directly back to the theory as action research emerged out of an assumption that theory can be directly expressed in action. This chapter first outlines distinctions between social constructionalism and social constructivism. However, following discussions regarding these areas it employs the term constructivism to identify a general paradigm which incorporates nuances relating to the different but complimentary perspectives. Based on the assumption that there is a distinction between the social and natural world, 'constructivist inquirers seek to understand contextualised meaning … the meaningfulness of human actions and interactions – as experienced and construed in a given context' (Greene, 2000: 986). Second, this chapter provides an overview of constructivism and identifies weak and strong perceptions of the paradigm of inquiry and it then relates the stronger variant to notions relating to the participatory paradigm. Finally, it introduces action research with clear indications of how the participatory paradigm underpins and informs this methodological approach.

Social Constructivism and Constructionalism

Social constructivism and social constructionalism incorporate different perspectives of how reality is developed and understood. The former consider that individuals develop and give meaning to the world while the latter argue that meaning is developed through social amelioration and agreement. They come from different directions but each amounts to a similar position in that reality is not external to human existence but determined and defined through social interaction. Symbolic interactionism identifies this process in terms of self and other defining the individual and community; 'through language and structure we become a generalised other … we attain consciousness of self as a generalised other' (Howell, 2000: 27).

Symbolic interaction is distinct to human beings because it is part of what makes us human, rather than simply reacting to human action we interpret or define it (Blumer, 1962). Humans have and are able to act towards self. Mead (1962) considered that the ability to react to self was the central mechanism of existence.

> This mechanism enables the human being to make indication to himself of things in his surroundings and thus to guide his action by what he notes. Anything of which a human being is conscious … he is indicating to himself … The conscious life of the human being . . . is a continual flow of self indications. (Mead, 1962: 180).

Fundamentally, 'the formation of action by the individual through … self-indication always takes place in a social context' (1962: 183). In other words, community and self are intrinsically linked and the distinction between self and community difficult to ascertain. Consequently, even though distinctions exist between social constructivism and social constructionism with an emphasis on the individual in the former and community in the latter, both meet in the formulation or construction of reality. Indeed, there are many differing definitions of what social constructivists and social constructionists entail so to determine the point where self and other congregate to define, determine and construct reality, this chapter will draw together these terms in a generic context (as a general paradigm of inquiry) and the term constructivism will be employed (see Denzin and Lincoln, 1994, 2000, 2005).

Constructivism

For constructivism, humanity alone is responsible for knowledge development and understanding is a matter of interpretive construction on the part of the active subject. 'Constructivism argues that any so-called reality is in the most immediate and concrete sense-the construction of those who believe that they have discovered and investigated it' (Watzlawick, 1984: 10). Guba and Lincoln posited that for the constructivist paradigm, the core assumption is that realities are not objectively 'out there' but are constructed by people, often under the influence of a variety of social and cultural factors that lead to shared construction (1989: 12). Guba and Lincoln subsequently concurred that such socially constructed realities are not independent of the 'observer' (constructor) but are absolutely dependent on him or her for whatever existence they have (1989: 13). An external ontology is far from the primary focus and as for certain phenomenologists reality is already in mind and verification of this reality entails a pre-conceptualisation of what exists. The main criticism of constructivism involves the relativist reduction and self-refutation; reality is constructed so all constructions are true realities. This given, can truth in one construction be truth for all or even another separate construction? Can any form of generalisation be realised? Truth can only be realised for a given situation and not for another; consequently, it can be true and false simultaneously. Furthermore, because the basis of two social structures are totally different each has an incommensurable worldview and comparative judgement between them is impossible; so how may distinctions regarding truth be assessed?

Guba and Lincoln (1985) considered key axioms were structurally configured into the constructivist paradigm. They defined axioms as 'the set of undemonstrated … "basic beliefs" accepted by convention or established by practice as the building blocks of some conceptual or theoretical structure or system' (1985: 37). Constructivist axioms involve holistic, multiple realities and the fact that multiple realities raise more questions than answers; prediction and causality are unlikely outcomes of constructivist research although levels of understanding (*verstehen*) can be achieved (Guba and Lincoln, 1985). Epistemologically in the constructivist paradigm, researcher and researched continually interact and influence one another and the research project involves limited possibilities regarding generalisation. Only temporal and context-bound working hypotheses (idiographic statements) are possible. As such, 'within the possibility of causal linkages … all entities are in a state of mutual simultaneous shaping; so that it is impossible to distinguish causes from effects. Finally, the enquiry is value bound' (Guba and Lincoln, 1985: 37). Overall, the axiological position involves subjectivity and the inclusion and acceptance of values and bias.

Constructivism contradicts positivism and rational reconstructions of scientific knowledge in terms of scientific statements (explanation and description through hypotheses, theories and observations). Similar to critical theorists, constructivists take up critical positions in relation to accepted or normal interpretations of the world or the way things are or seem. In contrast with critical theory constructivism does not elevate history, culture and tradition. Foundationalists consider that through assumptions of meaning, knowledge involves precise reflection of an independent reality; that is, knowledge, language and self interlock through a set of assumptions relating to meaning. These involve the following ideas:

- meanings of words relate to things or situations;
- language exhibits a logical structure that enables meaning;
- descriptive and evaluative aspects of language should not be confused.

These elements provide a picture or representation of an external reality and the existence of a bed-rock of basic beliefs (see Definition Box, below).

Definition Box

Foundationalism

Knowledge is justified through basic beliefs such a 'I think therefore I am.' 'There is no doubt that I exist ... one must ... take as assured that the proposition: I am, I exist, is necessarily true, every time I express it or conceive of it in my mind' (Descartes, 1968: 103). Basic beliefs provide support and justification for other beliefs. A basic belief does not require justification.

This perspective of ontology and epistemology is challenged by constructivists, who consider that the mind is active in the construction of knowledge and knowing is interactive with data rather than simply abstractions reflected by the mind. We construct knowledge through continual interaction and modification of constructions in a social environment. Understanding is constructed through interpretations in the world. Constructivism may also be termed perspectivism; this is where all knowledge claims or knowledge evaluation takes place through a conceptual framework by which the world is described and explained. Naïve realism is negated and empirical epistemology challenged; the idea that an external reality from an objective standpoint can be mirrored is negated. Potter (1996) considered that constructivism was linked with ethnomethodology and conversation analysis and that reality was formulated by the way we discuss, write and dispute issues in the world.

Constructivists take umbrage with what may be labelled 'meaning realism', which considers that meanings are fixed, external to the inquirer and discovered through research processes. However, in certain instances constructivism neither denies or affirms the existence of an external objective world out there. Gergen

(1994) argued that constructivism was agnostic regarding the idea of an objective reality but was certain that humanity gave language meaning through interaction. Ideas regarding meaning and coming into being are shared by Heidegger who would agree that we are self-interpreting entities and that language defines the entities we are (our very being). Where disagreement may occur relates to the extent that language (or discourse) is able to identify meaning and truth.

Types of Constructivism

A general assumption for constructivism is that knowledge is based in politics and interests; it is ideological and culture is based upon and determined through value. Schwandt (2000) identified a distinction between weak and strong constructivism. Both weak and strong constructivism involves the idea that knowledge was not abstract but socially bound and value laden. However, even though the weaker perspective shows the ideological and political dimensions of constructivism, there is an attempt to comprehend how the real world can constrain knowledge construction. Indeed, observations and experiential data are based in notions relating to hypothesis testing and validation and incorporate difficult elements to be challenged and dismissed.

Weak constructivism is linked with critical theory and attempts to unveil the ideological perspectives of knowledge discovery, generation and accumulation. Longino (1993a) argued that methods used to organise and analyse data and identify cause and effect are not epistemologically free from interference; they are 'contextual' and intersubjective in terms of assumptions, beliefs and culture. Indeed, these are 'the vehicles by which social values and ideology are expressed in inquiry and become subtly inscribed in theories hypotheses and models defining research programmes' (Longino, 1993a: 263). Consequently, as long as we think that knowledge is produced through individual cognition it will not be possible to take these variables into consideration. If research programmes accept contextual and intersubjectivity they can begin to deal with and critique background assumptions. Longino (1993b) outlines a set of criteria that would allow a transformation of critical discourse; these include:

- shared standards of evaluation;
- community response to criticism;
- equality of intellectual authority.

Furthermore, Longino (1993a) also considered that experimentation and observation were not totally under the control of the autonomous objective researcher; all is contextual, intersubjective and incorporates background assumptions. Background assumptions require criticism, which necessitates an understanding that objectivity involves social interaction and knowledge construction is a social activity. Only when these premises are activated and numerous alternative points of view deployed can background assumptions be critically evaluated. Such an approach enables the researcher to identify and challenge values and interests that can otherwise seem the norm and seen as necessary aspects of research programmes and processes. As with critical theory Longino (1993b) argued that situations should be organised and structured that facilitated critique, and that this critique should concentrate on the following issues:

- how communities react to criticism;
- the extent communities tolerate criticism;
- levels of shared evaluative standards;
- who has intellectual authority.

For weak constructivism, practical issues are interwoven with naturalistic scientific inquiry; that is, science is part of the process and objectivity an element within knowledge production. When certain scientific procedures are accepted and objectivity endorsed, the idea that any explanation or interpretation will do can be challenged and negated.

Strong constructivism developed through the recognition that language is part of social existence and that evaluation of beliefs depend on the language games from which said beliefs emanate. In this context, 'the meanings of different language games or different forms of life are incommensurable' (Schwandt, 2000: 200). When this is linked with the idea of many continually changing realities we are led to epistemological relativism; all knowledge is produced through social structures and truth, good or reality are formed by the different communities of interpreters that inhabit them. Consequently, all statements relating to values are community based so should be treated with suspicion and continually doubted. For certain thinkers this does not curtail knowledge development but leads toward greater democracy in thought and discussion and the enhancement of critique and reflection of the human condition (Gergen, 1994). In a similar way, Denzin (1997) rejects epistemological relativism when he argued that through experience the world can be accurately depicted. Through the individual's socio-historical position the world of experience may be studied and experienced (see Question below). However, he also agrees that 'ethnographic practices given to writing moral and allegorical tales … are a method of empowerment for readers and a means … to discover moral truths about themselves' (Schwandt, 2000: 200).

QUESTION

EPISTEMOLOGICAL RELATIVISM

- Given the absence of cross-framework criteria how can we decide which is the most democratic or best for human existence?
- Does the construction of moral tales assume a truth or morality?
- If so, which socio-historical position provides the most accurate interpretation?

Participatory Paradigm

This chapter also investigates and explains the emerging participatory paradigm of inquiry. The participatory paradigm is based on certain phenomenological positions as its ontology perceives reality as integrated with human existence and interaction between subjective and objective perspectives; there is a strong leaning toward being-in-the-world. Indeed, reality is co-created through mind and cosmos or external world. The epistemological position here involves critical subjectivity of the self in participatory transaction with the cosmos or other. Findings are co-created through practitioner attributes such as experience and practical knowledge. This means that methodology in this paradigm of inquiry encapsulates collaborative action and political participation through the primacy of practice and language grounded in shared experience and situational context. This latest paradigm rests on the belief that reality involves interaction between the world, self and inner historical being. The mind 'creatively participates with [the cosmos] and can only know it in terms of its constructs, whether affective, imaginal, conceptual or practical' (Heron, 1996: 10). Mind and cosmos interact in a creative process and what emerges as reality is the outcome of this process; reality involves the outcomes of iterative interaction between mind or selves and world or cosmos (Heron and Reason, 2000).

The participatory paradigm offers an alternative means for undertaking social research projects and programmes. It is based on liberation, neo-Marxist and liberal human rights (so in this context related to critical theory). The participatory paradigm differs from other approaches in the following ways:

- ownership of the research is shared (co-ownership);
- analysis of social problems undertaken by the community;
- community action.

Reason and Bradbury (2001: 6–7) described this paradigm as systematic, holistic, relational, feminine, experiential and participatory.

> Our world does not consist of separate things but of relationships which we co-author. We participate in our world, so that the 'reality' we experience is a co-creation that involves the primal 'givenness' of the cosmos and human feeling and construing; as we participate in creating our world we are already embodied and breathing beings who necessarily act – and this draws us to consider how to judge the quality of our actions.

These thoughts reflect ideas outlined by Heidegger in terms of becoming and Merleau-Ponty regarding being in the world. Furthermore, the judgement is already in formation as our action determines that to be judged and the actual judgement itself.

Skrbina (2001: 2) provided a description of this new paradigm and considered that the mechanistic worldview encourages reductionism and a dualist subject-object approach to reality, while the participatory worldview empha-sises a holistic cooperative perspective; the participatory worldview incorporates a strong axiological component while the mechanistic worldview is ethically neutral and detached. Where the mechanistic worldview investigates the world via positivism and quantitative methods, the participatory worldview uses new methodologies of participation and action research. Overall, 'the mechanistic worldview sees a world of dead inert matter while the participatory worldview sees an active, animated, and co-created reality' (Skrbina, 2001: 2).

For the participatory paradigm of inquiry, knowledge is organic and firmly based on the critical subjectivity and practical understandings of the researcher and researched; it is developed in communities of practice. The criteria of quality regarding the participatory paradigm involves the fit between experiential prac-tice (again similar to critical theory) and the extent this leads to transformational action and human improvement. Consequently, the values of the researcher and researched are included in the research process and these are used to reveal the actuality of the situations under analysis. Voice emanates through self-reflection and action with secondary voices made explicit through discourse, theory, song and dance etc. Facilitation is important in this paradigm because co-researchers are actively engaged in a learning process; empathy is required as is a democratic perspective and egalitarian skills base. The axiology or the relevance of knowl-edge incorporates practical knowing regarding growth of autonomous individu-als and a cooperative society in general is an end in itself. In such a way the participatory paradigm is closely related to both the critical theory and construc-tivist paradigms. As with constructivism both control of the research process is shared and validity incomplete without action. Many equal voices are apparent in the research and reflexivity is central. The research process relies on critical subjectivity, empathy and understanding of self in relation to others. Criticisms of the participatory paradigm include:

- absence of scientific rigour;
- dresses action up as research;
- researcher identification with communities under analysis;
- alienation from wider research community;
- confusion between social activism and research.

Table 6.1 Mechanistic and participatory worldviews

Mechanistic worldview	Participatory worldview
Reductionist and dualist in approach	Holistic perspective to research
Pursues a value-free approach	Values accepted and incorporated into the study
Positivist and quantitative	Phenomenological and qualitative
Studies inert and stable matter	Studies active, animated, changeable matter

Some consider that rather than research the participatory paradigm involves political agendas and is politically motivated; that communities are manipulated and exploited by researchers with agendas of their own. It is not communities that identify problems but researchers and through action the welfare of these communities are put at risk or alienated from their society.

Action Research

Action research is closely linked to the participatory paradigm of inquiry and concentrates on undertaking research with people rather than on or about them. Participants are involved in the research process and situation, which will usually take place in their own groupings or organisations. Participants are involved in the data gathering and analysis and plot the success and direction of the research; this means developing questions and answers as shared experiences in a group of co-researchers. This methodology attempts to overcome the power imbalance between researcher and researched and provide a democratic open environment. 'Action research aims to solve pertinent problems in given contexts through democratic inquiry in which professional researchers collaborate with local stakeholders to seek and enact solutions to problems of major importance to the stakeholders' (Greenwood and Levin, 2000: 96). However, there are numerous strategies relating to these themes; each similar but with differing levels of interaction and democracy and involves human beings creating reality through participation, experience and action (Denzin and Lincoln, 1994). Action research also allows for participation of other partners so that shared interpretations can be developed. Positivist and post-positivist paradigms and associated methodologies have a long established history and have their usefulness in certain situations; they are nonetheless inappropriate in a situation where the principal objective of the research is to seek and effect change. Greenwood and Levin label this '*cogenerative inquiry* because it is built on professional researcher-stakeholder-collaboration' (2000: 96). Indeed, action research requires five main tenets:

1 Knowledge cogenerated through interaction between researchers and participants within the research programme.
2 Meaning formulated in the research process becomes practice; findings lead to social action.
3 Further and new meaning is formulated through reflection on social actions.
4 Different experiences are perceived as means of enriching the research process and the following social action.
5 Research is contingent and contextual, based in the field or real world and deals with problems apparent within these situations. (Greenwood and Levin, 2000)

AN INTRODUCTION TO THE PHILOSOPHY OF METHODOLOGY

It is often the case that those who apply action research as a methodology involve practitioners who wish to improve understanding of their practice and can be:

- social change activists trying to mount an action campaign;
- academics who have been invited into an organisation (or other domain) by decision-makers aware of a problem requiring action research.

Research within areas relating to sustainability, the environment and socio-economic development recognise that resource management issues are not so much characterised by problems for which an answer is required, but rather by issues which need to be resolved and will inevitably necessitate one or more of the parties to change their views. Social change depends on the commitment and understanding of those involved in the change process. In other words, if people work together on a common problem clarifying and negotiating ideas and concerns, they will be more likely to change their minds if endeavours regarding joint research indicate such change is necessary. Action research involves participation in the research process where researcher and researched develop the research programme together so people can be provided with the interaction and support necessary to make fundamental changes in practice, which endure beyond the research process.

Overall, exploring the social process of learning about situations is inextricably linked with the acts of changing those situations. Results from surveys and other methods of social research assist interpretation. However, so does information regarding why individuals comprehend things as they do. It is by bringing these aspects into the open and stimulating debate between the different groups through action research that the social variables are brought into the process. Thus, the action research approach seeks to influence the phenomena being studied during the action research process itself, in the belief that the true nature of social systems (social, cultural and institutional considerations) become most evident when you seek to make changes to them.

Different Types of Action Research

There are a number of different approaches to action research, which include:

- critical action research;
- action learning;
- action science;
- industrial action research.

Critical action research involves intense reflexivity on behalf of all those involved in the research process. Issues relating to power relations, language usage and strategies for improvement are paramount when developing a research programme and undertaking the research. Participation is central as is a strong desire to uncover the emergence and existence of injustice, inequality and oppression in an industrialised world. There is some criticism of this methodological approach in that it may be used as a means of developing radical ideologies in local communities. However, this does perceive and consider those being researched or under investigation from a positivist perspective and denies the self-understanding and reflexivity components. That said this may simply be a mirage and there still exists imposition by researchers on malleable non-participatory individuals and communities.

Action learning involves bringing people together to deal with specific management problems; people learn together and the researcher is directly involved with this process (researchers get their hands dirty). Individuals congregate and learn from one another's experiences; each studies their own situation, identifies what needs to be dealt with and removes difficulties that detract from objectives. Overall, management efficiency is central. However, this is a major criticism of action learning because if the main concern is efficient management, then effective change and other work place issues may be ignored. If efficiency is paramount then wider values and purposes relating to organisations are dismissed. Action learning could be seen as the opposite of critical action research because learning is determined by the researcher and the consequent outcome complicity rather than critique.

The main principle for *action science* involves relationship construction between organisational psychology and actual practical difficulties as they are experienced in the situation under analysis. Distinctions between formal theories or theories in the abstract and substantive theories or theories in use are identified. This may be seen as differentiations between theory and practice and 'the gap' between these the point from where problems transpire (see Chapter 2 on theory, Chapter 9 on grounded theory and below for further on the distinctions between formal and substantive theory). Indeed, the point between theory and practice is where organisational cover-ups occur. Action science wishes to develop the reflective practitioner (RP) (Schon, 1983) and identify a distinction between the expert and RP the expert must have total knowledge even though uncertainties exist whereas the RP accepts and embraces uncertainty because this may become the source of new knowledge. The expert looks for deference and distance from the client but the RP pursues contact and connection so through recognition of expertise and knowledge respect can emerge and further develop as the project progresses (Schon, 1983). 'Judge the man rather than his knowledge. Challenge him and see how he responds to challenge. Look for the combination of confidence and humility, advocacy of a position and openness to inquiry which is a characteristic of reflective competence' (Schon, 1983:

301). Distance from the researched or 'client' ensures 'deference' and reinforces the expert 'persona'. The reflective practitioner embraces uncertainties as sources for further learning and even though he/she has some understanding of the situation they should not be considered founts of all knowledge. Understanding is a joint exercise and knowledge is 'discovered' as it 'emerges' from the context or research environment. Connectivity between researcher and researched demolishes the 'facade' of expertise and aloof objective perspectives that the professional approach engenders (Schon, 1983: 300).

Definition Box

The Reflective Practitioner

Embrace and utilise your own Ignorance
Source Risks of intended Outcomes
Seek out Multiple Views (Triangulate). (adapted from Schon, 1983: 301)

Industrial action research (IAR) is similar to action science in terms of reflection but is primarily based on consultancy with a drive to develop relationships between social sciences and organisational actors. Democratisation is an underpinning idea in terms of the workplace and the research process itself; rather than efficiency the emphasis for IAR is on organisational effectiveness and the improvement of employee relations. In general, 'participatory action research has evolved as an extension of applied research into practical social settings with participants taking on roles formerly occupied by social researchers from outside the settings' (Kemmis and Mctaggart, 2000: 572).

Conclusion

This conclusion draws these ideas together and indicates how through synthesising ontological and epistemological positions, post-positivism, critical theory, constructivism and participation may enable the synthesis of methodological approaches and theoretical frameworks when analysing social science phenomenon. The constructivist paradigm is closely linked with critical theory and displays certain phenomenological underpinnings. Constructivism understands reality as locally constructed and based on shared experiences, even though groups/individuals are changeable; ontologically, this identifies 'relativist realism'. Epistemologically, constructivism is similar to critical theory except that it considers that findings are created and develop as the investigation progresses. This means that results are created through consensus and individual constructions, including the constructions of the investigator. Theory in this paradigm is relative and changeable, reliability and prediction almost impossible and cause and effect difficult to identify. Furthermore, we have a new emerging paradigm or the participatory paradigm that again is linked closely with phenomenological approaches. The ontology here is participative, which incorporates co-creation of the world through mind and cosmos through both subjectivity and objectivity. The epistemology involves critical reflexivity and subjectivity through transactions between self and world. Findings are co-created through practical and theoretical knowledge in the context of becoming. Methodologically, this involves action research in its numerous forms and collaboration in terms of a practical and shared experience.

Closely linked to this emerging paradigm is action research which returns social research to the objective of 'knowing how' (*phronesis*) 'by acting on the phenomena, and away from *techne's* world of inaction and putative distance from the subject' (Greenwood and Levin, 2000: 97). Knowledge is cogenerated and aimed at developing strategies for social action and social change; knowledge generation through action research is closely related to action. Theory and practice become intimately related to one another, they interact, are iterative and provide an in-depth comprehension of specific situations. However, because research is specific to certain practical problems in precise situations, generalisation is difficult. This said, through theory-based evaluation of programmes related to social action, it is possible 'to contribute to generalisable knowledge about how social interventions work and the conditions and factors that enable and obstruct their success' (Greene, 2000: 993).

Further Reading

Burr, V. (2010) *Social Constructionism*. London: Routledge.
Critchley, S. and Schroeder, W.R. (1999) *A Companion to Continental Philosophy*. Oxford: Blackwell.
Denzin, N. and Lincoln, Y. (1994) *The Handbook of Qualitative Research,* 1st edn. Thousand Oaks, CA: SAGE Publications.
Denzin, N. and Lincoln, Y. (2000) *The Handbook of Qualitative Research,* 2nd edn. Thousand Oaks, CA: SAGE Publications.
Denzin, N. and Lincoln, Y. (2005) *The Handbook of Qualitative Research,* 3rd edn. Thousand Oaks, CA: SAGE Publications.
Reason, P. and Bradbury, H. (eds) (2001) *The SAGE Handbook of Action Research. Participative Inquiry and Practice*. London: SAGE Publications.

SEVEN

Postmodernism and Post-structuralism

Introduction

Modernism and aspects of structuralism relate to positivism whereas postmodernism and post-structuralism may correspond with aspects of phenomenology, critical theory constructivism and participatory paradigms of inquiry. For modernism the 'threat to (conventional) order comes … where conceptual categories change at a pace different from linguistic ones, the tensions are immediate' (McFarlane, 1976: 92–3). In a situation where the pattern that language and thinking impose on experience necessitates fundamental revision, and when the required discourse no longer reflects the situation, 'a crisis of culture and with it the inauguration of a wholly new "civilisation phase" is inevitable' (McFarlane, 1976: 92–3).

Lyotard (2004) uses the term postmodern to describe the condition of knowledge in occidental developed societies. Postmodernism identifies elements of occidental cultural transformation since the late 19th and early 20th centuries that have affected the 'game rules for science, literature and arts' (Lyotard, 2004: xxiii). Furthermore, modern is considered to 'designate science that legitimates itself with reference to a metadiscourse … making an explicit appeal to grand narrative, such as the dialectics of spirit, the hermeneutics of meaning, the emancipation of the rational or working subject, or the creation of wealth' (Lyotard, 2004: xxiii). 'Postmodern knowledge is not simply a tool of the authorities; it refines our sensitivity to differences and reinforces our ability to tolerate the incommensurable' (Lyotard, 2004: xxv). Lyotard (2004) argued that society should reject grand narratives or grand theory because by the second half of the 20th century they had lost their validity and credibility. Postmodernism is anti-authoritarian and enables arguments and techniques to formulate dissent and construct value judgements in the absence of authoritative narratives or grand universal theoretical frameworks. Postmodernism, 'provides us with the arguments and techniques to make (gestures) of dissent, as well as how to make value judgements in the absence of such overall authorities (Sim, 1998: 3).

Structuralism can be represented by the ideas of Ferdinand de Sausser (1857–1913), Claude Levi-Straus (1913–2009) and Roland Barthes (1915–80). Levi-Strauss considered that structuralism involved human beings defining and understanding the external world (like empiricists) through the senses. Consequently, the way we interpret the world and the characteristics we bestow upon it are ordered or structured by the way we interpret incoming data. Indeed, this data is ordered and structured through segmenting things or space into classes and time into sequential separated events. So, when we structure the human world or order society our comprehension of nature is imitated; culture is segmented and structured in the same way as we believe nature to be ordered.

Understanding of structuralism was further instigated through the work of Saussure who argued that language was a system and that this system of rules and regulations determined how language operated. Language involved a signifier (the word) and signifier (the concept or idea) and that these two elements made up the signs of language or meaning. Indeed, even though there was no natural relationship between signifier and signified, convention provided a level of stability between them which produced predictable meaning in a linguistic community. This allows generalisation to all subject areas and undermines the likelihood of variation. Narratives become very similar and the analysis of any given situation could be pre-determined. Indeed, this was the main criticism that post-structuralists had of the structuralist mechanistic approach. There was limited opportunity for the unexpected or creativity in the latter's approach; one could determine similarities between systems but difference and unpredictability were difficult to ascertain. For structuralism:

> one system (or narrative) comes to seem much like any other, and the analysis of its grammar becomes a fairly predictable exercise, almost as if one knew beforehand what one was going to find; one could even argue and post-structuralists did, that the analytical techniques being used by the structuralists determined the results. (Sim, 1998: 5)

This involved a level of determinism to the structuralists approach when undertaking research programmes and analysis (Sim, 1999).

Post-structuralism and postmodernism are used in different ways by different authors to challenge structuralist and modernist positions. One may consider post-structuralism as an aspect of postmodernism that concentrates on discourse and language patterns linked with subjectivity and identity. Derrida and the idea of deconstruction can be seen as post-structuralist or postmodernist. Deconstruction identifies proposed meanings of texts (the meaning the text wishes to portray), then exposes the contradictions on which supposed meanings are founded. Subsequently, deconstruction illustrates that the foundation on which the portrayal of meanings are based is unstable and complex. The text is not a unified entity with one meaning but many different contradictory meanings and interpretations.

Foucault may be seen as a post-structuralist and/or postmodernist. For instance, Margolis (1989) thought Foucault 'a typical example of a post-modernist' because he considered deconstruction parasitical and reactive in relation to texts and that a more holistic or rounded interpretation of history, power and controlling ideas were required. However, Foucault himself shied away from labels and did not relish being considered a postmodernist (Foucault, 1983). Roland Barthes was concerned with the relationship between the structure of a sentence and the more general narrative; he considered this structuralist approach useful but following Derrida and the idea of deconstruction, his work argued that not only signs and symbols were limited but so was the entire occidental dependency on ideas relating to constant ultimate standards.

▓▓▓▓▓▓▓▓▓▓▓▓▓▓▓▓▓▓▓▓▓▓▓▓▓▓▓ QUESTION ▓▓▓▓▓▓▓▓▓▓▓▓▓▓▓▓▓▓▓▓▓▓▓▓▓▓▓

STRUCTURALISM, POST-STRUCTURALISM AND POSTMODERNISM

- Levi-Strauss
- Barthes
- Foucault
- Derrida

Explain whether each of these thinkers is a structuralist, post-structuralist or postmodernist.

Identify the distinction between structuralism, post-structuralism and postmodernism.

One may argue that postmodernism deals with a more generic critique of culture and post-structuralists concentrate on method. 'For example, post-structuralists concentrate on deconstruction, language, discourse, meaning and symbols while postmodernists cast a broader net; they consider social existence and phenomenon in general' (Rosenau, 1992: 3).

Postmodernism

Postmodernism is a form of scepticism (scepticism of authority), which sets out to question and undermine theoretical frameworks claiming ultimate truth or knowledge. Scepticism is 'anti-foundational', which disputes the idea that discourse has valid foundations. 'Scepticism is an essentially negative form of philosophy, which sets out to undermine other philosophical theories claiming to be in possession of ultimate truth, or of a criteria for determining what counts as ultimate truth' (Sim, 1998: 3). Anti-foundationalists dispute the validity of the basis of truth and inquire into the extent that a foundation of truth can exist. 'What guarantees the truth of your foundation (that is, starting point) in its turn?' (Sim, 1998: 3).

Definition Box

Anti-Foundationalism and Scepticism

- Anti-foundationalism or non-foundationalism involves the idea that knowledge is not founded on some basic belief. That is x is justified by a basic belief or by a set or chain of beliefs that are justified by a basic belief.
- Scepticism begins with given indubitable truths then investigates rationales to dispute the grounds of these truths and involves a means of showing that the grounds identified fail to justify emergent beliefs.

That is how can foundations of truth or knowledge be guaranteed? In numerous works Nietzsche identifies this approach when he called for the 'revaluation of values'.

> What really is it within us that wants 'the truth'? – We did indeed pause for a long time before the question … until we came to a complete halt before an even more fundamental question. We asked after the value of this will. Granted we want truth: why not rather untruth? And uncertainty? Even ignorance? (Nietzsche, 1984: 18)

Fundamentally, everything was up for grabs. Except in extreme circumstances he denied that the search for knowledge has been the motor of philosophical and scientific endeavour 'but that another drive has here, as elsewhere only employed knowledge (and false knowledge!) as a tool' (Nietzsche, 1984: 19). Indeed, Nietzsche questions the modernist position when he considered that if something has been explained do we have further concern with this. 'What did god mean when he said 'know thyself?' Does this actually mean: 'Have no further concern with thyself! Become objective! – And Socrates – and the man of science?' (1984: 74). Nietzsche questions the edifice of foundationalism, scientific knowledge, grand theory and the modernist position; he takes a sceptical perspective and begins to demolish occidental ideas of knowledge and supremacy.

Postmodernism incorporates: 'that which denies itself the solace of good forms … that which searches for new presentations … to impart a stronger sense of the unpresentable' (Lyotard, 2004: 81). Artists and writers in the postmodern tradition take on the role of the philosopher and the works or the texts 'produced are not in principle governed by pre-established rules and they cannot be judged according to a determining judgement, by applying familiar categories to the text or to the work' (Lyotard, 2004: 81). Postmodernism is not about supplying reality but inventing allusions and questioning the quest for the complete entity. The Hegelian illusion of the whole has provided much terror in the 19th and 20th centuries, postmodernism challenges the realist, modernist authoritarian position and is closely related to constructivist and participatory paradigms of inquiry based on phenomenological perspectives.

Lyotard (2004) alludes to the authoritarian nature of knowledge generation and dissemination and argued that whoever controls knowledge has political control. Fundamentally, Lyotard is committed to ensuring that knowledge dissemination is kept as open as possible and is critical of grand narratives or theories that claim to explain everything. Grand theories are authoritarian and impregnable as they involve immutable truths and are beyond criticism. Consequently, Lyotard champions the notion of small theories or little narratives; these are structured by small groupings that do not attempt to deal with all of society's problems but aim at achieving specific objectives. Such groupings exist only for as long as it takes to acquire the set objective. In such a way, through constructivist and participatory paradigms, knowledge may be developed and disseminated through breaking down knowledge monopoly exercised by grand theories. Small theory or narrative generation searches for understanding, paradoxes and instabilities rather than construct a theory for general explanation. The main objective here is to undermine grand theory which is authoritative and represses the notion of individual creativity. Grand theory can no longer provide guides to action at either the public or private level. However, when we dispense with grand theory or central authority, difficulties regarding value judgements and subjectivity emerge. How can we construct value judgements that others will accept as just and/or reasonable? Lyotard further argued that value judgements can be realised without grand theory and based on case by case analysis (an inductive small theory generation approach). Where we build understanding on case by case basis; such relates to substantive theory and the formation of understanding through praxis which underpins the postmodern approach.

Foundations or absolute criteria for belief or truth are impossible to ascertain but this does not mean, that as proponents of grand narratives argue, social order should disintegrate. This anti-foundationalism rejects the idea that foundations to systems of thought and beliefs actually exist and are necessary for value judgements. Indeed, this identifies relativism and relates to arguments from antiquity; for example, in a meeting between the dialogue *Theaetetus* the idea of relativism or humanity as the measure is broached. Theodorus (an admirer of Protagoras) argues that 'truth and falsity are dependent upon individual impressions'. Socrates however considers that if everyone believed this to be the case, one is accepting the beliefs or truths which oppose his own; in other words, individuals are conceding that the truth they hold is wrong.

If it is true that humanity be the measure of all things then this statement is refuted by this very truth. This issue is one of authority of truth or objective knowledge. Socrates considers that ultimate authority does exist and that an ultimate arbiter external to humanity exists whereas Protagoras takes the solipsistic stance in that each human possesses their own truth. As we have seen with individual phenomenologists, this relationship between relativism and absolutism is central to the definition of ontology and the epistemological relationships between the researcher and researched.

```
┌──────────┤ Reflection Box ├──────────┐
```

Postmodernism

- Architectural styles
- Literary and artistic movements
- Assessment of Western civilisation
- State of knowledge and understanding

(Continued)

(Continued)

- Perception of science and scientific inquiry
- Philosophical approach
- General cultural perspective
- Restricted cultural perspective
- Post-war social epoch
- Media driven movement
- Mass consumption driven
- Distinction between high and low culture
- Intensified division of labour
- Collapse of communism.

Consider each of these rationales for the emergence of postmodernism. Synthesise perspectives and identify a coherent framework for comprehending postmodernism.

Post-structuralism

Post-structuralism does not denote a distinct body of work but involves a disparate network of interconnections which escapes precise delineation. Indeed, post structuralism is closely related to structuralism and the difference between these can be difficult to ascertain. For post-structuralists all categories are open to re-assessment and radical scepticism including literature or writing itself. If the categories and the study do not refer to things in themselves and all things are constructed through difference then the criticism that articulates the difference is of equal importance to the subject. For Derrida, the text would have no meaning without criticism; both categories within the text as well as the author should be subjected to such reasoning. Post-structuralism questions the notion of category as an independent entity.

Saussure (1974) argued that the sign consisted of the signifier and signified which were arbitrarily set through social contract. Once set, signifier and signified become fixed and inseparable and the sign's form and meaning are identical. Phenomenon are carved up by language and once the arbitrary signifier and signified were fixed they formed a stable one-to-one correspondence. Post-structuralists disputed this assumption because meaning is not as clearly present in signifiers or signifieds as this notion suggests. Any attempt to identify the meaning of a word involves a circular pursuit of signifiers. Take the word meaning in the *Oxford English Dictionary* where the meaning of meaning is indicated as 'what is meant; significance … ' 'meant' refers 'to mean'; 'to signify' and 'significance' 'to have meaning'. The meaning of meaning is not given as it slips beneath a circularity of signifiers. Post-structuralism considers that the sign is not a set entity but indeterminate and meaning slippage occurs in the shift between signifiers; meaning becomes unfixed and relative. Post-structuralism questions the idea that underlying structures provide a core to things which structuralism unveils to explain surface forms. Structuralism appeals to a form of meta-language, which provides meaning but does not overcome slippage and indeterminacy; a full final presence of meaning still cannot be achieved. Indeed, the meta-language itself is always open to another meta-language. Consequently, the idea that an explanation of the world may be achieved through the scientific investigation of signs is compromised.

The core characteristics of post structuralism involve the de-centring of identities and emphasis on the role of signifier over signified. It is a network of interconnected ideas and concepts primarily driven forward through two trajectories. These may be labelled the language trajectory and the discourse trajectory; the former developed and used by Derrida and the latter by Foucault. The former is primarily concerned with language in abstraction, the latter with its material significance within the world. Derrida was primarily concerned with deconstruction of the principles of ordering and the metaphysics of presence that are built into language. All language is made up of signifiers consistently tied up with textuality (a condition of being where signifiers consistently refer to other textual occurrences rather than pre-text). Foucault tends toward discourse which considers language as a practical concern closely connected with the context in which it appears. The sign is unstable for both trajectories but in the discourse it is continually fixed and unfixed at different moments in time (Foucault will be discussed in greater detail in Chapter 11).

Derrida and Deconstruction

'Derrida's deconstruction ... was directed against the system building side of structuralism and took issue with the idea that all phenomena were reducible to the operations of systems, with its implication that we have total control over our environment' (Sim, 1998: 5). Deconstruction transforms the marginalities of texts into centralities and uses methods involving irony, paradox and absurdity to accomplish this. As a methodological technique, deconstruction makes explicit, concealed weaknesses and fractures in the text that undermines its proposed unity. Indeed, deconstruction illustrates that the text fails to come to conclusions based on initial premises. Consequently, every piece of work is flawed and every crack indicates a flaw in the complete work; the true unity of the given text is not that asserted but one concealed and uncovered through the dismantling of the text. Such contradicts structuralism because the old unity of the text is replaced by that which was previously hidden. Deconstruction then takes another step or identifies a further problem that can then provide further development; deconstruction is an activity undertaken by 'texts which in the end have to acknowledge their own partial complicity with what they denounce' (Norris, 1993: 48). Each text is complicit in the disruption and denunciation of the text so should itself be open for similar treatment; that is the 'most rigorous reading ... is one that holds itself provisionally open to further deconstruction of its own operative concepts' (Norris, 1993: 48).

Reflection Box

Deconstruction

Step 1: the text is flipped on its head or the world is turned on its head and implicit meaning is made explicit. This involves the destruction of the dominating interpretation.

Step 2: opposite meanings of the text are undermined and displace both meanings with another notion or thought. This involves the destruction of both interpretations, their displacement and construction of a new wider entity within which the previous at best constitute special cases.

Relate this process to a text or piece of research of your choice.

Reflection Box

Writing

When it came to writing Theuth (a minor Egyptian God) declared: 'here is an accomplishment ... that will improve both the wisdom and memory. Theuth my paragon of inventors replied to the King (Thamus of Ammon; a major Egyptian God) ... those who acquire it will cease to exercise their memory and become forgetful; they will rely on writing to bring things to their remembrance by external signs instead of their own internal resources. What you have discovered is a receipt for recollection, not for memory. And as for wisdom, your pupils will have the reputation for it without the reality: they will receive a quantity of information without proper instruction, and in consequence be thought very knowledgeable when they are for the most part quite ignorant. And because they are filled with the conceit of wisdom instead of real wisdom they will burden society ... The fact is Pheudrus ... writing involves a similar disadvantage to painting. The productions of painting look like living beings, but if you ask them a question they maintain a solemn silence. The same holds true of written words; you might suppose that they understand what they are saying, but if you ask them what they mean by anything they simply return to the same answer over and over again' (Plato, 1976: Phaedrus, pp 96-7).

Relate this passage to deconstruction. What could it tell us about the Internet?

Derrida emphasised phonocentricism, which means that the spoken word has greater emphasis than the written; speech is more immediate and expresses meaning more emphatically. Furthermore, logocentricism stems from phonocentricism, which considers that all leads to logos (the divine ultimate world) and the occidental pursuit of attaining teleological finalities and goals based on logical rational origin. Consequently, the importance of the spoken word is inverted and the written word elevated in the hierarchical structure. The written word even with its isolation from the writer and his/her original meaning provides the basis for the unified written self-contained text. Speech is immediate and more straightforward in identifying the originator's intentions. Phonocentricism leads toward the idea of logocentricism where everything becomes the divine word or logos with the tendency to identify logic and rationality as well as objectives and end results. For Derrida, because the written word involved detachment from intended referents the privileged position of speech over the written word is eventually inverted.

Logos is Greek for reason or justification and implies that rational thought or logic is bound up with the spoken word. Logocentricism indentifies how Western philosophy prioritises reason and that anything which is not deemed rational is considered irrational and is subsequently peripherised. Derrida argued that logocentricism assumed a named and constant foundational entity such as 'God' or 'being'; the origin of truth has always been assigned to the logos (Derrida, 1976). Logocentricism involves the 'metaphysics of phonetic writing' for example the utilisation of the alphabet to impose ethnocentric power upon individuals and society, power that controls the concepts of writing, metaphysics and science or the means by which we search for truth and knowledge (Derrida, 1976: 6). Such provides a dominant mode of developing understanding through reasoning in terms of rational choice, calculation, deduction and measurement that excludes anything that does not develop through such a process. Phallocentricsm is linked with male domination or patriarchy and with logocentricism attempts the domination and mastery of all truth, knowledge and understanding. Derrida considered that such domination, based in calculation and measurement as unifying entities, brings about the disintegration of dissemination and continual disaggregation of knowledge. For Derrida, there existed a clear miscomprehension regarding what is signified (object) and the signifier (language) and that there is no clear relationship between them. Language does not clearly correspond with the world it attempts to clarify; it is not a means of providing an accurate depiction of reality. Indeed such a view elevates speech through presence over absence and explains how this 'does not depend on a choice that could have been avoided' but 'of economy ... of life ... of history ... of being as self relationship' (Derrida, 1976: 7). Fundamentally logocentricism is the 'the privilege of the phone' (Derrida, 1976: 7).

Derrida uses deconstruction to assess the pre-conceived rational perspective of knowledge generation and understanding which uses Husserlian cancellation and Heideggerian practice of crossing terms out in the text because their meanings cannot be identified precisely (erasure). Through his denial of logocentricism Derrida does not attack existing logic but wishes to question the extent that the practice of assertion and opposites can hold; he does not wish to deny all oppositions, for example, ideal/matter, specific/general, truth/false, but to question why there is a reification of such distinctions or contradictions. Derrida sees philosophy as a practice of critique with an emphasis on a close attention to the critique of language and the means by which it produces, directs and obscures our concerns about the world. Fundamentally, little can be objective as subjective tendencies continue to be involved with the very language we use to develop a research project and determine our interpretation of the world. Texts are linked with and emerge over a certain time or epoch; they are not separate entities but part of a body or fragmented transmissions distinct from the realities they purport to portray. Furthermore, through deconstruction Derrida interrogated Western philosophy in terms of otherness and that which had not been thought. Indeed the text as a representation of reality is questioned and its fractures and weaknesses made explicit.

Deconstruction involves *arche-writing* which is a precondition for both speech and writing. There is a difference, distance or deviation between what is thought, spoken and heard. Arche-writing involves 'that which exceeds the traditional (restricted) sense of the word in order to release all this hitherto repressed significations which have always haunted the discourse of logocentric reason' (Norris, 1987: 122). *Arche* is a Greek term and translates as origin (original and identical to self; not like anything else). Speech can be seen as an origin (self present and self identical), however, once the origin is written it becomes a representation of that origin and therefore no longer original itself. Consequently there is a breach between what is written and what the text conveys and is included in all attempts at conveying meaning, even the notion of self-presence. The text continually defers meaning – meaning is never present so never captured by the reader or critic, it is continually subject to the future and even if the future is incorporated alternative possible futures continue to obscure meaning. Texts are not even present for authors themselves – meaning is even deferred for the writer – 'there is nothing outside the text' (Derrida, 1976: 158). Derrida is contradictory in this context; he calls for the openness and undermining of closed systems while at the same time seeing nothing beyond the text, the text closed to the external world; texts may only refer to themselves. Writing does not exist as the servant of science, but as identified by Husserl it involves 'the condition of the possibility of ideal objects and therefore of scientific objectivity. Before being its object, writing is the condition of the episteme' (Derrida, 1976: 27). For Derrida, questions arise regarding the origin of writing and language because each is closely related to the other: 'What is writing? Means where and when does writing begin ... The question of origin of the origin of writing and the origin of language are difficult to separate' (1976: 28). In the Pheadrus, Plato attacks writing through the notions of presence and absence; 'writing lures language away from its authentic origins in speech and self-presence. To commit ones thoughts to writing is to yield them up to the public domain ... to the promiscuous wiles of interpretation' (Norris, 1993: 63).

┌─── **Definition Box** ───┐

Textuality and Intertextuality

- Textuality involves the arrangement of words in relation to a reader's interpretation of the text. It refers to attributes that give a text its distinctive nature (the text is the communicative process under analysis). Textuality brings about the meaning and being of the text in specific ways; the text becomes part of a network of meanings which transcends the text and places it in a wider abstract context.
- Intertextuality identifies how the meanings of texts are shaped through the meaning of other texts. Not transferred directly as with intersubjectivity but through mediated codes transposed through other texts.

Intertextuality can be seen as something Derrida labels différance which involves both difference and deferral. For structuralism the majority of world bound entities incorporate linguistic signs that generate texts, which allowed Derrida to play with the differences between signs. Furthermore, as identified in *arche-writing*, for all texts meaning is deferred infinitely. Derrida wanted to illustrate 'the instability of language and indeed systems in general. Signs were not such predictable entities ... and indeed there was never any perfect conjunction of signifier and signified to guarantee unproblematic communication. Some slippage of meaning always occurred' (Sim, 1998: 5).

Derrida considered that difference, which meant both difference and deferral, and the idea that absence was far more important than the idea of presence, which underpinned and incorporated all occidental metaphysical thinking. He argued that this involved an underlying presence in terms of something behind what exists, some hidden entity pulling the strings. Indeed, the Wizard of Oz is behind the curtain creating illusions but when unveiled he becomes human and illustrates that no hidden power exists only surfaces or the realisation of the human being through rewards for certain attributes, that is, medals, certificates and machines. 'Différance ... comes into play ... at the point where meaning eludes the grasp of a pure, self present awareness' (Norris, 1993: 46).

Presence in terms of social science may incorporate the presence of the rational being behaving in a certain way to ensure intentions and outcomes; the presence of the end in relation to the means the presence of effect in relation to cause. That the full meaning of a word is always absent, 'the metaphysics of presence ... is an illusion: différance always intrudes into communication to prevent the establishment of "presence" or completeness of meaning' (Sim, 1998: 6).

> Signs refer to what is absent so in a sense meaning is (also) absent ... Meaning is continually moving along a chain of signifiers, and we cannot be precise about its exact location ... No one can make the means (the sign) and the end (meaning) become identical. Sign will always lead to sign. (Sarup, 1993: 33)

Overall, because of the reliance on presence, Derrida criticised both positivism as a philosophical position and occidental thinking in general.

| **Definition Box** |

Différance

Différance incorporates an amalgamation of the following:

- Difference involves differentiation of entities from each other which creates opposites and hierarchies of meaning.
- Deferral means that signs and words may only be defined by deferring to another source. Definition may only be achieved through words or signs from which they differ; meaning is continually deferred.

As noted above, Derrida used the idea of *sous rature* or (under erasure) which occurs when the word is written and crossed out, for example, Heidegger used to write Being crossed out or deleted but with this deletion printed; this recognised that the word did not quite convey the necessary meaning but was all we had so a required necessity. Heidegger argued that Being incorporated 'the final signified, which all signifiers refer, the transcendental signified' (Sarup 1993: 33). Derrida identified différance as 'the movement according to which language or any code, any system of reference in general, is constituted "historically" as a weave of differences' (1982: 12–13). In such a way, différance and deconstruction are closely related and that even though both attempt to undermine traditional metaphysical statements one still has to end up making a statement. In a research project no matter how far one would wish the data to speak eventually the researcher or research community will comment; something will be said. What is said by the research is arrived at through the weaving of meaning, language or signs; a language that does not perfectly convey meaning in either logocentric or phonocentric contexts. For example, writing which corresponds identically with speech is available 'no purely and rigorously phonetic writing' exists; all writing includes punctuation and spaces (Derrida, 1982: 5). Overall, meaning is woven together through historicity, individual languages, symbols, experiences and interpretations.

Scientific and Narrative Knowledge: Lyotard

Lyotard (2004) interrogated the status of knowledge and the relationship between scientific and what he labelled narrative knowledge. Scientific knowledge involves a number of prescriptions that determined or regulated whether something is scientific or not. First, the sender should speak the truth, be able to provide proof or refute opposing statements. Second, the individual to whom truth is aimed at or the hearer will be a potential sender so will need to determine agreement or disagreement with the statement as they will also be expected to determine proof or refutation. Third, the referent requires conformity with what actually exists. However, what actually exists can only be determined through what is said and subsequently becomes problematic.

'The scientific solution to this difficulty consists in the observance of two rules ... which underlie what nineteenth-century science calls verification and twentieth-century science, falsification' (Lyotard, 2004: 23–5). However, 'a statement of science gains no validity from the fact of being reported ... it is taught only if it is still verifiable in the present through argumentation and proof. In itself, it (knowledge) is never secure from falsification' (Lyotard, 2004: 26). Accumulated knowledge is defined through acceptable statements and these may be continually challenged. Narrative knowledge involves 'non-scientific knowledge' and even though they encompass different types of knowledge both are 'composed of sets of statements: the statements are "moves" made by ... players within the framework of generally applicable rules ... specific to each kind of knowledge ... rules specific to each kind of knowledge' (Lyotard, 2004: 26). Narrative knowledge does not prioritise legitimacy and is not accepted by positivist discourse and scientific knowledge. That said, Lyotard is critical of grand narratives; impregnable theory does not exist and he considered little narratives provided the most appealing form of knowledge and most appropriate means for the dissemination of this knowledge. 'Postmodern science, Lyotard informs us, is a search for paradoxes, instabilities and the unknown rather than an attempt to construct yet another grand narrative that would apply over the entire scientific community' (Sim, 1998: 9).

Reflection Box
Purpose of Research
'The production of truth ... in which the goal is no longer truth but performativity – that is the best possible input/output equation. The State and/or the company must abandon the idealist and humanist narratives of legitimation in order to justify the new goal: in the discourse of today's financial backers of research, the only credible goal is power. Scientists, technicians, and instruments are purchased not to find truth but augment power' (Lyotard, 2004: 46).
Consider the distinction between truth and power in the development of knowledge.

Conclusion

As approaches to social science research, postmodernism and post-structuralism may offer some insight and benefit. For example, ideas relating to meaning and the emphasis on the subject as well as theoretical frameworks can enhance social research. Furthermore, the distinction between fact and literature in social science research and the production of text began to doubt the ability of linguistic capability to identify and explain a nïve or critical realism and determine meanings that language was supposed to provide. Rather than being able to give meaning in a literal and unequivocal manner, language becomes uncertain, metaphorical and evasive. Consequently, as language is central to conveying the meaning of the research process, the very basis of the objective position and reflection of external reality in a clear and rational context is undermined. Conversation and guidance among scholars take central stage and verification and explanation are relegated to a less important position in social research and theory generation. As with most paradigms within the phenomenological tradition, truth is not fixed and discovered, it is either historically or relatively constructed through the reflexivity of communities whereby the theorist and practitioner or researched and researcher become interchangeable within the research process and theory generation. However, this does cause some difficulty for the position of the researcher within the research process.

Can the researcher say anything about rationality, truth, theory or reality that is more incisive than that said by those involved in the situation under analysis? What about interpretation; can good interpretation and in-depth comprehension be achieved? We can question whether people ever really say what they think? Do attitudes and behaviour correlate? Do individuals have definite comprehensions of value systems and attitudes that are explicitly expressed? Consider an ideal situation whereby issues such as misinterpretation, the Hawthorne effect, dishonesty, are overcome and an environment exists in which respondents are able to express themselves in an open and clear manner. The difficulty is that for respondent's considerations to be meaningful, contingency must become part of the analysis, individuals say different things at different times and will be affected by what has been said at earlier points in time or by the way questions, interviews and conversations are organised. Fundamentally, post-structuralists would consider that language involves a metaphorical figurative stance that is contingent and does not easily reflect complex situations. Indeed, language does not give a mirror image of reality, it provides different perspectives from different positions in specific situations. Rather than pure reflection, or rather than give a mirror image, language provides a prism through which the observed may be understood or interpreted. Language outlines theories which reflect multifaceted perceptions of truth.

Discourse analysis also considers that individuals are inconsistent and language is contingent. Just because an individual says x or y on occasion a or b, it does not mean that any general inference may be drawn because on a different occasion another point of view may be taken. Individual accounts nearly always incorporate variation; separate people describe things in different ways and the same person describes things in different ways. Obviously this has implications for truth and generalisation and directs the researcher toward understanding and analysing what people say in relation to the specific situation. In this context, interviews or focus groups become part of the research rather than simply means of data collection. However, beliefs become contingent and what people really think uncertain, but through concentrating on certain questions some sort of reflected attitudes may be ascertained, these include:

- When and where are different perspectives expressed?
- How are these perspectives constructed?
- What functions do specific perspectives fulfil in specific situations?
- Which contexts are certain perspectives included within?

Postmodernism and post-structuralism identify difficulties relating to the way theories claim a certain authority, assumptions that exist within them, the way they are constructed and how the language used validates their supremacy. Denzin (1989) argued that postmodernism should strive to understand those being researched through immersion in people's lives and environments. Then produce contextualised interpretations and reproductions of local tales and histories propagated by individual members and the community in general. The consequence of this will give multi-voiced and dialogical interpretive theories based on what is implicit in native interpretations (Denzin, 1989: 20). The postmodern moment 'universalises itself in the lives of interesting individuals' (Denzin, 1989: 189). Postmodernism and post-structuralism identify and exemplify multiplicity, contradictions, variety and fragmentation rather than integrated frames and probable or immutable outcomes. Several voices should represent reality and the human experience is constituted in language and discourse; it is not external to language but embodied within it. 'What then is postmodern? ... A work can only become modern if it is first postmodern. Postmodernism thus understood is not modernism at its end but in the nascent state, and this state is constant' (Lyotard, 2004: 79).

Table 7.1 Modernism, structuralism, postmodernism and post-structuralism

Modernism	Usually denotes an expression of advanced (post-Enlightenment) or *avante garde* occidental art and thought.
Postmodernism	Challenges modernist perspectives in philosophy (dualism), physics, art, politics, regarding ideas that emerge from Enlightenment.
Structuralism	Normally describes a European movement that applied structural linguistics to social phenomenon. Considered that social and cultural phenomenon encompassed objects that were not simply physical but entities that involved meaning.
Post-structuralism	Originated as a critique of structuralism with the objective of becoming a framework that could provide overall comprehension of humanity through application in the human sciences.

Further Reading

Denzin, N. and Lincoln, Y. (1994) *The Handbook of Qualitative Research,* 1st edn. Thousand Oaks, CA: SAGE Publications.

Denzin, N. and Lincoln, Y. (2000) *The Handbook of Qualitative Research,* 2nd edn. Thousand Oaks, CA: SAGE Publications.

Denzin, N. and Lincoln, Y. (2005) *The Handbook of Qualitative Research,* 3rd edn. Thousand Oaks, CA: SAGE Publications.

Lyotard (2004) *The Postmodern Condition: a Report on Knowledge.* Minneapolis, MN: University of Minnesota Press.

Norris, C. (1987) *Derrida.* London: Fontana Press.

Rosenau, P.M. (1992) *Post-Modernism and the Social Sciences: Insights, Inroads and Intrusions.* Princeton, NJ: Princeton University Press.

Sarup, M. (1993) *An Introductory Guide to Post-Structuralism and Postmodernism.* Hemel Hemstead: Harvester Wheatsheaf.

Sim, S. (ed.) (1998) *The Icon Critical Dictionary of Postmodern Thought.* Cambridge: Icon Books.

EIGHT

Ethnography

Introduction

Chapter 8 investigates ethnography, which involves an important methodological approach for social science researchers. Furthermore, this chapter identifies examples relating to ethnographic research and discusses epistemological and ontological issues regarding this methodological approach. Ethnography can be defined as a methodological approach, which emerged through interest in the origins of culture and civilisation, describes social groups and was initially related to anthropology and study and analysis of so-called (primitive) societies. Anthropology attempts to comprehend groups in a social settings of other or alien communities. For conventional ethnographers, research is undertaken in the field and attempts to capture and understand social action and the meaning of this action. The researcher is not based in a constructed setting or experiment but part of the everyday natural situation within which those under investigation (or those involved with research project) exist. Ethnography does not involve a synonym for all qualitative research and concentrates on the role of human affairs or culture. That said, culture itself is a difficult term to pin down as it is used in many distinct ways; however, in the case of ethnography it may be used to identify ways of understanding social interaction in groups. Indeed, it may be conceived as an abstraction that may be applied to small or large groups, for example, people working in small companies, regions or even nation-states.

Ethnographic studies attempt to comprehend the group or societies' values and norms (culture) of one group or society through the norms and values of another cultural perspective. However, certain analysts argue that even though an emphasis on empirical observation exists ethnographers always use some form of theoretical framework to ensure some distance between the researcher and researched (Silverman, 1985).

Overall, the ethnographic approach involves pursuing shared understandings and meanings of the lifeworld (the daily existence) of societies and groupings through research undertaken over long periods of time. Obviously, if the place of study is related to the researcher's own environment or situation, then because he/she has knowledge of the situation the time period for the study can be shorter.

┌───┐
│   │ **Definition Box** │   │
│   │
│ **Culture**   │
│   │
│ Culture identifies acceptable behaviour and is intrinsic in determining how people think. │
│ Culture directs actions and consists of symbols, norms and values, it encapsulates world- │
│ views and is usually so in-built it remains covert and unrecognisable. Only when atten- │
│ tion is turned to the notion of culture does it begin to become explicit; in other words a │
│ level of intentionality is required. Overall, culture outlines acceptable modes of behaving │
│ and thinking in specific societies. Hofstede (2004) argued that culture is learned through │
│ mental programming. Mental programming goes on throughout our lives. However, most │
│ is undertaken in our formative years when we learn easier with fewer pre-conceptions. │
│ Culture is intrinsically linked with human nature and our social existence. │
│   Once patterns of feeling, thinking and acting have been established they are difficult │
│ to change. │
└───┘

Sources of learning lie in social environments, beginning with family and moving through other groups to class.

┌───┐
│   │ **Definition Box** │   │
│   │
│ **Ethnography**   │
│   │
│ • Assessment and analysis of ideas, norms symbols and values of local social settings │
│   and groups within wider social contexts. │
│ • Focuses on methods and the quality and quantity of data and data collection. │
│ • Acceptance that theories exist and use these to direct the research. │
│ • Approach the field with an open mind. │
│ • Analysis of numerous and comprehensive observations. │
│ • Involvement with the researched. │
│ • Close contact and personal involvement. │
│ • Triangulation and combination of qualitative and quantitative methods of data collection. │
└───┘

Hammersley and Atkinson (2007) argued that ethnography involved the following features: investigation of social phenomenon through inductive processes rather than deductive processes and hypotheses testing; a tendency to deal with data that is coded at the point of collection into categories, themes or typologies; investigation of small numbers of cases or one case in a very detailed fashion; and data analysis based on interpretations of meaning and action which involves the elevation of qualitative explanation over quantitative techniques. Ethnography is a contested methodology and encapsulates different ontological and epistemological positions but in all contexts it provides insight into groups of people and allows us to understand their different habitats or worlds. That said, in relation to a general or conventional perspective of ethnography there are a number of different perspectives that may be utilised in a research project, which include: positivist ethnography, critical ethnography and constructivist ethnography.

Even though in certain contexts the term social science has become unpopular, for example, the term science and its positivist connotations; it does provide a means of describing the interdisciplinary nature of study within the social domain. Indeed, ethnography can move beyond academia and influence policy as well as individuals' daily lives – it provides an opportunity for synthesising theory and practice (praxis). Scott-Jones (2010) argued that ethnography should be about changing people's lives. Indeed even though numerous texts define ethnography, Scott-Jones (2010) brings together diverse examples of ethnographic studies from social sciences that use or rely on different types of fieldwork. It is difficult to go into detail in a generic methodology text however, ethnography involves a little more than participatory observation from a reflexive perspective. This chapter identifies and outlines ethnography in terms of:

- historical roots;
- how it relates with social science research;
- different types of ethnographic methodology;
- why it is concerned with politics, power and ethical behaviour.

Table 8.1 Types of ethnography

Positivist ethnography	Incorporates positivist, ontological and epistemological perspectives so research should seek to accumulate knowledge through procedures similar to natural science. Objectivity and distance from the subject should be ensured; interaction with the subject will contaminate data and outcomes. Consequently non-participatory observation is the method usually employed.
Critical ethnography	Draws on critical theory, engages with analysis and includes ethical considerations. A critical viewpoint will question what is at stake when the researcher interprets and transmits information about others.
Constructivist ethnography	Requires a foundation-less detachment in terms of a phenomenological stream of becoming and the world continually shifting in relation to this becoming. The world is a social construction that relates to individuals and is defined and determined by ideology, power, politics and culture that are implicit in this construction.

METHODS OF DATA COLLECTION

- Observation
- Participatory observation
- Analysis of cultural and social artefacts
- Diaries and personal documents
- Life histories
- Key in-depth interviews
- Focus groups
- Discourse and language analyses.

How may these methods be used in an ethnographic study?

A Short History of Ethnography

Ethnography means the study of people; *ethnos* is a Greek term for people and graphic involves making something clear and/or the study of certain phenomenon. As noted, ethnography is based on anthropology and over 200 years the latter developed the methods to underpin the former and lend a distinctive means of undertaking research and understanding human beings in their own settings or situations. In the 19th century a survey was developed to enable non-professional researcher's record the activities of those they encountered on their travels so, 'those who were not anthropologist' could provide data for scientists wishing to undertake anthropological studies at home (*Notes and Queries on Anthropology, 1874*; cited in Tedlock, 2000: 456). However, it was considered that the document involved leading questions and simply gathered data that intensified pre-conceptions and prejudices. Such an approach was questioned by the scientific community and by the end of the 19th century direct participation in the lives of others was a necessary means of understanding the lives of subjects. When Malinowski (1922) argued that the ethnographer should understand the 'native's point of view' the emphasis for the ethnographer involved the idea that 'participant observation would lead to human understanding through a fieldworker learning to see, think and sometimes behave like an insider or native' (Tedlock, 2000: 456). That is, the ethnographic fieldworker should become a 'marginal native', 'professional stranger' or 'self denying emissary' (Tedlock, 2000: 457).

During the 19th century the term 'native' was considered to encompass the antithesis of European civilisation. Fiction in general during this period provided a negative portrayal of going native because it detracted from a pure European culture and spirit. Going native involved the fear that a contamination of culture would take place if colonisers were drawn into the degenerate other (savage cultures). Degeneration of this kind is explored in Joseph Conrad's novel *Heart of Darkness* and the character Kurtz who ultimately experienced what Europeans feared in themselves. *Heart of Darkness* identifies the line between the culture of European colonisers and foreign primitive non-occidental worlds.

Africa challenged the rationality of European colonialism; what is appropriate for Europe proved absurd in Africa. Such absurdity challenged the position and narrative of colonialism through which a crisis in authority for the European position arises. Kurtz was lost to his 'savage and superb lover' (Conrad, 1986: 137) who symbolised the African wilderness as he was lost to the wilderness itself. However, even though lost, throughout his journey he glimpses the nature of himself, European culture and humanity in general. Indeed, through going native Kurtz sees the terrifying nature or the 'horror' of humanity, which illuminates a fundamental comprehension of self. Through a descent into savagery Kurtz produces a 'narrative of degeneration that reveals the vulnerability of colonials in foreign lands' (Tedlock, 2000: 457). Going native in a research context involves a close proximity to the ideas, beliefs and moral perspectives of the individuals under investigation; this usually incorporates limited reflexivity regarding self and other. Willis (1977) became over involved in his research project through 'over-rapport' when he closely identifies with the culture of respondents and consequently fails to assess problems with the research findings. From a sub-culture perspective found in working-class school boys he extrapolated to working-class people in general. However, other working-class voices were marginalised and a flawed perspective of working-class consciousness emerged through research data and interpretation. Willis identified a sub-culture or counter-culture within a school and argued that this culture provided the basis of workplace culture for manual workers and suggested that those individuals that conformed to normal culture would less well adapt to manual work. Fundamentally, ethnographers are required to adopt numerous roles but the maintenance of a marginal position are necessary if the research is to ensure 'access to participant perspectives' while dealing with issues relating to 'over-rapport' (Hammersley and Atkinson, 2007: 88). The ethnographer encounters difficulties regarding the appropriate role to play when undertaking research in the field. The two extremes involve the complete participant and complete observer. However, even though such extremities are useful research positions when collecting data and undertaking analysis, less, well-defined roles, such as participant observer or observer as participant, allow a middle-range position between 'going native', and a scientific or positivistic position. The complete participant can be useful for undertaking covert research projects and programmes but becoming too close to those under investigation (going native) may lack a level of detachment, objectivity and reflexivity.

Going Native

'I had immense plans he muttered … I was on the threshold of great things. He cried in a whisper at some image at some vision – he cried out twice, a cry that was no more than a breath – 'The horror! The horror!'. (Conrad, 1995: 108-12)

Consider the relationship between imperialism, anthropology and early ethnographic studies. Contemplate what has happened to Kurtz and consider the implications for understanding ethnography. How may the researcher deal with issues relating to 'going native' and over-rapport?

The researcher should not 'go native' but ensure a degree of distance between subject and object; going native should be avoided because complete membership as top of the embraced culture could have devastating consequences; as it did for Kurtz in *Heart of Darkness* and the film based on this, *Apocalypse Now*. Complete membership in an autocratic context may undermine the thoughts of others and lead to misinterpretation, misconstrued understanding and incorrect or over-stretched generalisation. It has been posited that early ethnographic studies did not really tell us very much about the 'other' and revealed as much about occidental society as those under research. Interest in the 'other' was usually determined by exploitation in terms of labour, natural resources and territory. Fundamentally, concern for early ethnographers and anthropologists revolved around colonialism and imperialism.

Positivist Ethnography

During the 19th century a positivistic perspective of anthropology and ethnography predominated. This perspective emerged through the predominant social structure and gave rise to imperialist and colonial understandings of the 'other', which usually illustrated a superior cultural attitude and perspective. Initially, ethnographic studies were undertaken by 'Western missionaries, explorers, buccaneers, and colonial administrators' and encapsulated the view of the conqueror and civilisation (Vidich and Lyman, 2000: 5). Cultures were interpreted in relation to a superior occidental perception of the world. The difficulty with a positivist perspective of ethnography is that the researcher's worldview and his/her decisions about which data are important. When collecting data, ethnographic studies can be either positivistic or phenomenological; that is etic (values of the researcher are primary) or emic (values of the researched are primary) positions may be taken in relation to the situation/people under investigation where researchers either immerse themselves in the data or take a more objective, epistemological stance. Consequently, for early positivist ethnography an etic occidental perception of the world directed research activity, norms and ethics, which was clearly grounded in the predominant social science research perspective.

For western or occidental society ethnographic interest regarding the origins of humanity, society and civilisation stemmed from an analysis of (what were labelled) less civilised cultures than those exemplified in Europe. This notion emanated from imperial and colonial understandings usually perpetrated by explorers, missionaries and early entrepreneurs. Indeed, the initial conceptualisation of the West as benefactor (through natural and social science studies) was replaced by distinct ideas of evolutionary progress linked to the ideas of Charles Darwin (1809–1882) in *Origin of the Species* (1959) and Herbert Spencer (1820–1903) in *First Principles* (1862). This intensified the positivist ethnographic position of superior researcher analysing the 'other' from an objective standpoint. Indeed, this understanding of human relations can be based in the Hegelian perception of master-slave dichotomy and issues regarding mutual recognition in relation to self and other.

QUESTION

EVOLUTION

Identify and explain the theory of evolution? How would such a theory assist imperialism, colonialism and positivism?

Positivist ethnography adheres to empiricist notions of knowledge generation. Based in positivist ontological and epistemological positions there is a belief that social sciences deal with difficulties similar to those encountered in the natural sciences. Subsequently, social science research should seek to accumulate knowledge through procedures similar to natural science. Objectivity and distance from the subject should be ensured; interaction with the subject will contaminate data and outcomes. Causality should be sought; causal connections identify rationales for human activity, simplicity and idealisation pursued and a deductive approach identified. Prediction incorporated the bottom-line; when we can predict outcomes we encounter complete explanation so as to control outcomes through the most appropriate means as well as create desired results. Each of these procedures underpins the idea of the 'scientific method', which has been discussed in Chapter 3. Indeed, positivist ethnography is by its very nature ground in a specific mode of undertaking social science research.

However, these points made, there are a number of ways in which positivist ethnography fails to adhere to the scientific method procedures, which include:

- interaction between object and subject (objectivity and subjectivity);
- involvement in natural settings (lifeworld);

- explores meanings regarding the everyday (lifeworld);
- flexible open-ended methods (triangulation of methods);
- less structured research process (primarily inductive);
- measurement is not the primary objective (meaning and interpretation imperative);
- numerical data is not the most appropriate data (words take centre stage).

Consequently, many positivists and post-positivists criticise ethnography for its so-called non-scientific position and in many instances it is simply used at the exploratory stages of the research process. This has led positivist ethnographers to emphasise procedure, rigour and objectivity and argue that the approach was scientific. An external reality needed to be explained and the rigorous ethnographer could identify this and explain it. Through rigorous procedures ethnographers could capture and explain fixed realities. Others have abandoned elements of the positivist and post-positivist positions and define ethnography through a different form of social science research and employ the critical theory paradigm in the form of critical ethnography.

Critical Ethnography

Critical ethnographers draw on a social science mode of research related to critical theory and do not simply report analysis; they engage with analysis and include ethical considerations regarding the way people are represented. How people are represented is how they are treated, which puts an enormous amount of power and responsibility in the hands of those that undertake interpretations of groups societies and individuals (Hall, 1997).

When undertaking social science research through ethnographic studies, we meet people and learn of their experiences and cultures through the lens of an interpreter's interpretation. However, a critical viewpoint will question what is at stake when the researcher becomes the transmitter of information and the skilled interpreter in both presenting and representing the lives and stories of others. These are people that the researcher has come to know and who have given permission for the researcher to broadcast their lives, stories and cultures. Indeed, when involved in social science research the critical ethnographer explores a number of ethical issues when interpreting and representing the lives of others, which include:

- reflection and evaluation of purpose and intent;
- identification of consequences and potential harm;
- creation and maintenance of dialogue and collaboration between researcher and researched;
- specification of relationships between localism and generality in relation to the human condition;
- consideration of how the research may ensure equity and make a difference in terms of liberty and justice.

Positivist 'ethnography is criticised by advocates of critical ethnography for adopting an inappropriate theoretical perspective that neglects oppression and its causes and (even more importantly) for not being closely related to political practices designed to bring about emancipation' (Hammersley, 1992: 96). Critical ethnographers should view human behaviour from a critical position and develop emancipatory-based social science theory; they should concentrate on the constraints and/or repressive aspects of cultural environments in terms of injustice, inequality and control. Through a sceptical stance, ideas, norms, symbols and values, critical ethnographic methodology charts, assesses and analyses local social settings and groups within wider social contexts. Critical ethnography is firmly based and grounded in social science research, fundamentally, it is primarily concerned with social change and a critique of the human condition.

Critical ethnography focuses on the quality/quantity of data and data collection as well as the interpretation of this data through non-established modes of thinking; such involves, innovative methods of data collection and creative analysis. For instance, discourse should not be perceived as inane but in terms of power relations and the relationship between the researcher, researched and the research environment critically assessed with regard to power relations and responsibilities. Furthermore, the affect the researcher has on the data and research process should be critically assessed and the utilisation, reporting and validity of the research closely investigated.

The researcher should accept that social theories exist and these should be used to direct the social investigation while at the same time approach the field with an open critical mind (this is problematic and a dichotomy for most social science research projects; how may an individual researcher have theoretical pre-conceptions as well as an open-mind?). The main emphasis of the critical ethnographic approach should be the reflective analysis of numerous and comprehensive observations. Researchers must be willing to involve themselves with the researched; close contact and personal involvement is imperative. Triangulation is also an important element for critical ethnographic studies and a combination of qualitative and quantitative methods of data collection should not be discouraged. Such methods can include: non-participatory observation, participatory observation, analysis of cultural and social artefacts, diaries and personal documents, life histories, key in-depth interviews, focus groups, discourse and language analysis.

Definition Box

Critical

'Critical' as used by critical ethnographers derives from German philosophy and specifically that of Kant, Hegel and Marx. Marx adapted and adopted a view of the relationship between theory and practice initiated in the ideas and writings of Kant and Hegel, These

(Continued)

(Continued)

ideas are different from those espoused in antiquity, for example, for Aristotle, practice and theory were quite distinct from each other; practical knowledge was only probabilistic and displayed uncertain validity. Practical knowledge was not directed toward truth and concentrated on determining the good. In contrast, theory was concerned with the contemplation and understanding of eternal 'verities and of value in itself'. Kant elevated the practical domain and considered it in terms of ethical behaviour and metaphysical thought. Such was very different from reality investigated by theory, which concentrated on the natural sciences. Hegel overcame these distinctions by synthesising metaphysical reality and theory as being in the world; Enlightenment provided a historical circumstance when theory and reality were reconciled. Marx disputed such reconciliation and argued that history had arrived at the point where these distinctions could be overcome and this made explicit in the emancipation of humanity and that reconciliation was identified in historical materialism or his theoretical perspective (Hammersley, 1992).

Critical ethnography is flexible and unlike Straussian perspectives of grounded theory does not have set procedures for data collection; this provides opportunities for the pragmatic study to emerge (as noted by Glaser's approach to grounded theory) in relation to the data collection process and ongoing analysis (see Chapter 9 for an assessment of Strauss and Glaser's approaches to grounded theory). However, complete emergence related to an inductive approach is not primary because theoretical frameworks and ontological and epistemological standpoints guide critical ethnographic methodology. For critical ethnography, data and theory may not always completely correspond but even if it does not this provides indications regarding the explanatory capability of the theory in relation to the specific empirical study and analyses. Critical ethnography should not concentrate solely on data but ensure that the critical theory paradigm of inquiry and specific theoretical frameworks guide analyses. That said, it is difficult to integrate theory and empirical data and with the emphasis on reflection and concentration on theory in critical ethnography, the amount of data involved becomes problematic. Consequently, the critical ethnographer should concentrate on particular data or data that relate to the emancipatory or injustice elements of the situation under analysis.

The critical ethnographer should concentrate on close interpretation and theoretical analysis when dealing with empirical data. Negation should be continually employed, this can take the form of introducing counterfactuals or something that should be involved but is not or the denial of something which is apparent and looks straightforward but is not. If such a research process and stance to the data is taken, critical ethnography can overcome the problem of authority that a positivistic position encounters. An ethnography that did not pursue a non-critical perspective may admit that non-political positions can be taken but may not claim their work to be totally objective; subjectivity or bias is recognised. Value judgements may be considered from a Weberian perspective who considered that phenomenon is far from value-free but once identified, to discover the truth, the said phenomenon should be investigated through the suspension of practical value-judgements. The difficulty here of course is how does one suspend one's value judgements? Are they not with you continually? Postmodern ethnographers went further than the critical theory paradigm and developed perspectives of social science research based in constructivist and participatory paradigms of inquiry, each of which may not take a critical stance but accept the inclusion of subjective tendencies.

Postmodern/Constructivist Ethnography

Distinctions between approaches to social science research that involved positivist understandings of ethnography toward the critical theory and constructivist researchers identified the postmodern ethnographic method which should be 'dedicated to understanding how this (postmodern ethnography) universalises itself in the lives of interesting individuals' (Denzin, 1989, 1994: 42, 120, original parentheses). Postmodern ethnography requires a sort of foundation-less detachment to the world; there exists a phenomenological stream of becoming and the world continually shifts in relation to this becoming. In such a way, the world is a social construction that relates to individuals defined and determined by ideology, power, politics and culture that are implicit to this construction.

History, values and ethical perspectives are deconstructed and deemed as self-serving facts selected by power brokers or different groupings within the structure. All universal understandings or grand theories as representations of reality are rejected. Through deconstruction human existence is formulated and social science understood at the local level with limited generalisations available. Indeed, even the local is relative and open to continual change. Generalisation is put to one side and 'thick description' and 'thick interpretation' pursued (Geertz, 1973; Denzin, 1989). Furthermore, general history is pushed to the periphery and local histories given explicit meaning in relation to the situation under analysis.

Definition Box

Deconstruction

Deconstruction identifies the supposed meaning of a text (the meaning the text wished to portray) then exposes the contradictions on which this supposed meaning is founded. Subsequently, deconstruction illustrates that the foundations on which the portrayal of meanings based are unstable and complex. The text is not a unified entity with one meaning but many different contradictory meanings and interpretations.

Some researchers consider that the postmodern ethnographic approach merely presents the words of respondents and accepts their perceptions of reality; there is limited social scientific research involved. Others argue that this is not the case and it involves analysis of respondents' words. While respondents' voices can be pre-eminent in analysis; these voices should not be reported, analysed and interpreted uncritically. Obviously, as well as criticisms regarding validity, levels of generalisations also come into question. Denzin (1989) and Denzin and Lincoln (1994) suggested a means of overcoming this argument or dilemma for postmodernist ethnography, which included:

- immersion of self in the lives of subjects involved in the investigation;
- achieve a deep comprehension of the subjects through rigorous effort;
- produce contextualised reproduction and interpretation of the subject's stories.

A postmodern ethnographic study involves social scientific research because it encompasses the synthesis of theoretical and the empirical (practice/experience). The 'final interpretive theory is multi-voiced and dialogical. It builds on native interpretations and … articulates what is implicit in those interpretations' (Denzin, 1989: 120). Postmodern ethnography recognises that the world is shared by all those that exist within it and each responds to it in a specific way. Consequently, understanding the common situation becomes problematic but not the impossibility identified in pure postmodernism.

Social science research in this context ultimately involves interaction between the individual and what is sought in relation to values embedded in the research environment as well as other individuals involved in the investigation. Indeed, for postmodern ethnography (as with the phenomenologists Heidegger and Merleau-Ponty) that which is sought gives direction to the research and investigation. Researchers are caught up in their own social, historical and cultural histories which need to be made meaningful in a general context. Fundamentally, research becomes meaningful in relation to existing and historical theoretical frameworks and ongoing present day research in relation to that under investigation by the individual researcher. The main method in this form of social science research or constructivist ethnography is participatory observation and reflexivity where the researcher becomes a working member of the group and reflects on the activity of self and group interaction, which closely resembles action research.

⌐ Definition Box ⌐

Participant Observation

Participant observation was originally forged as a method in the study of small, relatively homogeneous societies. An ethnographer lived in a society for an extended period of time, learned the local language, participated in daily life and steadily observed.

AN INTRODUCTION TO THE PHILOSOPHY OF METHODOLOGY

Participant observation implies simultaneous emotional involvement and objective detachment (Tedlock, 2000).

| Reflection Box |

Observation of Participation

Kurt Wolff (1964) describes how, during his field research in a northern New Mexico village, he opened himself to the risk of being hurt by becoming so totally involved and identified with the community that everything he saw or experienced became relevant to him. 'It was years before I understood what had happened to me: I had fallen through the web of culture patterns and assorted conceptual meshes into the chaos of love: I was looking everywhere, famished, with a ruthless glance' (cited in Tedlock, 2000: 466). Compare and contrast the experience outlined here with the 'horror' identified by Joseph Conrad in the *Heart of Darkness*.

Conclusion

This chapter has dealt with social science research through a number of different interpretations of ethnography (positivist, critical theory and postmodernist) as well as overviewed its occidental roots and relationship with colonialism, imperialism and early anthropology. Eventually, there was a move away from the overt occidental and positivistic positions and recognition of the integrity of cultures in the developing world. Indeed, with the softening of the positivist approach and emergence of the critical and constructivist perspectives there was a recognition of 'other' and emergence of a relationship between subjective and objective and that interpretation and understanding was subjective and relative. This latter perspective related closer to phenomenological conceptions of ethnography and saw the researcher as part of the research process rather than removed from and external to it.

Positivist ethnographers consider they went beyond descriptions of perspectives and behaviours and provide in-depth explanations of situations. Furthermore, they do not bring in ideas relating to emancipation because to do so will simply make them critical ethnographers. In an axiological context, critical theorists challenged positivist ethnography for its adherence to the value-free context professed by natural scientists where behaviour can be described from a neutral or value-free position and an objective stance. Such a position fails to see the importance of the researchers' values in relation to the research as well as the ever present values involved in the political and cultural environments.

The difficulty is that the researcher's worldview and decisions about which data is important, and which are not, guide observations. Fundamentally, research is value laden. The question is by whose values are observations to be guided? As noted, observations may be either be etic or emic, a further problem involves how one comprehends the observed when their values are different to one's own (a difficulty with the colonial comprehension of the so-called primitive practices observed from a Christian value-laden perspective). Furthermore, one may argue there are problems relating to postmodernism in terms of generality and validity.

Based on the phenomenological perspectives, the critical theory and postmodern constructivist ethnographic approaches consider human understanding to be subjective and relative. Ethnographic studies should define humankind and provide social scientific descriptions of people and their cultural bases; in such a way we can develop comprehensions of 'self' in relation to 'other' in terms of becoming. A constructivist ethnographic study should represent an integrated synthesis of theory and experience. Indeed the, 'final interpretative theory is multi-voiced and dialogical. It builds on native interpretations and articulates what is implicit in those interpretations' (Denzin and Lincoln 1994: 120). As noted, Denzin considered that the ethnographic method for this period (postmodern) should be 'dedicated to understanding how this historical moment universalises itself in the lives of interesting individuals' (1994: 189). 'Experience is intersubjective and embodies not individual and fixed, but social and processual. Intersubjectivity and dialogue involve situations where bodies marked by social … that is, by difference … may be presented as partial identities' (Tedlock, 2000: 471). Critical ethnography argues that positivist ethnography describes micro-based situations in a common-sense manner that fails to take into consideration wider political and social frameworks. The constructivist ethnographic study should represent an integrated synthesis of theory and experience. Each ethnographic approach involves a separate perspective of social science research and different understanding regarding validity and knowledge generation but each is committed to these endeavours in their own but very different ways. Furthermore, each of these approaches is not totally discrete and synthesis of these methodological or ethnographic approaches may be utilised to enhance social science research projects.

Further Reading

Denzin, N. (1989) *Interpretive Interactionism.* Thousand Oaks, CA: SAGE Publications.
Denzin, N. and Lincoln, Y. (1994) *The Handbook of Qualitative Research,* 1st edn. Thousand Oaks, CA: SAGE Publications.
Denzin, N. and Lincoln, Y. (2000) *The Handbook of Qualitative Research,* 2nd edn. Thousand Oaks, CA: SAGE Publications.
Denzin, N. and Lincoln, Y. (2005) *The Handbook of Qualitative Research,* 3rd edn. Thousand Oaks, CA: SAGE Publications.
Hammersley. M. (1992) *What's Wrong with Ethnography?* London: Routledge.
Hammersley, M. and Atkinson, P. (2007) *Ethnography: Principles in Practice.* London: Routledge.
O'Reilly, K. (2009) *Key Concepts in Ethnography.* London: SAGE Publications.

NINE

Grounded Theory

Introduction

This chapter outlines grounded theory and explains how this methodological approach constructs theory and provides in-depth insight and understanding of the area or situation under investigation. Grounded theory builds theory through data collection and analysis in relation to pre-existing theory and practice. Grounded theory suggests that there is an over-emphasis on quantitative research and wishes to demote the idea that the discovery of relevant concepts and hypotheses are a priori to research. For further see (Bryant and Charmaz, 2007a, 2007b; Charmaz, 1983, 2000, 2006; Clarke, 2002; Corbin and Strauss, 1990; Cresswell, 2007; Glaser, 1978, 1992; Glaser and Strauss, 1967; Goulding, 2002; Hood, 2007; Strauss, 1987; Strauss and Corbin, 1990, 1994). Grounded theory posits that theory is derived from data and cannot be divorced from the process by which it is developed. Subsequently, questions, hypotheses and concepts are generated through the data and worked out during the course of the research (Glaser and Strauss, 1967). Strauss and Corbin (1998) argued that grounded theory provided methodological lenses for seeing and comprehending the world and involved the following characteristics: first, on the one hand, the means for critical analysis of events and situations from an objective stand point, while on the other hand the capability for recognising subjective tendencies. Second, abstract thinking and openness to useful criticism as well as empathy and sensitivity when dealing with the actions and discourse of those involved with the investigation. Finally, there should be immersion and absorption within the research, analysis and data collection process. Fundamentally, grounded theory allows the direction of the research and analysis of the data to be guided by an empowered researcher. Indeed, because of the flexibility of the approach, grounded theory is used by researchers from a range of different subject areas and disciplines and deployed in eclectic and distinct ways. It is used in areas as diverse as business, nursing, political studies, psychology, sociology and many areas of social science in general. Furthermore, when using grounded theory a number of philosophical issues in terms of ontological and epistemological positions may be ascertained. This chapter accepts that this methodological approach is primarily concerned with data collection, analysis and theory construction but because of the philosophical underpinning as well as eclectic areas that utilise grounded theory, it is worth identifying its roots and evolution as a useful tool or mechanism for undertaking qualitative research.

Philosophical Underpinnings of Grounded Theory

Even though there is a phenomenological underpinning to interpretations of grounded theory, Glaser and Strauss (1967) primarily drew on the US pragmatist tradition of Dewey (1950) and symbolic interaction approach of Mead (1962) and Blumer (1969). Dewey (1950) argued that 'flowers can be enjoyed without knowing about the interactions of soil, air, moisture and seeds of which they are the result. But they cannot be understood without taking just these interactions into account and theory is a matter of understanding' (1950: 12). Theory cannot answer questions 'unless we are willing to find the germs and roots in matters of experience' (Dewey, 1950: 12).

│ Definition Box │

Pragmatism

Pragmatism defines truth as those tenets that prove useful to the believer or user. The verifiability of truth exists to the extent that actuality or things correspond with state-ments and thoughts. Objective truth cannot exist because it needs to relate to practice; both subjective and objective dimensions are necessary.

In the acquisition of knowledge, an essential element 'is the perception of relations, especially the relations between our actions and their empirical consequences' (Scheffler, 1974: 197). In such a way, the world around us and individuals take on deeper meaning; in this context, humans need experience and the means of storing that experience. However, as with phenomenology experience is more than 'a passive registering or beholding of phenomena; it involves deliberate interaction with environmental conditions, the conse-quences of which are critically noted and fed back into the control of future conduct' (Scheffler, 1974: 197). Pragmatists considered that from 'the child's exploration of its environment to the scientist's theorising about nature the pattern of intelligent thought is the same: a problem provides the initial occa-sion of inquiry ... Experiment ... is, experience rendered educative' (Scheffler, 1974: 196).

Through these pragmatist foundations grounded theory can be understood in terms of symbolic interaction, where the 'individual enters as such into his own experience only as an object not as a subject; and he can enter as an object only on the basis of social relations and interactions' (Mead, 1962: 225). Through the language and structure of roles we become a generalised other; we attain a consciousness of self as a generalised other. This may allow the individual to take an impartial and general standpoint in observing and evaluating one's own conduct when one becomes a generalised other or the object of one's own reflection. At this point one has become self, which reflects the phenomenological underpinnings of Hegelian recognition and being in the world.

Blumer (1962, 1969) also built on the work of the pragmatist tradition and considered that, 'ordinarily human beings respond to one another, as in carrying on a conversation, by interpreting one another's actions or remarks and then reacting on the basis of interpretation' (Blumer, 1969: 71). Grounded theory builds on this understanding and considers that research should be grounded out of reality and that the researcher should enter into the field and discover/comprehend what is going on. People have an active role in shaping the world and through interrelationships in terms of meaning, action and conditions the nature of experience continually evolves, which creates continual re-interpretation of phenomenon (Corbin and Strauss, 1990). Indeed, grounded theory is primarily inductive and pursues the interpretations of those involved in the situation that is being researched and the interpretations of the researcher in relation to the data. Through this process, grounded theory is enacted and substantive theory constructed. Symbolic interaction is distinct to human beings, it is part of what makes us human because we 'interpret or define each other's actions' rather than simply react to them (Blumer, 1962: 179). Furthermore, humans have and are able to act towards self. Mead considered that the ability to react to self was the central mechanism of existence.

This mechanism enables human beings to indicate to themselves things in their surroundings and thus guide action through what is noted. 'Anything of which a human being is conscious … he is indicating to himself … The conscious life of the human being … is a continual flow of self indications' (Blumer, 1962: 180). Such is similar to phenomenology in terms of being in the world and intentionality. Fundamentally, 'the formation of action by the individual through … self-indication always takes place in a social context' (Blumer, 1962: 183); as does the background or environment (fore-structure) which indicates possible ways of questioning (Heidegger, 1962/1984). Additionally, Stern considered that grounded theory was an interpretative method and was underpinned by 'phenomenology that is methods that are used to describe the world of the person or persons under study' (1994: 213).

Furthermore, with distinct linkage to Heidegger and later Merleau-Ponty, interpretation 'is grounded in something we have in advance . . . understanding operates in … an involvement whole that is already understood'. Effectively the environment or background determines possible ways of questioning. However, interpretation is also 'grounded in something we see in advance – in foresight' (Heidegger, 2004: 191). Additionally, interpretation is made on the basis of those interacting with the researcher; in this context, the individual is both subjective and objective. The researcher is interpreted by self in relation to society and interpreted by society in relation to self through self-indication. 'Self-indication is a moving communicative process in which the individual notes things, assesses them, gives them a meaning, and decides to act on the basis of meaning' (Blumer, 1962: 183). However, to accomplish this some foresight is necessary, even if this is only a comprehension of language or culture. This foresight takes into consideration the theories that already exist or more formal theories. Additionally, the researcher brings to the analysis expertise, knowledge and theoretical sensitivity. Effectively, objectivity is continually pursued through the recognition of subjective influences throughout the research process. As with phenomenology there are relationships between reality and the human mind. Indeed, the 'research findings constitute a theoretical formulation of the reality under investigation rather than consisting of a set of numbers or a group of loosely related themes' (Corbin and Strauss, 1990: 24).

'One now regularly takes an impartial and general standpoint in observing and evaluating one's own conduct … (however) … The organised community or social group which gives to the individual his unity of self may be called the generalised other which is the attitude of the whole community' (Blau, 1952: 162–3, original parentheses). Interpretations of situations change as individuals change (this includes the researcher and the researched). Indeed, with the knowledge that pure objectivity cannot be attained the research can become more objective, for example, through accepting subjectivity one can become more objective. Grounded theory attempts to understand social patterns and construct social theory. 'Grounded theory involves soliciting … emic viewpoints to assist in determining the meaning and purposes that people ascribe to their actions' (Guba and Lincoln, 1994: 110). 'Grounded theory methodology incorporates … assumption(s) … concerning the human status of actors whom we study. They have perspectives on and interpretations of their own and other actors' actions. As researchers we are required to learn what we can of their interpretations and perspectives' (Strauss and Corbin, 1994: 280, authors' brackets).

| Reflection Box |

Pragmatism, Phenomenology and Symbolic Interaction

Demonstrate where similarities exist between pragmatism, phenomenology and symbolic interaction.

Indeed, such identifies aspects of being in the world and intentionality outlined by Heidegger and Husserl. The rest of this chapter will outline what grounded theory entails and explain how it may be applied. It then discusses the different perceptions of grounded theory displayed by Barney Glaser and Anselm Strauss as well as the subsequent variants that evolved from these distinctions.

Using Grounded Theory

Grounded theory is a way of collecting data and through comparative analysis and coding a means of generating or building substantive theory. Grounded theory is about building theory through the collection and analysis of rich data; that is data that exists below the surface of the social entity being investigated. To achieve rich data some persistence and creativity in the inquiry process is required. Initial questions the researcher may first attempt to develop include:

- What research problem should be studied?
- How may the project be undertaken?
- Which methods should be used in the collection of rich data?

The research problem should emanate through work or ideas generated through previous studies; issues that have become apparent following the writing of a report, essay, dissertation or academic paper. Furthermore, when identifying the research problem, issues regarding access and participant numbers requires some consideration. If the right participants are located and access to these allowed, then the first hurdles for accumulating rich data have been overcome. Such data will illuminate further detail regarding the research question or issue and enable new insight into what may initially have seemed mundane concepts. Grounded theory is social science based and involves research about and with people. Rich data enables insight into the veiled and sometimes opaque feelings, ideas and beliefs of the individuals involved in the investigation as well as those investigators will undoubtedly carry themselves. Grounded theories are developed or built through the comparative analysis of rich diffuse data (data collected from different places and through separate methods). Through writing thick description based on field-notes, observations, personal diaries and accounts of events as well as interviews and secondary data, detailed narratives may be formed.

Fundamentally, grounded theory attempts to improve theory as one can only replace existing theoretical frameworks with improved or enhanced theories (Glaser and Strauss, 1967). 'Grounded theory is based on the systematic generation of theory from data, and itself is systematically obtained from social research (and) offers a rigorous orderly guide to theory development that at each stage is closely integrated with a methodology of social research' (Glaser, 1978: 2). Through comparative analysis, grounded theory creates theories made up of general categories. It is not necessary to know the empirical or specific situation better than those involved; the researcher simply wishes to develop theory that applies to relevant behaviour. Theory is never complete but always under development. Theory generated from data means that ideas or hypotheses are not only derived from this but worked out in relation to the data as the research progresses.

While positivism seeks to verify deduced hypotheses, grounded theory implies steps prior to discovering what concepts and hypotheses are relevant to the area of research should be made explicit. Ultimately, the relationship between categories and sub-categories which are discovered during the research should be as a result of information contained within the data or from deductive reasoning which has been verified within the data, but not from previous assumptions which have not been supported (Howell, 2000).

Grounded theory offers a rigorous approach to research in terms of:

- interactive iterative nature of data collection and analysis;
- comparative methods;
- conceptual analyses through memo writing;
- refinement of emerging ideas through sampling;
- theoretical framework derived from and integrated with both data and theory.

Glaser (1978, 1992) identifies the following criteria:

- Fit
- Work
- Relevance
- Modifiability.

Theoretical categories must emerge and be developed from data analysis; they must fit. Grounded theory should order the data so as to explain the phenomena; it should work. It should have relevance in terms of dealing with actual problems and processes located in the research setting. In addition, through accounting for variation grounded theory is durable and flexible.

Glaser and Strauss (1967) challenged the division between theory and data as well as the perceived lower importance of qualitative techniques in relation to quantitative. Furthermore, they also synthesised data collection and analysis and critiqued ideas that qualitative research was unsystematic and relied heavily on impressions. Overall, they argued that qualitative research could go beyond descriptive case studies and engender theory development. Glaser used his training in positivism to develop a rigorous form of qualitative analysis. Strauss brought a pragmatic perspective that built on ideas relating to symbolic interaction. Glaser (1992) clearly states that he used the statistical analytical method as a model for the qualitative method in grounded theory. Consequently, a model for quantitative analysis provided the basis for a unique qualitative approach.

The other side of the equation that is symbolic interaction involved a number of underpinnings for grounded theory. These include:

- pragmatism (close relationship between theory and practice);
- idiographic as opposed to nomothetic research;
- qualitative research as primary rather than secondary;
- exploration as a central function;
- creation of worldviews through sensitising concepts (empathy and judgment are central);
- social action rather than structuration as the main focus;
- symbols are relayed between actors through agency;
- intersubjectivity is central;
- interaction between self and other is central for humanity;
- self is a world of meaning not an external structure (primarily cognitive).

Open and axial coding examines phenomena through comparing and categorising data. This text will break down coding procedures and explain the processes and activities involved in each of the procedures. The initial objective for grounded theory is to identify categories and properties which are relevant to the theory and allow a level of integration. 'The goal of the analyst is to generate an emergent set of categories and their properties which fit, work and are relevant for integrating theory. To achieve this goal the analyst begins with open coding' (Glaser, 1978: 56). Attention should be fixed on a category and the properties that emerge continually coded and analysed as the initial basic steps. Fundamentally, the researcher constantly compares and continually categorises data and concepts.

Theoretical Sampling

Theoretical sampling is undertaken on the basis that 'concepts have *proven theoretical relevance* to the evolving theory' (Strauss and Corbin, 1990: 176). *Theoretical sampling* involves three processes: *open sampling*, which relates to *open coding*; *relational and variational sampling*, which is associated with *axial coding*; and *discriminate sampling*, which is linked to *selective coding* (coding processes are discussed below). *Proven theoretical relevance* identifies concepts that are significant enough to be considered *categories*:

> they are deemed significant because (1) they are repeatedly present or notably absent when comparing incident after incident (2) through coding procedures they earn the status of categories ... The aim of theoretical sampling is to sample events, incidents, and so forth, that are indicative of categories, their properties and dimensions, so that you can develop and conceptually relate them. (Strauss and Corbin, 1990: 177)

The sampling is undertaken purposefully which encompasses choosing individuals and documentation that demonstrated variations in the categories and what happened when change occurred. As with the coding (see below) the distinction between relational and variational sampling and discriminate sampling became unclear. *Discriminate sampling* is direct and deliberate. 'In discriminate sampling, a researcher chooses the sites, persons and documents that will maximise opportunities for verifying the story line and relationships between categories' (Strauss and Corbin, 1990: 187). Sampling in grounded theory studies is concerned with the ' representativeness of concepts in their varying forms. In each instance of data collection, we look for evidence of its significant presence or absence, and ask why?' (Strauss and Corbin, 1990: 190) (see Table 9.1). Grounded theory studies look 'for incidents and events that are indicative of phenomena' (Strauss and Corbin, 1990: 187). They pursue density and:

> the more interviews, observations and documents obtained, then the more evidence will accumulate, the more variations will be found, and the greater the density will be achieved. Thus there will be wider applicability of the theory, because more and different sets of conditions affecting phenomena are uncovered. (Strauss and Corbin, 1990: 190–1)

Open, Axial and Selective Coding

Grounded theorist code data as it is collected. Coding defines and categorises data. Codes are created as the data is studied. Data should be continually interacted with and questions continually posed as the analysis develops. It should not fit into pre-conceived codes but codes that have emerged through the researcher's interpretation of the data. Coding is iterative and interactive and line by line coding can ensure that the researcher's beliefs are not imposed on the data and interpretation.

Glaser (1978, 1992) stressed continual comparative methods, that is, comparing:

- views, action environments, narratives, discourse, beliefs and stories;
- data from the same individuals at different points in time;
- situation with situation;
- incident with incident;
- data with categories;
- categories with categories. (Charmaz, 1983; Glaser, 1978, 1992)

Strauss and Corbin (1990) are more structured and developed new procedures:

- dimensionalisation;
- axial coding;
- conditional matrix.

These are supposed to make emerging theory thicker or denser, complex and rigorous.

Through memo writing, coding provides the very bedrock of grounded theory; the essential relationship between data and theory is a code, which conceptualises the underlying patterns of the data. Consequently through 'generating a theory by developing the hypothetical relationships between conceptual codes (categories and their properties), which have been generated from the data as indicators, we discover a grounded theory' (Glaser, 1978: 55).

Charmaz (1983) considered that coding incorporates 'the initial phase of the analytical method (and) is simply the process of categorising and sorting data. Codes then serve as shorthand devices to label, separate, compile and organise data. Codes range from simple concrete, and topical categories to more general, abstract conceptual categories for an emerging theory' (Charmaz, 1983: 111). Indeed, in 'grounded theory research there are three basic types of coding; open, axial and selective' (Corbin and Strauss, 1990: 9). Through memo-writing, coding requires researchers to re-assess what may seem like an obvious perspective of the phenomenon under investigation; the data should undergo analysis from different standpoints and it should be continually critiqued and questioned. Comparison is a central technique and the researcher should continually compare memos with codes and data with data and codes. Through coding interviews, documentation, observations, focus groups and secondary data, categories emerge through data segmentation on which labels may be placed. Coding involves interpreting the data and moving from concrete to more abstract conceptualisations; through coding one takes the first tentative steps towards theory generation. Coding involves the very framework of the analytical process and identifies the bridge between the data and emergent substantive theory. Coding involves microanalysis (detailed close line-by-line attention) and involves a dynamic fluids process; categories and properties are created and relationships assessed through open and axial coding.

Definition Box

Microanlysis

Microanalysis can involve word by word coding of the data which forces the researcher to concentrate on specific meanings incorporated in the text; this means the way the sentences are structured and flow as well as distinct contexts. Line-by-line coding which comprises of labelling each line read (not sentences but each line); this throws up unexpected themes and ideas that one may not detect when coding sentence by sentence. When dealing with empirical difficulties accounted through observations, focus groups, interviews or documentation, line-by-line coding is particularly useful as it details and reveals opaque issues, problems and situations. This coding procedure investigates underlying meanings and actions as well as clarifies the significance of ideas through identifying and comparing deficiencies in the data.

Indeed, open and axial coding are undertaken together in the formation of categories and properties, however for the purpose of explanation we will now separate these activities and explain the processes individually.

Memo Writing and Open Coding: A Practical Example

Initially, grounded theory is inductively derived from the study of the phenomena it represents. Data collection, analysis and theory are reciprocal; one does not start with a theory, which is then tested but with an area of study from which what is relevant to the area is derived through data collection. Induction is grounded in social phenomena or observations and experience; hence the strong link between inductive procedures and grounded theory. Glaser and Strauss (1967) and Charmaz (1983) proposed that data collection and analysis were undertaken simultaneously and interpretations formed through data discovery. This process which simultaneously led back to the data (the researcher resides in the field of discovery) allows for emerging ideas because it provides for further data collection. A main strength of the grounded theory approach is that data and ideas are derived through the research rather than through a priori deduction. Verification is secondary to understanding, not simply understanding the phenomenon, but an understanding of social life as process.

> As such, theoretical analyses may be transcended by further work either by the original or later theorists. In keeping with their foundations in pragmatism, then, grounded theorists aim to develop fresh theoretical interpretations of the data rather than explicitly aim for any final or complete interpretation of it ... Although every researcher brings to his or her research general preconceptions founded in expertise, theory, method, and experience, using the grounded theory method necessitates that the researcher look at the data from as many vantage points as possible. (Charmaz, 1983: 111–14)

Data is analysed as it emerges or collected and through coding, 'order created' (Charmaz, 1983: 114). It is given that researchers have pre-understandings through their expertise, experience, theoretical frameworks, and for grounded theory these are important elements of analysis and important perspectives to be taken into consideration when dealing with the data; it is important that data be considered from many different perspectives or positions

With grounded theory, data collection procedures and strategies are continually refined; flexible guidelines are outlined rather than dogmatic prescriptions. Methods that deal with research questions should be targeted and followed in an investigative manner; methods of data collection affect the extent phenomenon will become important and how when and where this will be observed. Indeed, methods of data collection determine how we make sense of the phenomenon investigated. Coding for grounded theory involves posing analytical questions. Memos provide a record of the research process and include modes of 'analysis, thoughts, interpretations, questions, and directions for further data collection' (Strauss and Corbin, 1998: 110).

Strauss and Corbin (1998) give an example of an interview they undertook with a drug user which homed in on the term 'use' as it is specifically used by people when speaking of drugs. Usually when the term used is employed it means that something is employed in a specific way 'that an object or person is used for some purpose' (Strauss and Corbin, 1998: 110). When one uses something one considers that the user is in control and when one reassesses the term drug user in this context, even though it specifically means to consume, remnants of these ideas may also be included in the term; 'for example, being used for some reason, having control over what one does' (Strauss and Corbin, 1998: 111). Rather than simply taking drugs the term drug user takes on a number of connotations in terms of 'self-control over usage … purposeful … directed act that serves as an end and has a desired effect' (Strauss and Corbin, 1998: 111) Consequently, even though such issues may not be explicit in the data during the initial stages, this code or idea is something that may be kept in mind and used as the analysis and further data collection progresses (ibid). So the memo 'user' arises and directs the researcher to think in more detail about this term, for instance, one does not usually employ the term an 'alcohol user' and if one did what would this actually mean? Think of the reasons you may use alcohol; do you use it to cook, get to sleep, get drunk, take to dinner parties or provide for individuals invited to your home, do you use alcohol in bars, the park, at home, what type of alcohol do you use spirits or wine, do you drink alone or only with company, does it relax you and assist sleep, for how long does someone and how often do they use alcohol? Each of these questions raise certain properties regarding alcohol use 'such as frequency, duration, type, purpose, way of using and place of use' (Strauss and Corbin, 1998: 111) Consequently, in subsequent interviews issues regarding these properties may be further explored in terms of, reasons for usage, place, type, environment, levels of usage. Indeed, the category use or user is beginning to emerge and the properties relating to this may be placed on a 'dimension' with say 'usage' at one point and 'reason' at the other with the other terms placed on this dimension in relation to these two extremities. User emerges into a category with properties representing property locations along the continuum. For example, alcohol usage in terms of alcoholism and social drinker may be identified in terms of frequency and type (the number of times one gets drunk and strength of alcohol) will distinguish between these properties within this category. However, we may wish to clarify what we mean by social drinker and identify distinctions regarding drinking alone or not and the type of alcohol consumed. Further delineations may emerge in terms of binge drinking and how this may differ from alcoholism or social drinking; through such a process, property patterns begin to emerge and congregate on the dimension. Dimensions involve the 'range along which general properties of a category vary, giving specification to a category and variation to the theory' (Strauss and Corbin, 1998: 101). Obviously, through further data collection and analysis this dimensionalisation may be further developed and/or transformed.

Axial and Selective Coding

Axial coding involves the re-structuring of the whole process by finding connections between the data. Axial coding pulls the analysis together and provides a means of unifying the data into a coherent whole. It indicates how the categories created by open coding fit together and how they congregate around a core category. This type of coding provides a means of organising large amounts of data as the analysis details and understands the development of a major or core category. Fundamentally, axial coding links categories and sub-categories through diagrams as it pursues the development of substantive theory. It uses a set of terms to denote the process which include: *causal conditions* and *phenomenon*, which involve the environment of the researched in terms of circumstance or specific situation and the entity under analysis as well as the *context* or the more general historical and social/cultural situation within which the research or investigation is undertaken. The intervening conditions which pull together answers relating to questions regarding why, where, what, when, how? This portrays the need for *action/interaction* between entities in terms of the reason certain ideas and events occurred, for example, whether these be strategic or routine responses made to certain conditions, phenomenon or questions; action and interaction correspond with questions relating to whom and how. Finally, the *consequences* are the outcome of the process especially the success or failure of the action/interaction between entities. Consequences are denoted through questions relating to the outcome of actions and interactions, for example what would happen if *x* or *y* occurred? In 'axial coding we continue to look for additional properties for each category and to note the dimensional location of each incident, happening or event' (Strauss and Corbin, 1990: 114–15).

│ Definition Box ┌

Axial Coding

Axial coding is illustrated through:

- causal conditions;
- phenomenon;
- context;
- intervening conditions;
- action/interaction;
- consequences. (Corbin and Strauss, 1990: 96–7)

Axial coding can be used as a framework to encourage the emergence of categories which provide insight into the core category and the substantive theory.

Glaser considered that axial coding 'undermines and confuses the very method that he (Strauss) is trying to build' (1992: 61). This process forces the data and negates theoretical coding. The grounded theorist should code categories and properties and allow theoretical codes to emerge where they will. Strauss and Corbin (1990) argued that axial coding allows a more focused means of discovering and relating categories. Strauss and Corbin develop categories (phenomenon) in relation to the underlying conditions that enable its development, and through identification of properties the location of this phenomenon on a dimension (dimentionalisation), the context and the action/interaction strategies used to 'handle, manage, and respond to this phenomenon' (1990: 61).

Selective coding illustrates how the phenomenon fits around a core category and involves the process by which emerging categories are organised and unified around a core category (Corbin and Strauss, 1990). Core categories incorporate central phenomenon of research projects as they are identified through questions such as: 'What is the main analytical idea presented in this research? What does all the action/interaction seem to be about? The selection of data and the creation of other categories are processed with the core category in mind which are identified and unified through axial coding.

Between these three coding procedures exists 'process' through which changes to the data are monitored and made explicit. Process is also built into the theory. Process analysis involves 'breaking phenomenon down into stages, phases, or steps. Process may also denote purposeful action/interaction that is not necessarily progressive, but changes in response to prevailing conditions' (Corbin and Strauss, 1990: 10). Even though initially inductive, grounded theory also involves a deductive component, which is primarily used during the identification and pursuit of process. 'As you have probably noticed while coding we are constantly moving between inductive and deductive thinking' (Strauss and Corbin, 1990: 111). When process is difficult to identify, the researcher may turn to deductive analysis so as to identify, possible situations of change, 'then go back to the data or field situation and look for evidence to support refute or modify that hypothesis' (Strauss and Corbin, 1990: 148).

Theoretical Sensitivity

Grounded theory research should be approached with an objective demeanour, pursed with an open mind and primarily through inductive processes. That said, one must acknowledge that objectivity, an open mind as well as a completely inductive position are difficult to attain. Everyone is instilled with subjective tendencies and pre-conceptions, that said recognising these tendencies is part way to dealing with them. To overcome these tendencies one may use one's theoretical sensitivity, which allows the researcher to remain sensitive and 'record events and detect happenings without first having them filtered through and squared with pre-existing hypotheses and biases' (Glaser, 1978: 3). As identified in the phenomenology of Heidegger and Merleau-Ponty individuals have pre-determined ideas and different levels of sensitivity, which depend on 'previous reading and experience with or relevant to the area ... Theoretical sensitivity refers to the attribute of having insight, the ability to give meaning to data, the capacity to understand, and the capability to separate the pertinent from that which isn't ... It is theoretical sensitivity that allows one to develop a theory that is grounded conceptually dense' (Strauss and Corbin, 1990: 40–1). Glaser expanded on his earlier definition of theoretical sensitivity and argued that it 'refers to the researcher's knowledge, understanding, and skill which foster his generation of categories and properties' (1992: 27).

QUESTION

THEORETICAL SENSITIVITY

What is theoretical sensitivity? How does this relate to ideas outlined by certain phenomeno-logical positions?

Surveys in Grounded Theory

Within the grounded theory methodology the role surveys and quantitative data play is ambiguous. 'The sociologist whose purpose is to generate theory may of course collect his own survey data, but, for several reasons, he is more likely to analyse previously collected data called secondary (data)' (Glaser and Strauss, 1967: 187). However, the researcher should give him/herself the 'freedom in the flexible use of quantitative data or he or she will not be able to generate theory that is adequate . . . (and) in taking this freedom ... be clear about the rules he is relaxing (Glaser and Strauss, 1967: 186). Such flexibility will allow the richness of qualitative data to become apparent:

> and lead to new styles and strategies of quantitative analysis, with their own rules yet to be discovered ... For example, in verification studies cross-tabulations of quantitative variables continually and inadvertently lead to discoveries of new social patterns and new hypotheses that are often ignored as not being the purpose of the research. (Glaser and Strauss, 1967: 186)

Grounded theory relaxes rules of verification and accuracy of evidence to enable further theory generation 'the way they are relaxed for purposes of generating theory could apply to many styles of analysis' (Glaser and Strauss, 1967: 187). 'One might use qualitative data to illustrate or clarify quantitatively derived findings; or, one could quantify demographic findings. Or, one could use some form of quantitative data to partially validate one's qualitative analysis' (Strauss and Corbin, 1990: 18–19). This outcome may be realised through triangulation. Consequently, although surveys are not grounded theory techniques in the purest sense, used in certain ways they may benefit theory generation. In this context, they may be utilised in a grounded theory study and eventually they may be considered as part of the technique. This, one may speculate, is the direction in which Glaser and Strauss (1967) pointed toward and Glaser (1992) makes clear. 'To repeat, qualitative analysis may be done with data arrived at quantitatively or qualitatively or in some combination' (Glaser, 1992: 11) All methods are acceptable and how they may be used 'together effectively . . . depends on the research' (Glaser, 1992: 12).

EXAMPLE

USING A SURVEY

To supplement categorisation and provide further coding a survey can be conducted to investigate further perceptions. The survey questions can be formulated in relation to ...categories dimensions and properties (developed through previous coding) and emphasised basic questions such as When? Where? What? and How Much? (Howell, 2000).

Substantive and Formal Theory

Glaser and Strauss (1967) argued that grounded theory was concerned with two types of theory: substantive and formal. They emphasised that theory generation was accomplished through the collection, coding and analysis of data and that these three operations, as far as was possible, were undertaken together. Collection, coding and analysis should interact throughout the investigation as their separation hinders theory generation and set ideas stifle it.

Definition Box

Substantive Theory

Substantive theory necessitates four central criteria. Fit, comprehension, generality and control: first, theory should be induced from diverse data and be faithful to reality (it should fit). Second, the fit should be comprehensible; third, the data should be comprehensive and interpretations conceptually wide (there should be generality). Finally, in relation to generality, it should be made clear when conditions apply to specific situations and phenomenon (there should be control) (Corbin and Strauss, 1990).

Grounded theory generates substantive theory through comparative analysis and coding. It does not attempt to undermine theory but improve it 'a theory's only replacement is a better theory' (Glaser and Strauss, 1967: 28).

Grounded theory is based on the systematic generation of theory from data, and itself is systematically obtained from social research. Thus, the grounded theory method offers a rigorous orderly guide to theory development that at each stage is closely integrated with a methodology of social research. (Glaser, 1978: 2)

Through the general method of comparative analysis, grounded theory wishes to create a theory made up of general categories.

> A formal theory is composed of a model plus an indefinite number of interpretations, and there is a sharp distinction between model and interpretation. A model is not affected by any of its interpretations, but can be understood and studied in abstraction from all of them … A substantive theory … is … about something in the real world. (Diesing, 1972: 31)

Consequently, substantive theory needs to be verified and if changes to the theory are to be made there must be references to empiricism. The formal theory 'can be understood and studied in abstraction . . . one can . . . make deductions, search for inconsistencies, study the effects of changes in those postulated, and add new terms without referring to anything empirical' (ibid). Formal theories are more abstract and may be broken down into meso (middle range), grand or meta theories (philosophies); as discussed in more detail above. Substantive theory relates to a practical situation and through accumulation of substantive theory can develop and become meso, grand and eventually meta theory.

This chapter acknowledges that it is easy to find a problem with a theoretical concept by identifying that certain data is missing. This could be the charge against most analyses. However, as Glaser and Strauss put it: 'If each debunker thought about the potential value of comparative analysis … he would realise that he has merely posed another comparative datum for generating another theoretical property or category' (1967: 22). Despite what those concerned with evidence may say, nothing has been disproved, only another comparison created (Glaser and Strauss, 1967). Theory is never a finished product, but always under development. Generating theory from data means that most of the ideas or hypotheses are not only derived from the data but are worked out in relation to the data as the research progresses.

QUESTION

GROUNDED THEORY

Identify why and then how you might undertake a grounded theory approach for an upcoming research project. What would you consider the major strengths and weaknesses of this approach?

Theory building is an important element within the phenomenological tradition or approach. Made explicit in grounded theory qualitative research allows substantive frameworks to emerge through the categorisation of data. Substantive theory is concerned with a specific domain or area of inquiry and closely related to practical situations. Substantive theories are developed to illuminate nuances of human interaction; they are embedded in the relationship between theories and practice (praxis).

Categories are continually synthesised to form a theoretical framework through the continual attention to the relationship between memos and existing theoretical ideas. Memos and ideas are continually coded and through weaving these together substantive theory gradually emerges. Coding data and memo-writing are central to the grounded theory technique of constructing substantive theory; memos may be written representations, diagrams, tables, matrices or vignettes. Through such a process substantive theory will gradually emerge. Furthermore, a core category may be identified around which peripheral categories revolve. Core categories require the following dimensions: they need to relate to other categories in some form or another in qualitative (depth of relations) and quantitative (number of relations) contexts, be recurrent in the data, maximise variations and build theory with implications for pre-existing formal theory. In relation to these approaches substantive theory may also involve a model or a diagram of the framework identified through the core category and related peripheral categories. The substantive theory should identify how the separate categories are integrated within the theory; it needs to be conceptually dense and integrated. However, density and integration require intimacy with the data and close proximity to those being researched and analysed which may fall into the trap of simply stating the obvious. Consequently, the substantive or emergent theory needs to relate to formal or pre-existing theoretical frameworks. 'A substantive theory generated from the data must be formulated, in order to see which of diverse formal theories are, perhaps, applicable for furthering additional substantive formulations' (Glaser and Strauss, 1967: 34).

Substantive theory is developed in relation to an empirical situation whereas formal theories either pre-exist or are built with regard for a formal or conceptual area. Glaser and Strauss (1967) argued that both substantive and formal theories exist between models and grand theory but in the main they take the form of meso theories and allow a bridge between lower range theories and philosophical perspectives. Formal theory may be generated directly from the data but it is more conducive to develop substantive theory and from this move onto more formal applications.

Disputation in Grounded Theory:
Barney Glaser and Anselm Strauss

For many years there existed a dispute between Glaser and Strauss, which revolved around differences regarding the emergence and forcing of data. Glaser considered that Strauss and Corbin's 'pet theoretical code violates relevance and forces data' (Glaser, 1992: 28). He contended that such a structured outlook undermines the emergent, empirical and endless ways of relating substantive codes. 'The researcher must be aware of the vast array of theoretical codes to increase his sensitivity to their emergence in the data' (Glaser, 1992: 28). However, in their work Strauss and Corbin address their book to those 'who are about to embark on their first qualitative analysis research project and who want to build theory at the substantive level' (Strauss and Corbin, 1990: 8). In other words, it is a simplification, which may lead the researcher into the more difficult nuances of grounded theory.

Verification also seems to be a sticking point between the scholars. However, on closer examination neither is pursuing pure verification; each wishes for it to add to theory generation not to negate or disprove 'but add variation and depth of understanding' (Strauss and Corbin, 1990: 109). Glaser argued that the 'two types of methodologies should be seen in sequential relation. First we discover the relevance and write hypotheses about them, then the most relevant may be tested for whatever use may require it' (1992: 30). Whereas, Strauss and Corbin saw it as an aspect of the grounded theory method; they considered that statements should be verified against data, not to 'necessarily negate our questions or statements, or disprove them, rather … add variation and depth of understanding' (Corbin and Strauss, 1990: 108–9). It is just as important to 'find differences and variation as it is to find evidence that supports our original questions and statements. The negative or alternative cases tell us that something about them is different so we must move in and take a closer look' (Strauss and Corbin, 1990: 109). However, each considers that it is possible to utilise verification as part of theory generation, the latter as part of grounded theory and the former as a methodology in its own right (see Strauss and Corbin, 1990: 107–9, Strauss, 1987: 11–15 and Glaser, 1992: 27–30).

Strauss (1987) makes his position clear where he contends that induction, deduction and verification are the very basis of grounded theory. 'Because of our earlier writing in Discovery (1967) where we attacked speculative theory – quite ungrounded in bodies of data – many people mistakenly refer to grounded theory as "inductive theory" (however), as we have indicated all three aspects of inquiry … are absolutely essential' (Strauss, 1987: 12 author's brackets). 'Grounded theory is of course inductive; a theory is induced or emerged after data collection starts. Deductive work in grounded theory is used to derive from induced codes conceptual guides as to where to go next for which comparative group or sub-group, in order to sample for more data to generate the theory' (Glaser, 1978: 37–8).

Glaser and Strauss' disagreements are based around their emphasis on deductive and inductive processes; Strauss considers that induction, deduction and verification are essential elements of grounded theory. Induction is primarily based on experience with the same kind of phenomena at some point in the past. It may be apparent because of personal experiences, exploratory research into phenomenon, previous research or because of theoretical sensitivity (knowledge of technical literature). 'As for deduction: Success at it rests not merely on the ability to think logically but with the experience in thinking about the particular kind of data under scrutiny' (Strauss, 1987: 12). This means drawing on experience as well as thinking about the phenomenon and may include comparative analysis to further the deductive powers (Strauss, 1987: 12). He also indicated that experience and learned skills are very important for verification. 'If ... experience and associated learned skills at verification, deduction and induction are central to successful enquiry, do not talent-gifts-genius contribute to that success?' (Strauss, 1987: 13).

Strauss and Corbin (1990) proposed that in grounded theory there is a continual movement between inductive and deductive thinking and that their statements are deductively proposed and verified. There is a continual comparison of incidents 'there is a constant interplay between proposing and checking. This back and forth movement is what makes our theory grounded' (Strauss and Corbin, 1990: 111). Glaser posits that it is at this point that Strauss and Corbin indulge in 'full conceptual description by forcing the data and leaving the emergence of grounded theory out completely' (Glaser, 1992: 71). The sticking point is the confusion between induction and deduction. Glaser charged that he (Strauss) 'confuses induction with testing deductive hypotheses which are forced on the data (and) that it is not inductive to say the data disproves a hypothesis, it is simply a verification' (1992: 71). However, Strauss and Corbin contended that it is necessary to continually verify 'concepts and relationships arrived at through deductive thinking must be verified over and over again against actual data ... we are building grounded theory and it is the grounding or verification process that makes this mode of theory building different' (Strauss and Corbin, 1990: 111–12). In response to this Glaser argued that Strauss and Corbin are developing a verification method. 'It simply tests forced conceptual hypotheses' (Glaser, 1992: 92). It is not a method that generates theory but one that verifies; it is a theory that forces the data rather than allowing it to emerge. For Glaser it was crystal clear that Strauss and Corbin had created a verification method.

Glaser argued that 'grounded theory is multivariate. It happens sequentially, simultaneously, serendipitously and scheduled' (1998: 1). Grounded theory is suitable for dealing with many research problems and requires that the researcher let go (pursue induction) and not attempt to force models onto the data. 'Grounded theory requires a tolerance for feeling out of control while generating the beginning of a relevant main concern, a core category and sub-categories' (Glaser, 1998: 11). It is a revolving step-method that starts the researcher from being 'know nothing to becoming an expert who will later become a theorist with a publication and with a theory that accounts for most action in a substantive area' (ibid, p 13).

Glaser (2001) further argued that as the most widely used methodology in the social sciences grounded theory provides a set of steps that are closely linked or underpinned by the rigours of good science. Grounded theory was identified by Glaser (2001) as an approach to both qualitative and quantitative data collection and analysis in response to positivistic attempts to force theory on data which created misfit and irrelevance. Glaser (2005) reassesses grounded theory analysis and identifies the differences between data gathered in everyday life and that collected for scientific study. Glaser and Holton (2007) are predominantly concerned with what they label 'exampling' (that is providing case studies or examples of research where grounded theory was used) and how this offers a learning experience no matter how experienced in grounded theory the researcher may be. Exampling identified 'the power and scope of classical grounded theory ... the global reach of the methodology and the varying levels of methodological maturity of the authors ... exampling ... provides a rich range of theories that have emerged largely from novice efforts at applying the methodology. They are theories from which all may learn about the application of grounded theory' (Glaser and Holton, 2007: 1).

▓▓▓▓▓▓▓▓▓▓▓▓▓▓▓▓▓▓▓▓▓▓ QUESTION ▓▓▓▓▓▓▓▓▓▓▓▓▓▓▓▓

GLASER AND STRAUSS

Discuss the main differences between Glaser and Strauss. Which approach to grounded theory would best suit your research project?

Charmaz (2000) considered that even though Glaser and Strauss were not quantitative, each of their perspective involved a post-positivist ontological position. Even though both Glaser and Strauss were deeply divided regarding a number of issues relating to grounded theory, both identified an external objective reality and neutral observer. Each argued for unbiased data collection, differing levels of technical procedures and means of representing respondents as accurately as possible. That said, both Glaser and Strauss have similarities with critical theory and constructivism when they wish to give voice to their respondents and acknowledge how their views differ from those of the researcher. They also consider that art as well as science should be utilised as an analytical tool.

Constructivist grounded theory assumes a relativism of multiple realities and the co-creation of knowledge. It emphasises natural settings and develops a non-post-positivistic stance. To enable this grounded theory, research should not be rigid or prescriptive, should focus on meaning to intensify interpretive understanding and desist from using a purely post-positivist approach. Charmaz (2000) juxtaposes constructivist and post-positivist perspectives to grounded theory but qualifies this when she acknowledges that this methodological approach may be used with elements of both paradigms of inquiry and that distinctions between the two exist on a continuum.

Identifying the Nature of Grounded Theory: Further Distinctions

Charmaz (2006) invites the reader to accompany her as she ascends the levels of analysis and theoretical conceptualisation while ensuring one is firmly adhered to the data on the ground or in the field. She identifies the main distinction between Glaser and Strauss in terms of positivism and pragmatism; Glaser more aligned with the former and Strauss closer to the latter. Glaser incorporated empiricism and rigorous coding and emphasised emergent properties and discoveries, whereas, Strauss emphasised human agency, subjectivity and emergent processes. That said, both believed in the emergence of theory and relationships between objectivity and subjectivity; Glaser was more inductive and less rigid or more phenomenological and Strauss and Corbin more prescriptive and positivistic in process. However, Strauss based his perspective on symbolic interaction (see above) which as discussed incorporates elements of pragmatism and phenomenology. Most grounded theories are substantive because they deal with specific issues in delimited areas. However, these can become formal theories 'through generating abstract concepts and specifying relationships between them to understand problems in multiple substantive areas' (Charmaz, 2006: 8).

Following the conflict between Glaser and Strauss and Corbin regarding the nature of grounded theory, others involved themselves in the debate and devised their own understanding of grounded theory. For example, Denzin and Lincoln (1994) considered that grounded theory can be post-positivist and/or constructivist. Annells contended that our understanding of grounded theory is based on an 'awareness of the method's ontological, epistemological and methodological perspectives' (1996: 379) and that these may be broken down into four paradigms of enquiry; positivism, post-positivism, critical theory and constructivism. Indeed, that understanding of methodology and consequently grounded theory are determined by one's metaphysical assumptions. Through their own epistemological positions scholars formulated their own understandings of grounded theory with most agreeing that it was not a unified framework. Indeed grounded theory should be seen as a family of methodologies that are distinct from other qualitative methodologies and share common characteristics (Bryant and Charmaz, 2007a, 2007b; Charmaz, 2006; Creswell, 2007; Goulding, 2002; Hood, 2007). These differences between grounded theory involve what has been identified as the holy trinity; that any grounded theory study requires theoretical sampling, emerging categories through the constant comparison of data and the development of substantive theory through the theoretical saturation of categories (Hood, 2007)

Definition Box

Grounded Theory

A grounded theory methodological approach requires:

- theoretical sampling;
- emergence of categories through comparative analysis;
- substantive theory development.

A number of perspectives exist but the three main influences in the new streams of grounded theory emanate from the social constructivist position (Charmaz, 2000, 2006), postmodernist situational analysis (Clarke, 2002) and anti-post-positivist position (Bryant, 2002; Bryant and Charmaz, 2007a, 2007b). Each transcends the post-positivist dimensions of both Glaser and Strauss; each places a premium on the relationship between the researcher and researched and the multiplicity of those involved in the construction of reality or theory (Charmaz, 2000, 2006). Furthermore situational analysis focuses on social situations, the co-construction of knowledge and interaction between researchers and researched (Clarke, 2002).

Conclusion

This chapter has dealt with grounded theory and identified that it involves developing theory through data collection and analysis; it mainly uses qualitative data and recognises the close connection between theory and practice. It has also outlined that some disputation exists regarding the nature of grounded theory and identified that Glaser and Strauss considered that 'grounded theory be flexibly interpreted and that researchers should use it in their own way that is, as it fits their investigation' (1967: 9). Charmaz viewed grounded 'as a set of principles and practices ... (which) can complement other approaches to qualitative data analysis, rather than stand in opposition to them ... grounded theory serves as a way to learn about the worlds we study and as a method for developing theories to understand' these worlds and phenomenon (2006: 9). Glaser and Strauss (1967) argued that theory is discovered as it emerges through the data. For Charmaz (2006) neither 'theories nor data are discovered they are part of the same world as ourselves and we construct our grounded theories through our past and present involvements and interactions with people, perspectives and research practices' (2006: 10). Theoretical perspectives offer an interpretive portrayal of the world under study and analysis not an extant picture (2006: 10). Substantive theories are ontological constructions and grounded theory involves phenomenological, interpretivist positions with pragmatist underpinning. Charmaz (2000; 2006) deals with re-assessing meanings or interpretations of theory in relation to methodology: positivist and constructivist types of grounded theory are juxtaposed to illustrate how different modes of analysis stem from contrasting starting points. Finally, reflection is dealt with in terms of grounded theory processes.

Furthermore, grounded theory raises difficulties regarding precise definitions of induction and deduction and the point where the former begins and the latter ends (and vice versa) and the grey area between the two. Alfred Marshall argued that '(y)ou make all your contrasts rather too sharply for me. You talk of the inductive & deductive methods: whereas I contend that each involves the other

& that historians are always deducing, & that even the most deductive writers are always implicitly at least basing themselves on observed facts' (Marshall, cited in Coase, 1995: 169). Ultimately, Marshall wished to emphasise the mutual dependency of induction and deduction. Strauss and Glaser aimed to do the same but each with different weightings. As with the problems of delineation between induction and deduction the same may be said in respect of emergence and forcing. Ultimately, one may consider that grounded theory should be interpreted as it was by Glaser. 'By its very nature grounded theory produces ever opening and evolving theory on a subject as more data and new ideas discovered. This nature also applies to the method itself and its methodology' (Glaser, 1978: ix). Grounded theory is a flexible methodological approach and should be applied to specific research projects. Ideas will emerge from data through interpretation but theoretical sensitivity and pre-conceptions will also ensure a level of forcing; as with inductive and deductive approaches, pure emergent or forced studies are impossible. Because of the nature of human existence and ontological and epistemological relationships with phenomenon, a certain level of forcing as well as subjectivity in relation to interpretation and emerging ideas necessarily must exist. That said, grounded theory takes into consideration these difficulties and provides a methodological approach that may be used in a post-positivist, critical theory or constructivist/participatory fashion.

Further Reading

Bryant, A. and Charmaz, C. (eds) *The Sage Handbook of Grounded Theory.* Thousand Oaks, CA: SAGE Publications. pp 1–28.

Charmaz, K. (2006) *Constructing Grounded Theory: A Practical Guide Through Qualitative Analysis.* London: SAGE Publications.

Denzin, N. and Lincoln, Y. (1994) *The Handbook of Qualitative Research,* 1st edn. Thousand Oaks, CA: SAGE Publications.

Denzin, N. and Lincoln, Y. (2000) *The Handbook of Qualitative Research,* 2nd edn. Thousand Oaks, CA: SAGE Publications.

Denzin, N. and Lincoln, Y. (2005) *The Handbook of Qualitative Research,* 3rd edn. Thousand Oaks, CA: SAGE Publications.

Denzin, N.K. (2007) 'Grounded theory and the politics of interpretation', in A. Bryant and K. Charmaz (eds), *The Sage Handbook of Grounded Theory.* Thousand Oaks, CA: SAGE Publications. pp. 454–71.

Glaser, B. and Strauss, A. (1967) *The Discovery of Grounded Theory.* New York: Alpine.

Glaser, B. (1998) *Doing Grounded Theory: Issues and Discussions.* Grounded Theory Institute: Sociology Press.

Howell, K.E. (2000) *Discovering the Limits of European Integration: A Grounded Theory Approach.* New York: Nova Science Publishers.

Strauss, A. and Corbin, J. (1998) *Basics of Qualitative Research: Techniques and Procedures for Developing Grounded Theory.* Thousand Oaks, CA: SAGE Publications.

TEN
Hermeneutics

Introduction

This chapter deals with hermeneutics, which derives from the idea that Hermes (the messenger of the Greek gods) could interpret and explain their wishes; consequently in this context, hermeneutics can clarify issues under analysis. However, Hermes also conveyed falsehoods and represents the misleading as well as clarifying relationship between humanity and phenomenon or the world. Hermeneutics derives from the Greek word *hermeneuin*, which means to interpret; as noted by Heidegger, hermeneutics involves 'the business of interpretation' (Heidegger, 2004: 7). Furthermore, *Peri hermeneias* or On Interpretation by Aristotle is concerned with the way sentences and words may be understood and interpreted. Hermeneutics is about interpretation and involves the 'classic discipline concerned with the art of understanding texts' (Gadamer, 2004: 157). Freidrich Schleiermacher (1769–1834) argued that the principles of hermeneutics may be used for the study of all humanity and not confined to either Classics or the Bible. Indeed he considered that hermeneutics were as 'universal as language' (Vedder, 1999).

Berlin considered that Vico discovered a means of knowing that clearly identified embryonic 'German historicism *Verstehen* (understand, interpret and participatory examination) – empathetic insight, intuitive sympathy, historical *Eifuhlung* (feeling into) and the like (1979: 116, original parentheses). However, not 'until the days of Dilthy and Max Weber … did the full … implications … of Vico's theses about the imaginative resurrection of the past begin to dawn upon some of those who, in their turn, resurrected him' (Berlin, 1979: 119). Wilhelm Dilthy (1833–1911) was concerned with the distinction between natural and human or social science and the ways in which they may be studied and analysed. He rejected using natural science methodologies to comprehend social phenomenon because they investigated cause and effect and the particular to general; whereas, the social sciences were more interested in the relationship between the parts and the whole. Dilthy considered that social science analysis would benefit from a combined approach but recognised that even though both emanated from the phenomenological lifeworld each reacted to it differently; natural science denied and negated the lifeworld and social science embraced it. Dilthy re-interprets Husserlian ideas when outlining the basic structures of consciousness in relation to comprehending historical existence; the basis of his hermeneutics involved lived experience in a historical manner. Following on from the work of Freidrich Schleiermacher, Dilthy coined the term hermeneutic circle, which incorporated the continual interaction between the implicit and explicit, and between the particular and the whole. Indeed, the hermeneutic circle could be a useful tool when analysing or undertaking research in the social sciences; Dilthy thought that hermeneutics involved an *organon* of social sciences. In other words, he argued that hermeneutics entailed a methodology for the social sciences in general that contrasted with the more empirical approaches utilised in the natural sciences. He outlined a clear distinction between causal explanation and understanding; causal explanation incorporated the objective of the natural sciences and understanding that of the social sciences. Fundamentally, Dilthy wished to understand 'other' through immersion within situations and minds while at the same time ensuring distinction between 'other' and the researcher. Furthermore, existence is not an abstraction but ground in historical contexts and self is realised through a temporal process and inner and outer elements of consciousness distinguished. The relationship between the individual and cultural or social existence remains a pivotal point in the development of self (Dilthy, 1989). Through objective spirit (a term gleaned from Hegel) that incorporates what it means to be human, for example, expressions of communication, human actions, human thought and the means by which these activities occurs humanity may be understood (Dilthy, 2002; Makreel, 1999). Max Weber (1864–1920) uses the term spirit in his historical assessment of the *Protestant Ethic and the Spirit of Capitalism* (2004) and explains at the outset of the text that we need to come to know what is meant by the spirit of capitalism in relation to or as the analysis progresses. Such is embedded in the 'nature of historical concepts which attempt for their methodological purposes not to grasp historical reality in abstract general formulae, but in concrete genetic sets of relations which are inevitably of a specifically unique and individual character' (Weber, 2004: 14). In this work, there is a close relationship between individual ethical and religious existence and the historical emergence of a capitalist spirit.

Definition Box

Max Weber And Methodology

Weber's methodological position was ground in the historical tradition of Germanic thinking. He emphasised that subjectivity was a necessary aspect of the research process; that is, human culture and behaviour should be involved in the research findings rather than negated. As with Dilthy, he considered that explanation and understanding must

(Continued)

---

take place within a historical context and involved genetic sequences. Each sequence was considered unique and could not be compared with others. He does not deny theoretical categories and considers these as necessary for the social as they are for the natural sciences.

Indeed, being human and meaning are community entities and render understanding a social activity. When analysing a text it should be conceived of as part of the community from which it emanates and deeper comprehension directed toward specific socio-cultural activity. So to fully comprehend nuances identified by Dickens or Trollope it is necessary to have an understanding of specific cultural traditions activities and events in 19th-century England. Only once these areas have been fully explored would Dilthy consider the inner being of the author. Overall, Dilthy's hermeneutic objective was not to try and comprehend writers of texts exactly as they understood themselves (if they ever achieved this), but comprehend them better (in greater depth) than they understood themselves. Through historical distance (retrospect or the benefit of hindsight) researchers are better placed to understand a novel, play or other work of art. Retrospection allows greater depth when understanding the relationship between artists and historical circumstance and gives an overall understanding of the meaning of the work (Makkreel, 1999).

Dilthy pursued a level of objectivity and was criticised for this by more subjective orientated individuals developing hermeneutical approaches, for example, Gadamer argued that Dilthy failed to extend beyond the methodological differences between social (motivations underpinning occurrences and events) and natural sciences (general laws). Even though he eventually criticised Dilthy's approach, Heidegger was highly influenced by the idea of lifeworld. Heidegger felt that the notion of Dasein or the being becoming-in-the-world failed to fully identify what lifeworld entailed. Indeed, initially Heidegger, and later Gadamer, both considered lifeworlds were historical and finite, consequently they were culturally bound so could never provide absolute science.

Identifying Hermeneutics

Initially, hermeneutics dealt with ancient scriptures and involved paying close attention to historical and social contexts that surround actions when interpreting a text. Two strands of hermeneutics developed one from a theological and the other a more humanistic tradition. Each involved rediscovery of hidden meaning; 'Classical literature though constantly present as material for humanistic education, had been completely absorbed within the Christian world. Similarly, the Bible … (although) constantly read … the understanding of it was determined … and obscured by the dogmatic tradition of the church' (Gadamer, 2004: 175–6, author's parentheses). However, to become a truly useful tool in the context of uncovering understanding, hermeneutics needed to move beyond this narrow remit and develop understanding for historical texts in general. Furthermore texts needed to be understood in relation to the context of the 'historical reality to which each individual historical document belonged' (Gadamer, 2004: 178). Ultimately, hermeneutics involves historical research as every sentence can only be understood in relation to its context (Gadamer, 2004). 'World history is … the collected work of human spirit, written in the language of the past, whose text it is our task to understand' (Gadamer, 2004: 178). Furthermore, hermeneutics involves 'the operations of understanding in their relation to the interpretation of texts'; with text involving the written word and discourse (Ricoeur, 2008: 51).

Hermeneutics assumes a relationship between conscious description and social structures and that the meaning of a text is continually interpreted with reference to context. Hermeneutics can be used to analyse law, literature or any subject that needs to uncover historical meaning. Dialectic process and hermeneutics are forms of traditional cultural discourse that are also counter-cultural. For according to Kidder they 'are dedicated to grasping cultural meaning from within, but also to finding critical resources within that universe of cultural meaning' (1997: 1191). Dialectics involves understanding history as process and that aspects of the past as well as future possibilities exist in the present.

Reflection Box

Dialectics

Consider the term dialectics and apply to a piece of research or daily occurrence you have encountered. Identify a phenomenon and explore its historical context.

Hermeneutics seeks mutual understanding across different cultural horizons and involves a 'continuous dialectic tacking between the most local of local detail and the most global of global structure in such a way as to bring both into view simultaneously' (Geertz, 1973: 239). Arguably in this context, the fusion of the most local of local and the most global of global structure transcend into global interpretation as different cultural horizons and different cultural periods emerge into simultaneous views and interpretations of historical data.

Hermeneutics enables one to interpret historical data by providing a situated context within which one engages through the process of interpretation. Through

---

hermeneutics, the past can be interpreted and understood and the validity and truth of this be realised. Hermeneutics considers that understanding is perceived as interpretation and the basis of the human condition rather than an outcome of procedural processes; understanding is based in life experience of community and not an isolated human activity. We are always taking something as something. That is the primordial givenness of our world orientation, and we cannot reduce it to anything simpler or more immediate (Hess and Palmer, 1970). In addition, historical understanding and cultural being should not be isolated from the research but incorporated within it so as it interacts with the very process of interpretation and understanding. Attempting to remove tradition, culture and history is like trying to remove self from the research process. Consequently, understanding requires engagement with self which involves including pre-conceptions, subjectivity and bias. Pre-conceptions allow understanding of everyday thought and discourse. 'The point is not to free ourselves of all prejudice, but to examine our historically inherited and unreflectively held prejudices and alter those that disable our efforts to understand others and ourselves' (Garrison, 1996: 434). In this context hermeneutics reflects the critical theory paradigm and is an ideal methodological approach when taking this perspective.

Furthermore, understanding is developed through interaction and participative dialogic process. Understanding requires interaction with what is alien to us, that which makes claims upon us and opens up our prejudices, subjectivity, biases and pre-conceptions. Through such a process understanding is discovered and produced. Meaning involves making sense of the situation, text or social action and is temporal and processional (it is becoming) or coming into existence through understanding; the process is phenomenological. The meaning of text or action is negotiated through mutual interaction; interpretation is mutually negotiated not simply discovered.

Empathy is also perceived as an important aspect of hermeneutics. If understanding and the context of understanding are to be realised then it is necessary for researchers to live-like or put themselves in the situation and act-like the agent to fully comprehend the meanings of the act or text. Researchers must empathise with the researched if an in-depth comprehension of the person, situation or text is to be realised. 'Hermeneutics watches language at work, so to speak language as it is used by participants to reach a common understanding or a shared view'. That said, the idea that observation of language will provide meaning 'obscures the fact that language in its performative use is embedded in relationships' (Habermas, 2007: 25). The main objective of hermeneutics is to understand communities/individuals better than the agents themselves and to achieve this, the researcher should use intuition to understand the innermost aspects of individuals. Intuition and empathy involves self-consciousness; one must understand one's self to understand others and understand other to understand self. Indeed, the distinction between subjective and objective, empathy, intuition and self-consciousness

Table 10.1 Hermeneutical Approaches

Objectivist hermeneutics	A clear distinction exists between objectivity and subjectivity; an objective stance exists.
Alethic hermeneutics	Objectivity and subjectivity are always subsumed; researchers are historically and culturally bound so an objective stance is impossible. Understanding is pre-determined by our historical and cultural pre-conditioning.
Phenomenological hermeneutics	Rejects the notions of subjective and objective positions; the researcher continually exists in the world. Worlds and individuals are merged prior to any reflection, thinking or construction.

as well as the level of part and whole led to the emergence of three distinct herme-neutical approaches: objectivist, alethic and phenomenological.

Objectivist Hermeneutics

Based on the Renaissance analysis of religious texts and antiquarian litera-ture, objectivist hermeneutics requires linkage between parts of the whole of the text (there is an iterative and interactive process between sentences, chapters and complete text). Objectivist hermeneutics involves understand-ing the relationship between the part and the whole. This means that cer-tain verses in the Bible can only be understood in relation to the Bible in its entirety. The hermeneutical circle indicates a continual dichotomy; the part can only be understood in relation to the whole and the whole may only be comprehended in relation to its parts. Furthermore, the idea of the part and whole extended as hermeneutics was used to study more than religious texts or antiquity. Eventually, hermeneutics incorporated the study of the spoken word, texts in general and ultimately included the author. Once authors were included, then their social and cultural backgrounds could not be ignored. Eventually, it becomes necessary to involve world history in its entirety in any hermeneutical study and analysis.

Hermeneutics deals with this dichotomy through developing a spiral approach where the researcher moves between parts and the whole. This requires con-centration on a part and its relationship with the whole through which certain illuminations of the whole occur. The researcher then returns to the part under analysis and repeats the process. Alternation between parts and whole progres-sively develops deeper comprehension. This approach is undertaken by objectiv-ist hermeneutics whereas alethic hermeneutics developed its own circle based on pre-understanding and understanding.

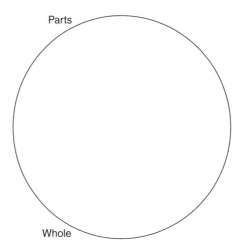

Parts

Whole

Hermeneutic Circle

Objectivist hermeneutics takes its starting point from a neo-Kantian or an anti-positivist position. In this context, positivism should be banished from the realms of social science and humanities and confined to areas of natural science. Causality should be the main objective of the natural sciences and understanding and meaning that of the social sciences. Through the development of hermeneutics the sciences could be given equal value; social science would use comparative method, generality and intuition to provide insight and understanding. However, the objectivist hermeneuticians also retained the distinction between the objective and subjective position. To a degree objectivity still existed. Ricoeur (2004) argued that this distinction needed to be abandoned because such a method of understanding retains an idea of objective knowledge. Hermeneutics should take a phenomenological position and move 'outside the enchanted circle of the problematic of subject and object and question oneself about being' (Ricoeur, 2004: 7). To do this one must question the Dasein of the being that is undertaking the understanding of beings in general. 'Understanding is thus no longer a mode of knowledge but a mode of being which exists through understanding' (Ricoeur, 2004: 7).

QUESTION

HISTORICAL CONTEXT

Should hermeneutics reconstruct the past or integrate it with the phenomenon under investigation? That is, should we attempt to reconstruct the work and understand it as originally constituted? Does a text provide true significance in the context it originally belonged? Or is such an endeavour futile because the past is the past and may never be re-constructed?

AN INTRODUCTION TO THE PHILOSOPHY OF METHODOLOGY

Historical Context

Hegel considered that the restoration of historical context was futile when he argued that texts and art 'are now what they are for us – beautiful fruits torn from the tree. A friendly fate presents them to us as a girl might offer those fruits. We have not the real life of their being – the tree that bore them, the earth and elements, the climate that constituted their substance, the seasonal changes that governed their growth. Nor does fate give us with those works ... their world, their spring, their summer and the moral life in which they bloomed and ripened but only the veiled memory of this reality' (Hegel, *Philosophy of Spirit*, cited in Gadamer, 2004: 160).

Given the previous Question Box, consider the point Hegel is making in this quote. Do texts remain fruit torn from the tree?

Alethic Hermeneutics

Alethic hermeneutics strongly disagrees with the position taken up by objective hermeneutics. The distinction between subject and object indicates correspondence between the researcher (subject) and researched (object) because this reflected the explanation and causality elements of positivism, which ultimately provides understanding through scientific procedures. For alethic hermeneutics understanding was not developed through procedures but by the very basis of everyday existence. Consequently, the baseline position was that to start an investigation the researcher must comprehend that the understanding or explanation within the social and natural sciences are secondary objectives.

Researchers are historically and culturally bound as they are products of a given space and time. Rorty argued that the:

> notion that there is a permanent neutral framework whose structure philosophy can display is the notion that the objects to be confronted by the mind, or the rules which constrain inquiry, are common to all discourse ... Thus epistemology proceeds on the assumption that all contributions to a given discourse are commensurable. Hermeneutics is largely a struggle against this assumption. (2009: 316).

By commensurable Rorty meant that through set process or rules rational agreement may be reached. This indicated that hermeneutics should pursue a rule free demeanour and break with the objectivist stance.

Alethic

Alethic refers to the extent that something may be true e.g. possible or impossible, probable or improbable. How far is it possible to uncover and reveal the truth?

Alethic hermeneutics is about revelation of the concealed rather than correspondence. Alethic hermeneutics denies the distinction between subjective and objective whereas phenomenological hermeneutics considers that the something concealed or hidden is something at the core of our being and buried so deep within; something that has been forgotten. Truth involves the discovery and revelation of this core property; in essence our very being. Although distinctions between objectivist and alethic hermeneutics exist, there are areas where overlap may occur in a specific research project; that is they may be used in a complementary fashion. This idea closely links with phenomenology especially that of Heidegger and truth as something at the very core of Dasein.

Phenomenological Hermeneutics

Phenomenological hermeneutics is based on the work of Gadamer and Ricoeur and inspired or underpinned by Husserl, Heidegger and Merleau-Ponty. As discussed in Chapter 4, Heidegger's phenomenological approach involved the very basis of a methodological approach for social science (Heidegger, 2004; Ricoeur, 2008). One understanding of interpretivism involves the researcher engaged in critical analysis of people (human action) or texts through the deliberations of the uninvolved observer. Phenomenological hermeneutics challenges this approach; it argues that in the first place understanding is not rule based or a procedure it the very fact of being human 'understanding is interpretation' (Ricouer, 2004: 194). Gadamer argued that comprehension is not 'an isolated activity of human beings but a basic structure of our experience of life. We are always taking something as something. That is the givenness of our world orientation, and we cannot reduce it to anything simpler or more immediate' (1970: 87). In this context Gadamer reiterated Heidegger and human experience expressed through pre-conceptions or prejudice. Indeed, it is from Heidegger that Gadamer 'receives the conviction that what is called prejudices expresses the structure of anticipation of human experience' (Ricoeur, 2008: 70).

Heidegger illustrates a fore structure and circular nature of understanding through the temporality of Dasein. For Heidegger the hermeneutical circle should not be 'reduced to the level of a vicious circle, or even a circle which is merely tolerated' the circle conceals our basic mode of understanding and this is realised only when we continually interpret without 'allowing fore-having, fore-sight and fore-conception to be presented to us by fancies and popular conceptions. Fore-structures should unsure scientific procedures and be worked out in relation to the phenomenon under investigation' (Heidegger, 2004: 153). Heidegger identifies that the hermeneutical circle 'possesses an ontologically positive significance' and that all interpretation limitations of thought and 'arbitrary fancies' must be negated and the investigation concentrated on the phenomenon or thing itself and this incorporates 'the first, last and constant task' (Gadamer, 2004: 269). All questioning and understanding involves a hermeneutical circle because any attempt to question something involves some notion regarding the nature of the matter or situation investigated; that is, some notion of the question in relation to the subject matter must primarily be understood. Questions do not emanate from nowhere, they are not born out of total ignorance, they already exist within what is to be studied and self and the answers to these questions cause us to re-assess the perspectives we originally held; such then involves further questions. Consequently, we have a hermeneutical circle that is embedded in the ontological position of temporal Dasein.

'A person who is trying to understand a text is always projecting' (Gadamer, 2004: 269). Projected meaning for the complete text is proposed as soon as reading and interpretation begins and initial meaning emerges (Gadamer, 2004). Each fore-projection is able to project a new projection before itself and this constant process of projection constitutes the movement of understanding and interpretation (Gadamer, 2004). Being-in-the-world and understanding are developed through the circle as it is part of meaning and how we necessarily interpret and understand things. So when we perceive something like a motor vehicle or more specifically a car we do not see this and then interpret it as a car from some objective viewpoint. We encounter entities as beings-in-the-world with things already interpreted through a web of connected possibilities that distinct phenomenon possesses, that is, the car is a type of motor vehicle and a specific type of car but we comprehend this web of possibilities before we interpret the car as a car and consequent type of car. In all situations and cases 'interpretation is grounded in something we have in advance – in a for-having, fore-sight, pre-grasp or fore-conception' (Heidegger, 2004: 191, 150). Indeed it is the dichotomies and fit and non-fit between expectations regarding advance knowing and actuality that provides the mechanism of the circle or interpretation and understanding. Assessing and analysing projections in relation to the entities in themselves incorporates the constant task of understanding (Heidegger, 2004: 267, 252).

In a similar vein, Werner Sombart (1863–1941) considered that all understanding incorporated immanent realisation and that one could only understand through what already existed within a given community, which is the connection point for understanding. Sombart asks what it means to understand and argues that it gives insight into meaning. However, the question then emerges what is meaning? Meaning involved connection with a spiritual totality which required the correspondence of object and subject. Both subject and object are identified in terms of spirit; culture involves objective spirit whereas individual human being's motivations, objectives and thinking involve aspects of individual spirit. Such a relationship between immanent realisation and the relationship between the individual and culture identifies a circular process and reflects Gadamer's understanding of the relationship between the individual and culture. He argued that every person who moves from natural to spiritual being 'finds in the language, customs and institutions of his people a pre-given body of material, which as in learning to speak, he has to make his own' (Gadamer, 2004: 13); through a circular movement there exists a return to the self. Indeed, the idea that humanity and humans were becoming and forming understanding through the hermeneutical circle was central for Gadamer.

Gadamer inquires into what hermeneutics actually entail and presents an argument involving two forms of alienation; the first being the alienation of aesthetic consciousness and the second alienation of historical consciousness. The former involves human relationships with artistic forms and how judgements are made regarding these. The second incorporates means by which humanity has in an incremental way 'perfected the art of holding ourselves at a critical distance in dealing with witnesses to past lives' (Gadamer, 1966/2008a: 4). When we consider a work of art a classic do we mean it will endure the test of time? 'Is it not always already determined in this way what will be significant? (Gadamer, 1966/2008a: 8). Indeed the self and our existence involves an entity 'resonates with the voices … that are preceding all explicit aesthetic judgement' (Gadamer, 1966/2008a: 8). The same point may also be made regarding historical consciousness and even though some form of critical distance is apparent for historical research study and analysis, the past still influences our thoughts in relation to present and future. Indeed, Heidegger identifies the importance of the future in our recollection and retention of history in relation to the hermeneutical circle 'where it is not so much our judgements but our prejudices that constitute our being' (Gadamer, 1966/2008a: 9). For example, if we are attempting to comprehend 'historical phenomenon from the historical distance that is characteristic of our hermeneutical situation, we are already determined by history. It determines in advance both what seems to us worth inquiring about and what will be the object of investigation' (Gadamer, 2004: 300). In this context, prejudices are not entities that undermine truth but involve valid means by which historical experiential is directed and understood (Gadamer, 2004). 'Prejudices are biases of our openness to the world. They are simply conditions whereby we experience something – whereby what we encounter says something to us' (Gadamer, 1966/2008: 9).

Gadamer (1970) identified and purported that in the main, interpretive perspectives concentrated on the role of the interpreter. This is where an individual's comprehension of self as having no effect on the study as this would be considered a form of bias; the interpretivist approach is based on the researcher as uninvolved observer. Phenomenological hermeneutics challenges this epistemological position: first, understanding is perceived as interpretation and the basis of the human condition rather than an outcome of procedural processes. Based on the work of Heidegger, Gadamer (1970) explained that understanding was not an isolated activity of human beings but a basic structure of our experience of life. We are always taking something as something. That is the primordial givenness of our world orientation, and we cannot reduce it to anything simpler or more immediate.

Phenomenological hermeneutics should clarify the situation within which our understanding exists. However, these conditions do not encompass a methodological procedure brought to the research situation or text; phenomenological hermeneutics clarifies what is understood through the act and process of understanding. The objective is to understand what is involved in the act of comprehension itself. Overall, phenomenological hermeneutics argued that the distinctions between subjective and objective positions were redundant.

Conclusion

Hermeneutics necessitates dialogue with the text, which should not be revered but approached as an equal entity; individual researchers should listen to what the text has to say while at the same time interrogate it. Each of these techniques enables interaction with the text and enables the act of interpretation and discovery of meaning. One must listen to the text with a sensitive ear so as to hear answers as they emerge. In asking different or the same question constantly and iteratively, understanding emerges; we continually interrogate the text until no new perspective emerges. That said it is not about finding the definitive answer but developing through the process; undertaking and learning from the journey. In addition, it is imperative that the text is fully interrogated while at the same time we ask questions of ourselves. Phenomenological hermeneutics questions the text line by line and on occasion puts the same question continually; this technique eventually gives insight and like the persistent visitor is finally admitted.

Penetration is an important aspect of hermeneutics. 'A good interpretation should be penetrating in that it brings out guiding and underlying intention of the work, in this way making the author's various works or statements intelligible by seeing them as attempts to resolve a central problematic' (Madison, 1988: 29). Heidegger saw this technique as harming the text because the text is asked an unspoken question; something is said that is beyond the text. Investigators should go further than listening and interrogating, they need to go beyond the boundaries of the text; interpretation here could be considered arbitrary but in some instances the hidden problematic of a text may emerge. Indeed in most texts there is that which is unsaid and that which may be tacitly understood.

As with critical theory, constructivist and participatory paradigms, herme-neutics negates naïve realism and the idea that immutable laws can be realised or that a final interpretation can be reached. Meaning is negotiated and in a con-tinual state of becoming. In this way understanding is a practical experience. It is existential as it is who we are in the world in relation to our historical situation. Understanding 'is capable of contributing in a special way to the broadening of our human experiences, our self-knowledge, and our horizon, for ... understanding is mediated along with ourselves' (Gadamer, 2008b: 110).

In addition, as with the critical theory paradigm, hermeneutics considers that historical circumstance should not be marginalised in the pursuit of clear comprehension. Historical situation, culture and tradition are not considered externalities that should be admonished but should be accepted and utilised in the analysis. Tradition enters the analysis which shapes and determines why and how we interpret the world as we do. *'Consciousness of the history of effects'* involves a 'consciousness of being exposes to history and its action' (Gadamer, 2008b). We exist within history so cannot view it from an objective position; we cannot remove ourselves from the flow of history and observe. To move outside of tradition and culture would be to move outside of our-selves. Subjectivity and the prejudice involved provide pre-understanding and sensitivity to situations. We should not attempt to free ourselves of histori-cal circumstance but reflect on how this affects meaning and interpretation. Belonging to a historical situation and cultural tradition will to some sense govern our interpretations.

Understanding is participatory and involves discourse; it is bound with lan-guage and is produced, not reproduced, by the researcher analysing and inter-preting the data. Meaning is temporal and involves process; meaning is in a continual state of becoming and therefore illustrates a non-objectivist perspec-tive of meaning: people, action, the text and so on are not external entities requiring an objective interpretivist stance, but a construct with which the interpreter continually negotiates meaning and understanding. Understanding is mutually negotiated rather than discovered. Finally in the act of understand-ing there are two steps: understanding is a practical experience itself which identifies the types of entities we are in the world. Understanding is existential or part of our existence. We define ourselves as existence comes before essence. This form of phenomenology pursues clarification of the conditions in which understanding takes place and what understanding itself involves. Meaning involves making sense of the situation, text or social action and is temporal and processional (it is becoming) or coming into existence through under-standing. The meaning of text or action is negotiated through mutual interac-tion; interpretation is mutually negotiated not simply discovered. Indeed, it is Dasein; becoming-in-the-world.

Further Reading

Bauman, Z. (1978) *Hermeneutics and Social Science*. New York: Columbia University Press.

Critchley, S. and Schroeder, W.R. (1999) *A Companion to Continental Philosophy*. Oxford: Blackwell.

Denzin, N. and Lincoln, Y. (1994) *The Handbook of Qualitative Research,* 1st edn. Thousand Oaks, CA: SAGE Publications.

Denzin, N. and Lincoln, Y. (2000) *The Handbook of Qualitative Research,* 2nd edn. Thousand Oaks, CA: SAGE Publications.

Denzin, N. and Lincoln, Y. (2005) *The Handbook of Qualitative Research,* 3rd edn. Thousand Oaks, CA: SAGE Publications.

Gadamer, H.-G. (2008b) *Philosophical Hermeneutics*, trans. D.E. Ling. Berkeley, CA: University of California Press.

Ricouer, P. (1987) *Hermeneutics and the Human Sciences*, ed. and trans. J.B. Thompson. Cambridge: Cambridge University Press.

Ricoeur P. (2008) *From Text to Action*. London: Continuum Press.

ELEVEN

Michel Foucault

Introduction

One of Foucault's main objectives was to formulate an archaeological method which broke with positivist correspondence theory and the idea of deeper meaning linked with hermeneutics. Archaeology encompassed a description or uncovering of the unconscious ideas and thoughts he labelled *epistemés*. He focused on the relationship between knowledge and power and attempted to trace epistemés that he considered to be linked with the discourses of an epoch. Such discourses did not reflect a correspondence with truth (as with Husserl, Foucault bracketed truth) and through a radical phenomenology continued this Husserlian position by concentrating on meaning. Indeed, as a student of Merleau-Ponty, it is not surprising that Foucault leaned toward phenomenology.

Epistemés involved historical a priori of a given epoch (or period of time) and draw together common sense or practical everyday occurrences with a theoretical dimension. Archaeology involves digging into the historical thought of different epochs and tracking meaning through historical changes identified in epistemés, which are transferred and transformed through discourse. Foucault's archaeology challenges the idea that history is irregular through a focus on three aspects of human existence, these include:

- humanity in a biological context; as living beings (natural history);
- humanity in a socio-economic context; as productive entities (analysis of wealth);
- humanity in a cultural context; as a speaking species (general grammar).

Indeed, at the most intense level the regularity between these areas renders them isomorphic in terms of structural similarities; there exists a synthesis of structures within each epistemic situation or phase. That said, epistemés are more than perceptions of the world, they exist in our innermost being in a deep layer of unconsciousness. As with phenomenological positions what is sought and discovered resides at the very core of being; to understand the world we must comprehend ourselves.

Foucault (1981) argued that the world or reality does not have meaning that we discover, or that we decipher. We find order and regularity through discourse and the imposition of this upon the world; we create meaning and order. Consequently, regularities of reality are not anonymous but the outcomes of discourse that we impose on the world; discourse in this context restrains perception, everything is constructed and understood through the lense of discourse.

Foucault's Development

Foucault's initial works concentrated on the human sciences or as they are more normally known now, the social sciences. In his works he concentrated on questions regarding the extent social science is possible and the consequences of their existence. He was the Professor of the History of Systems of Thought and by thought he meant 'the forms of theoretical and conceptual reflection developed within philosophy of social sciences as well as the forms and means of rationality embedded in the everyday practice of administration' (Patton, 1999: 537). Through studies relating to 18th-century phenomenon Foucault assessed and critiqued how social sciences in a modern context were constituted in relation to humanity as both the object and subject of knowledge. For example in *Madness and Civilization* (2002b) the idea of madness, poverty, disability and unemployment start to come under the auspices of the state. Each is perceived as a social problem which the state is required to deal with; there is a new understanding of the role of the state. During the Renaissance so-called mad people roamed the land and, in the same way as Tom Bedlam lived in King Lear, existed on the peripheries of towns. During the 17th and 18th centuries madness or the insane take on the mantle of the other (outsider) and the state deals with these individuals as moral scapegoats through incarceration and stigmatisation. Physical confinement involved two objectives as it hid the poverty endured by the unemployed and negated social upheaval. Confinement indicated that madness and poverty were unacceptable forms of social existence and people were obliged to work as ethical values were closely linked with labour; these values meant that madness, poverty and unemployment were unacceptable and necessitated confinement and concealment. The unemployed were not banished or explicitly punished but at the cost of individual freedom confined by the state and forced to work (in the workhouse). Within this change we locate rational ideas relating to the mad, unemployed and poverty that perpetuate in collective thought as natural with no recourse to previous conceptualisations as these have been rendered irrational.

Foucault's ideas developed in relation to the political changes taking place during the 20th century. Indeed the student uprisings of the 1960s and their anti-authoritarian flavour had much influence on the evolution of his thinking and theoretical designs. Such anti-authoritarianism began to widen the political boundaries and social science disciplines, such as psychology, sociology and so forth, became explicitly political. As a member of the French Communist Party Foucault was explicitly political himself; like many intellectuals during the early 1950s Foucault was a Marxist who supported the Soviet Union. However, his support for the regime was shaken with the invasion of Hungary in 1956 and the condemnation of homosexuality as a bourgeois practice. That said, Foucault continued a complex relationship with Marxist ideas for the remainder of his days. Marxist influences informed his work on power and inequality and social structures. However, he did not agree with the state-centred stance and economic determinism adhered to by Soviet Marxism. Foucault considered that many Marxist ideas belonged in the 19th century and for him that is where they should have remained. There is little clarity regarding Foucault's political position and he himself did not wish to be judged and classified in this context. He argued that for politics to be progressive then historical and practical conditions needed to be understood, only then may they involve sound transformations; progressive politics challenge primeval teleological destination and advance the sovereign subject. Foucault moves away from abstract notions developed in political discourse and grounds this discourse in the local interactions of everyday life; all is political and the operation of power in a political context everywhere. In a practical context this took the form of involvement in many political causes where oppression was apparent such areas included: education, prisons, Tunisian students, Basque separatists, racism, Vietnam, Polish trade unionism, gay pride and human rights. However, he remained vehemently anti-Soviet Union and the ideas of communism propagated by the regime.

These beliefs provided the canvas on which Foucault's work emerged as an intellectual assessment of ideas relating to values, behaviour, common sense and policymaking in a newly invigorated radical social mix. Indeed, Foucault may be considered the doyen of a general challenge to authority that arose during the 1960s, through radical assessments of established ways of behaving and thinking, his work articulated this dissent. However, on the one hand, Foucault would have been loath to use the interaction between his personal history and text as he did not consider the role of criticism was to define the relationship between text and author whereas, on the other hand, he commented that the reason he concentrated on specific subjects was not simply based on theoretical interests but in personal historical experiences. Personal experience and empirical processes continually impacted on his theoretical work; there always existed an interaction between what was apparent to him in a practical context and the institutions on which he concentrated. One may argue that much of his work displayed an element of autobiography. Indeed, he is not only concerned with analysing social conditions and institutions but in the very bases of our means of analysing these entities where there exists a relationship between experience (of the researcher), the way a research project is approached and what will be discovered. In such a way it is necessary to analyse individual modes of analysis in relation to experience as well as the subject under investigation. A form of pre-understanding exists that determines what the study or researcher will concentrate upon and the subsequent analysis which provides the basis for what will be revealed by the research project.

Later in his life Foucault argued that his programme of work involved a historic-philosophical critique of modernity; it identified the historical conditions regarding occidental development in relation to the present and the historical roots of western rationality and how this is displayed in the spirit of modern western culture. Rather than trace a line of inevitability between past and present Foucault attempts to distinguish separateness and differentiation between the historical data and the interpretation of this in the present. In a Nietzschean manner Foucault argued that the historian should begin with the present situation, then trace this back into history until difference (or a break is located); then proceed forward from this juncture ensuring that discontinuities as well as connections are rendered explicit. Differing practices and discourses are explored in such a way that taken for granted rationality is undermined, what has been considered as irrational about the past is challenged and in many instances present day assumptions regarding past phenomenon found to be misunderstood. Indeed such distinctions may be found in distinct epistemés and the discourse that reflected the dominant ideas of these distinct periods. Human beings are not universal timeless entities but become or emerge in relation to historical situation and discourse of a given epistemé.

Foucault, Epistemé and Discourse

Foucault argued that the history of epistemés and history of science or history in general are very different things and there is no amalgamation of historical thought, simply an understanding of discontinuity between four distinct epistemés. These epistemés included:

- pre-classical (ancient to mid-17th century);
- classical (mid-17th to late 18th/early 19th century);
- modern (early 19th to the mid-20th century);
- contemporary (mid-20th century to the present day).

Only the ancient and classical are discussed in any detail in the 'Order of Things' whereas the latter two are dealt with rather fleetingly and the causes of epistemic change do not interest Foucault; rather than causality he concentrated on description.

Such disinterest in causality points to Foucault's distaste for system building and his emphasis of those marginalised (in specific situations) by social change and discourse. He contended that since the Renaissance difference has been marginalised through social norms imposed by dominant groups. In the *History of Sexuality* Foucault identified that in Greek and Roman culture discourse relating to homosexuality and heterosexuality made no reference to difference. Indeed, sexual inclinations were treated on an equal basis. This was in contrast to contemporary society where the latter is elevated to a norm and other sexualities considered deviations. Such an authoritarian approach for Foucault delineated the expression or epistemé of modern society. Take for example what constituted legitimate partners; 'it would appear that, in contrast with Greek and Roman societies, Christianity drew the line at monogamous marriage … Or the disallowance of relationships between individuals of the same sex: it would seem Christianity strictly excluded such relationships while Greece exalted them and Rome accepted them' (Foucault, 1992: 15). However, even though fundamentally, ideas regarding same sex relationships were historically bound and contextual.

Definition Box

Epistemé

Epistemé does not wish to legitimise a concept. For example in assessing the idea of science epistemé accepts that this exists; however, it does interrogate the rationale for science being seen as science. Epistemé investigates the point that science becomes

---

separated from other forms of knowledge. Epistemé accepts the fact of science but asks the question what it actually means for that science to be a science. It does not question the right for science to be considered science but why and how it actually exists. And the point it separates itself from all other types of knowledge is not related to the authority of an original act of giving (Foucault, 2002a).

Foucault (2002a) argued that humanity became apparent to itself in relation to discourse or discursive practice. Humanity is not universal and timeless but emerges in relation to historical situation and discourse of a given time. Equally, a historically constructed humanity defined by discourse can easily disappear or be re-shaped by changing historically located practices (with discourse as an aspect of this). Indeed, such practices not only produce the subject they also act as means of division. As noted, Foucault makes this point *in Madness and Civilization* where those considered mad are excluded and in *Discipline and Punishment* where the delinquent is excluded to the periphery. Indeed, existing discourse encompasses what is said but more importantly what is not said, what is omitted; 'The first theme sees the historical analysis of discourse as the quest for ... an origin that eludes all historical determination; the second sees it as the interpretation of hearing of an already-said that is at the same time a not-said ... Discourse must not be deferred to the distant presence of the origin, but treated as and when it occurs' (Foucault, 2002a: 28).

Definition Box

Discourse and Statements

- Discourse involves 'the general domain of all statements sometimes as an individualised group of statements', which refers to discourses such as sexuality or feminism.
- Discourse also incorporates 'regulated practices that account for a number of statements', that is, norms and values that are unwritten but underpin our conversations, statements and daily existence.
- Discourses are predictable regulated combinations of sets of statements that lead to the circulation of certain ideas and combinations of utterances. (Foucault, 2002a: 90)

Discourse is the difference between what could be said at one point and what is actually said at another. Hajer identifies discourse as 'a specific ensemble of ideas ... that is produced, reproduced and transformed in a particular set of practices and through which meaning is given to physical and social realities' (1995: 44) It is not neutral or optional but already exists as a thought or entity. 'In discourse something is formed, according to clearly definable rules ... this something exists, subsists, changes, disappears, according to equally definable rules;

in short ... alongside everything a society can produce (alongside: that is to say in a determinate relationship with) there is the formation and transformation of things said' (Edkins, 1999: 46).

Epistemé is the historical a priori that grounds knowledge and its discourses within a particular epoch. A number of epistemé may co-exist and interact at the same time and make up power-knowledge systems. It is like an unconscious underpinning and based on fundamental assumptions that go unnoticed by individuals existing in a particular epoch. Epistemé is the 'epistemological unconsciousness' of an era. Can this be seen in pervading ideas or is it deeper than this and made up of the spirit of an epoch? Furthermore, discourse acts as the point of resistance to prevailing ideas through the formulation of counter discourses. Discourse concentrates on why one statement rather than another appeared.

Foucault attempts to describe the relations among statements, in particular statements in discourse that involve the science of humanity. Indeed, he achieves this through genealogies which involve historical analyses that identify and trace social and historical development; this requires a conceptualisation and understanding of a given time and discourse that provides meaning for that time. Genealogy also involves the investigation of things we consider to simply exist without recourse to historical process, for example, sexuality. Genealogy does not pursue the origin of a given entity or some form of linear development but illuminate plurality and the extent power has influenced and or determined our understanding of truth. However, Foucault was keen to point out that 'genealogies are ... not positivistic returns to a form of science that is more attentive or more accurate. Genealogies are, quite specifically anti-science ... They are about the insurrection of knowledge' (Foucault, 2004: 9). Science must be disputed and if some form of knowledge considers itself a science then what type of knowledge is disqualified; that is, downgraded to a second tier understanding of knowledge. Foucault asks what we actually mean by science and how the difference between science and non-science is demarcated.

Power/Knowledge: Individuals and Institutions

Foucault concentrated on power in terms of the relationship between the individual and the institution; through a number of texts including *Birth of the Clinic, Sexuality, Discipline and Punishment, Power/Knowledge*, he assessed the extent to which institutions exert power over individuals and the role of people in relation to this power (acceptance or resistance to this power). Fundamentally, he analyses the way power works in everyday situations between people within institutions. 'Foucault considers how historically and culturally located systems of power/knowledge construct subjects and their worlds' (Gubriem and Holstein, 2000: 493). These systems involve discourses that 'are not merely bodies of ideas, ideologies or other symbolic formulations, but are also working attitudes, modes of address terms of reference, and courses of action suffused in social practices' (Gubriem and Holstein, 2000: 494). Such an emphasis on discourse as social practice in institutions (asylum, prison, hospital) underlines the importance subjectivity plays in the formulation of meaning and understanding.

Based on Husserl, Schutz (1970) lived experience (lifeworld) is constructed through discourse. 'World of daily life shall mean the inter-subjective world ... at any given moment (humanity) finds a stock of knowledge ... that serves him as a scheme of interpretation ... This stock of knowledge has its particular history. It has been constituted in and by previous experiencing activities of our consciousness, the outcome of which has become our habitual possession' (Schutz, 1970: 73–4) As Husserl noted the process encompassing the sedimentation of meaning; Deleuze (1999) argued that Foucault's social ontology encompassed an 'amorphous mass of turbulent social raw energies in time and space. These are structured into free-floating strategies and power plays, which in their turn are sediment into strata of the "visible and sayable" that is discursive and non-discursive formations of practices which are permeated by knowledge and power' (Alversen and Skoldberg, 2009: 256).

Foucault converted phenomenology into epistemology when he considered that when we see and speak, we do not necessarily see what we speak about nor speak about what we see and when we observe an entity this is always defined in relation to what it is not (Deleuze, 1999). Intentionality is denied and everything is knowledge 'it is irreducibly double, since it involves speaking and seeing, language and light, which is the reason why there is no intentionality ... (as) phenomenology itself surpassed intentionality as the relationship between consciousness and its object' (Deleuze, 1999: 90). There is a move from intentionality to the idea of the being moving toward and becoming being toward the 'fold of being' (Deleuze, 1999: 90). Eventually phenomenologists perceived no distinction between fold and being (being is the fold) and it was 'Merleau-Ponty who showed us how a radical "vertical" visibility was folded into a Self-seeing, and from that point on made possible the horizontal relation between seeing and a seen' (Deleuze, 1999: 91) Merleau-Ponty argued that he was determined by nothing external to him, not because nothing acted upon him but because he was the starting point, external to himself and 'open to the world' (1999: 456). 'We are *true* through and through, and have with us by the mere fact of belonging to the world, and not merely being in the world in the way that things are, all that we need to transcend ourselves' (Merleau-Ponty, 1999: 456).

Foucault argued that power did not simply concentrate on oppression, (for example, through class or the state) but that it permeated all levels of society (all social relations), which provided explanation and understanding of the normal day-to-day environments within which power is enacted. Such enabled an analysis of individuals in specific situations as active agents rather than entities that are or were acted upon. Power in this context becomes an active process rather than a possession; 'power operates in and through discourse ... Discourse not only puts words to work, it gives them their meaning, constructs perceptions, and formulates understanding and ongoing courses of interaction'. As well as representing a practical subject power 'simultaneously constitutes the kinds of subjects that are meaningfully embedded in the discourse itself' (Gubriem and Holstein, 2000: 294–5). Power functions in a chain-like manner, it is in circulation and is 'employed and exercised' through networks. For Foucault 'individuals are the vehicles of power, not its points of application' (1980: 98).

Power involves social relationships between individuals; it is not simply about oppressor and oppressed. As with the Hegelian master–slave dichotomy, power does not simply reside with the master; a power relationship exists between the two. Consequently, individuals are not where power resides but entities within which power is actualised; where it is enacted and people play a role in relation to others within institutional settings. This means that rather than being achieved, power is continually performed as a set of relationships which permeates society. 'Foucault shows that power ... is less a property than a strategy, and its effects cannot be attributed to an appropriation "but to dispositions, manoeuvres, tactics, techniques, functionings"; it is exercised rather than possessed ... In brief, power is not homogeneous but can be defined only by the particular points through which it passes' (Deleuze, 1999: 22–3). Foucault argued that even though modern states were founded on a disciplinarian basis, discipline did not reside with particular institutions because it involved a form of power that transcended state institutions. The origin of power is no longer located in a privileged or limited place; power is no longer local or localised. Power incorporates two distinct different meanings; power is specific to context rather than universal but never specific to context because it is diffuse. 'In short, it is a question of orienting ourselves to a conception of power which replaces the privilege of law with the viewpoint of the objective, the privilege of prohibition with the viewpoint of tactical efficacy, the privilege of sovereignty with the analysis of a multiple and mobile field of force relations, wherein far reaching, but never completely stable, effects of domination are produced' (Foucault, 1998: 102).

Power does not dominate and impose itself on individuals but it is rather implicit and permeates everyday life in terms of family relations and through organisational or institutional structures. Power relations are concealed within society and to understand these we must excavate and uncover these concealed relationships that exist within the economic system, governmental structures and everyday existence. Foucault is interested in localised power rather than that embodied by the state and that which is performed in a contingent manner rather than something continually possessed; power which develops human action and behaviours rather than a structure that inhibits individual liberty.

Foucault considered that in certain contexts power involved a positive force and it was 'precisely these positive mechanisms that need to be investigated and here one must free oneself of the juridical schematism of all previous characterizations of the nature of power. Hence a historical problem arises ... why the west insisted ... on seeing the power it exercises as juridical and negative rather than as technical and positive' (Foucault, 1980; cited in Rabinow, 1991). Indeed, this positive aspect of power concentrated Foucault's mind on revolution and how people take power in certain situations; this can be seen occurring today in terms of African counties and recent uprisings. People have taken to the streets in their thousands with calls for democracy in Tunisia, Egypt, Libya, Syria, Bahrain, and time after time once seemingly all powerful dictators toppled. However, these are not Marxist proletarian revolutions and do not encompass challenges to capitalism as an ideology. People simply wish to change the codified power relations that exist within dictatorships or autocracies to those which incorporate democracy and meritocracy. In this way the state should not be perceived as an entity that possesses power but a structure or conduit that constructs power relationships.

Foucault is not so much interested in what is actually known or understood as what are the conditions of knowing; what led something to be known or understood at a certain point in time? Why are certain concepts elevated and understood as knowledge in the form of facts while other comprehensions languish in the doldrums? He focuses on the power relationships embodied within knowledge and that power could not be enforced or exercised without knowledge and that knowledge would always produce power. That by producing knowledge individuals are making a bid for power; power and knowledge are not identical but different sides of the same coin, one does not exist without the other. Consequently, when there exist imbalances of power, one or other party has greater knowledge than the other. Such a perspective can assist social research in general especially where reflexivity is undertaken and the subjective human element is included. Through power, knowledge is able to differentiate between things and determine between the deviant and normal. Consequently, understandings and the regulation of the self are determined through science (as a body of knowledge and way of comprehending the world) and other powerful social institutions. Power exists in knowledge; the exercise and development of power interact with each other through a level of institutional control. Within the institution we can identify the relationship between power and knowledge in the form of control, for example, prisons, hospitals, private and public companies or social and natural scientific disciplines and so on. In this type of research the objective is to identify truth within the interactive relationship between power and knowledge rather than distinguish between scientific knowledge (as truth) and ideology or inclinations and prejudices. Foucault (1998) identified four rules, 'methodological imperatives', that underpinned his approach:

- Rule of Immanence
- Rule of Continual Variations
- Rule of Double Conditioning
- Rule of the Tactical Polyvalence of Discourses.

Rule of Immanence

As noted, power and knowledge are different sides of the same coin. 'Between techniques of knowledge and strategies of power, there is no exteriority, even if they have specific roles and are linked together on the basis of their difference' (Foucault, 1998: 98). Areas for analysis do not exist (spheres of knowledge) unless they have been brought into existence by power. 'One must not suppose that there exists a certain sphere of sexuality that it would be the legitimate concern of a free and disinterested scientific inquiry were it not the object of mechanisms of prohibition brought to bear by the economic or ideological requirements of power' (Foucault, 1998: 98). Studies begin with discourse regarding local relationships between power and knowledge in the form of reflexivity, 'self-examination, questionings, admissions, interpretations and interviews' (Foucault, 1998: 98).

Rules of Continual Variation

Through agency direction the relationships between power and knowledge shift continually; they encompass 'matrices of transformation'. The investigator should concentrate on processes and relationships regarding power rather than with whom it resides 'We must not look for who has power ... We ... seek ... the patterns of modifications which the relationships of force imply' (Foucault, 1998: 99).

Rule of Double Conditioning

Local centres must eventually relate to the general and generalities continually relate to localities. 'There is no discontinuity between them, as if one were dealing with different levels (one microscopic and the other macroscopic); but neither is there homogeneity (as if the one were only the enlarged projection of the other)' (Foucault, 1998: 99–100). The tactics employed in the local study must take into account the relationship with the broader strategy and the broader strategy must have some identification in the local situation. Foucault (1998) identifies relationships between the family (as the local centre) and Malthusian population control as the macroscopic (the general or strategic). The family did not exactly represent the state or society in general as society does not mirror the family. However, 'because the family was insular and heteromorphous with respect to the other power mechanisms (it) was used to support the ... Malthusian control of the birth-rate, for the populationist incitements, for the medicalization of sex and psychiatrization of its nongenital forms' (Foucault, 1998: 100).

Rule of the Tactical Polyvalence of Discourses

Through discourse, power and knowledge are intrinsically linked; discourse is multiple and no hierarchical structure exists in relation to it. Discourse is neither a 'uniform or stable' entity and no distinction exists between 'accepted discourse … excluded discourse … dominant discourse and the dominated; but as multiplicity of discursive elements that can come into play in various strategies' (Foucault, 1998: 100). Discourse must be seen as not simply an instrument of power but also as a means of challenging power. Foucault points to the discourse relating to sodomy and homosexuality and the changes that take place during the 19th century. that is 'there is no question that the appearances in the nineteenth century of discourses … on homosexuality … made possible strong controls into this area of perversity … it also made possible the formation of a reverse discourse: homosexuality began to speak in its own behalf, to demand that legitimacy or naturality be acknowledged' (Foucault, 1998: 100). Indeed, this social control and call for legitimacy may use similar vocabulary and the distinction between the two appears opaque at the edges. 'There is not, on the one side, a discourse of power, and an opposite to it another discourse that runs counter to it' (Foucault, 1998: 100). Rather than identifying discourse as simply an expression of the general; the contingent position and the relationship between local tactic and general strategic positions of the discourse requires continual examination.

Conclusion

Foucault outlines the problem of the unity and discontinuity of discourse. How can one isolate the unities with which one is dealing: 'What is a science? What is a theory? What is a concept? What is a text?' (Edkins, 1999: 46). 'Discontinuity is one of those great accidents that create cracks not only in the geology of history, but also in the simple fact of the statement; it emerges in its historical irruption; what we try to examine is the irreducible – and very often tiny – emergence' (Foucault, 2002a: 31).

Foucault challenges the modes of grouping and divisions even those that seem most obvious like the book. 'The frontiers of a book are never clear-cut: beyond the title the first lines and the last full stop, beyond its internal configuration and its autonomous form, it is caught up in a system of references to other books, other texts, other sentences: it is a node within a network' (Edkins 1999: 46). By liberating discourse of what are assumed to be 'natural, immediate, universal unities one is able to describe other unities' and through 'analysis of their co-existence, their succession, their mutual functioning, their reciprocal determination, and their independent or correlative transformation' (Foucault, 2002a: 32).

Foucault's approach to research involves uncovering individual experiences in contingent contexts. It is not anti-theoretical but pre-theoretical in that it explores how a theoretical position came into existence and what it is and what it might become. While the parallel goal involves identifying the social context and base of the realities that theory reflects. However, the latter remains a parallel objective as Foucault himself omitted social interaction and illustrated change through discourse that contrasted social forms in relation to the birth of new ones; through the archaeological process of uncovering, new entities are identified. That said, the actual technologies by which these changes are achieved are all but omitted from his work. Foucault denies that he had formulated a theory of power or even that he had begun to construct a theory of what power involved. If power incorporated fluidity 'or derived from a particular source' then a theory regarding the mechanisms and procedures of power may be uncovered. Indeed only through 'an analysis of the mechanisms of power' could an embryonic theory of power be realised (Foucault, 2007: 1–2).

Reflection Box

Human Science and the Order of Knowledge

Social sciences emerged in relation to theoretical and practical problems or obstacles. Industrialisation, democratisation and urbanisation identified new and very different norms for individuals and society. Consequently, psychology, sociology and economics (social sciences) emerge as human beings became the object of scientific inquiry. Foucault considers this emergence as an 'event in the order of knowledge' (Foucault, 2003: 376).

Consider the sentiments identified and determine what is meant by an 'event in the order of knowledge'. How can human beings encompass the object of scientific inquiry?

Foucault provides a mechanism for distinguishing between local or subjective perspectives and the separate worlds of experience through an understanding of the interplay between institutional discourses; he provides a distinction between what is said and what is experienced (between the articulated and the substantive). This distinction allows the research project to concentrate on the relationship between what people say and the conditions in which they say it when assessing and analysing social order. The central question becomes; how do individuals go about doing things? Actions and interactions predominate. Foucault argued that discourses construct meaning in specific situational temporalities and through this the everyday, usual or normality is captured. Consequently, the researcher should concentrate on a genealogy of epistemé and discourse to uncover true meaning of experience and lifeworlds. However, while concentrating on epistemés and discourse the researcher continually needs to recognise the power–knowledge relations beneath the immediate surface. For example, take the confession; this 'is a ritual of discourse … that unfolds within a power relationship … the authority who requires the confession, prescribes it, and intervenes in order to judge, punish, forgive, console, and reconcile … a

---

ritual that produces modifications in the person who articulates it; it exonerates, redeems and purifies' (Foucault, 1998: 61–2).

Self is central to the method pursued by Foucault; the central question becomes who am I? And the active creation of the subject occurs within the research process. However, the self is not a primarily a social construction but a construction of self through self-reflexivity in an attempt to oppose the imposition of accepted power–knowledge norms. There exists an uncertain, permanent and continual conflict between power–knowledge and subject which can never be totally understood in advance and never be completed or finalised. In such a way, by being converted in the nearest point (self), the furthest point becomes the interior. 'This is the central chamber, which one need no longer fear is empty since one fills it with oneself. Here one becomes a master of one's speed and relatively speaking, a master of one's molecules and particular feature, in this zone of subjectivation: the boat as interior of the exterior' (Deleuze, 1999: 101). Fundamentally, 'we are caught up in the world and we do not succeed in extricating ourselves from it in order to achieve consciousness of the world' (Merleau-Ponty, 1999: 5).

Further Reading

Deleuze, G. (1999) *Foucault*, (ed. and trans.) S. Hand. London and New York: Continuum.
Edkins, J. (1999) *Poststructuralism and International Relations: Bringing the Political Back In. Critical Perspectives and International Relations*. Boulder, CO: Lynne Rienner.
Foucault, M. (2002) *The Archaeology of Knowledge*. London: Routledge.
Foucault, M. (2003) *The Order of Things*. London: Routledge.
Mills, S. (2003) *Michel Foucault*. London: Routledge.
Rabinow, P. (1991) *The Foucault Reader*. Harmondsworth: Penguin.

TWELVE

Reliability, Generalisation and Reflexivity: Identifying Validity and Trustworthiness

This chapter examines, reliability, generalisation and reflexivity as well as validity and trustworthiness. Chapter 12 also outlines a number of mechanisms relating to phenomenological or qualitative methodological approaches, which include worthiness, credibility, transferability and fairness. Reliability involves replication and asks how far another researcher could repeat the research undertaken at a given time. Replication is important for positivist and post-positivist approaches to research. A positivist and post-positivist study will usually use numerical data obtained through surveys from a particular sample population. Obviously, there are difficulties regarding replication but in such a study it is easier to repeat the experiment than it is to undertake observations on two or more occasions and come to the same understandings or interpretations reached during the previous studies. Indeed, reliability is a less important criterion for phenomenologists who follow criterion and procedures relating to trustworthiness and authenticity.

It is difficult to ensure high levels of both reliability and validity because if one is to accurately identify what is actually occurring in specific situations, it is necessary to go beyond the survey and involve oneself in the context of the research. Furthermore, it is more straightforward to generalise from a sample population to the population as a whole than it is to generalise from situation x to all situations. Consequently, it may be posited that generalisation is easier or more straightforward within a positivist or post-positivist research project. Within a positivist research project it is normally assumed that generalisation from sample to population should involve an intrinsic part of the research project. However, for a couple of reasons this does not always follow; on occasion one may be interested in specific cases alone because this has social significance in itself and/or it is important to understand that some research does not concentrate on generalisation but is more interested in theoretical inference. Reflexivity involves examining different conceptualisations of self when collecting and analysing data. This chapter assesses each of these areas in more detail then the next chapter relates these to methods of data collection in terms of surveys, interviews, focus groups and observations.

Reliability

For positivism, reliability is concerned with the extent that an experiment can be repeated or how far a given measurement will provide the same results on different occasions. Experimentation should reflect stability and ensure that any investigation of an individual or group at a given point in time can be repeated in exactly the same manner at another point in time. However, this is difficult to ascertain because one is never certain whether intervening factors during the two periods of time have changed the phenomenon and affected reliability. Given this problem it is useful to employ 'equivalence validity' and compare situations on separate occasions so as to determine whether different measurements of the same phenomenon correlate with each other. Phenomenological positions regarding reliability are concerned with whether observations made in an earlier research project can be observed in different or later projects; that is, projects in the future. Reliability may be sought through categorisation and a synthesis of a positivistic and phenomenological position. Grounded theory attempts this through coding procedures, but this approach does have its shortfalls. For instance, even though an objectivist position is pursued through procedures and coding these can become extremely complex. Also the categories and procedures may alienate the reader from the research. Diagrams and conceptual maps can again complicate matters and obscure experience. Grounded theory may also make analysis opaque. Conversely, coding and categorising help to preserve images of experience as well as sharpen and direct questions.

Definition Box

Reliability

- Stability: determines whether the measure is stable over time which provides confidence that the measure for a sample is consistent.
- Internal reliability: consistency of indicators that involves the scale or index.
- Inter-observer consistency: insurance that subjective judgements or the recordings and categorisations of data are consistent.

Reliability is extremely difficult for phenomenological studies as the ability to repeat research projects' programmes is difficult to realise when individual situations in relation to multiple interpretation underpin the research process. Reliability is more easily realised when a structured, positivistic approach to the research programme is prioritised. In such a context, theory involves prediction so necessitates reliability through specified criteria and requires some form of hypothesis testing. Indeed, from a positivist perspective, validation requires a similar grounding to this as does the generalisation that follows in terms of laws that are immutable or remain until falsified. However, if we re-assess these positions from a phenomenological perspective different criteria emerge. For example:

> credibility, validity and reliability in action research are measured by the willingness of local stakeholders to act on the results of the action research, thereby risking their welfare on the 'validity' of their ideas and the degree to which these outcomes meet their expectations. (Greenwood and Levin, 2000: 96)

The positivist position provides an image of a scientist in a lab with the work outlined in organised reports regarding concepts, evidence and procedures. Conversely, the phenomenological position identifies the image of the writer or storyteller balancing theoretical interpretation with aesthetics. With a phenomenological, critical theory or/and postmodern approach the reader is provided with an interpretation of the stories uncovered during the research.

Generalisation

As noted above, it is more straightforward to generalise using a positivist approach than it is when undertaking a phenomenological-based research project. The main point of a positivist investigation involves identifying relationships between samples and the general population, this is not the case for phenomenological, constructivist or participatory studies.

> A generalisation of qualitative … studies is often called into question or regarded as infeasible, something which has weaknesses compared to quantitative set-ups … Only a statistical study that can establish the probability of the findings have not emerged by chance is … justified to make generalisations. (Alvesson and Skoldberg, 1999: 21)

However, this means that we must accept that a study of 'surface regularities' will provide identical patterns time after time. If it is accepted that non-observable phenomenon impact on the forms patterns take, such a position becomes untenable. Fundamentally, for a positivist research project generalisation involves the probability that patterns observed in a sample population can be extrapolated to a wider population from which the sample population is taken. Whereas a phenomenological project will be more concerned with generalisation from one setting to another; the extent that theoretical frameworks developed in one setting can be applied to other situations.

Difficulties for the social sciences have involved criteria for natural sciences being imposed upon it; generalisation is one such criteria. Positivism and post-positivism are based on empiricism, which as discussed in Chapter 3, was perceived as the correct and only way of undertaking scientific studies; a position that not only distorted social science but painted a false picture of how the natural sciences themselves actually worked. Given the necessities determined by natural science and quantitative perspectives, generalisation of phenomenological studies is often thought unrealistic. If simplified surface regularities are the benchmark then it is probable that such can be generalised from sample population to total population. It is probable that the findings are reliable and do not come about by some fluke or chance. However, this assumption depends on one's interpretation of theory in relation to epistemological and ontological positions as well as what is considered to incorporate generalisations. There is a debate regarding the level natural science preconditions should be imposed on the social sciences, especially when underpinned by different paradigms of inquiry in terms of critical theory, constructivism and participatory.

Strauss and Corbin (1998) argued that generalisation from sample to population encompassed only one type of generalisation and a study may generalise from situation to situation. However, how may one generalise from stories? An answer is mainly through empathy and understandings that provide the basis for an acknowledgement of socialisation and the fact that we are human beings investigating human beings. Generalisation may be achieved through assessing how individuals feel in different situations and how they may act in certain circumstances. Consequently, given the dislocated nature of reliability and validity (see below) within the phenomenological approach a number of interpretations and subsequent generalisations may be forwarded in relation to a specific study. There must be connections between the researcher and researched as well as the intended, and in some contexts, unintended audience.

Reflexivity

The core of reflection incorporates reflexivity and involves how we are constructed in a social construct while at the same time acting as constructing agents. Without a constructed constructing self within a construction all is meaningless; through interpretation meaning is constructed. Construction requires something to be constructed, the researcher as a constructing subject and an object or a community that constructs the researcher. Reflexivity involves acknowledging the constructive elements without giving precedence to any part of the process; construction requires a continuum of interaction, a form of symbolic interaction or Hegelian recognition. Consequently, the relationship between selves and others provides the foundations for social constructivism. However, a concentration on reflexivity can conjure criticisms regarding 'narcissistic self-centredness', 'self-absorption' and 'self-reflective isolationism'. One way of dealing with these criticisms involves researchers recognising themselves as elements of the wider social and political context and that we ourselves are caught up with and intrinsically linked to these contexts; others consider that the link between context and self should be negated. 'The very idea of reflexivity … is the … ability to break away from a frame of reference and to look at what it is not capable of saying' (Alvesson and Skoldberg, 2009: 270).

Reflexivity involves thinking critically about different conceptualisations of self; in a research project, self as researcher and respondent and wider self as learner, manager, parent, sibling and so on. Reflexivity involves a critical subjectivity in terms of coming to know self through the research process. For example, a doctorate is not simply about the completed thesis, it is also about the changes involved in students as they become active researchers; this is achieved through reflexivity undertaken during studies and the thinking required for the research process and successful completion of the thesis. In other words, the research project is as much about changes to the individual as the impact the research may have on the wider environment. 'Self' is brought to the research situation while at the same time self is developed through the research process. Indeed, types of self can be broken down into three categories: selves based around the role of researcher; selves formed through socio-historic existence; and selves determined by the situation or research environment (Reinharz, 1997). Each self requires interrogation regarding relationships with and formation of the research process. 'We must question our selves ... regarding how ... binaries and paradoxes shape not only ... identities called forth in the field ... but also our interactions with respondents, in who we become to them in the process of becoming to ourselves' (Guba and Lincoln, 2000: 183–4). Furthermore, through reflexivity researchers are able to locate themselves in the research; that is identify their socio-historical location and become aware that they carry a historical perspective of the situation or problem under analysis. Findings are co-created with researcher and researched involved in a saturation of the study with these juxtapositions of selves, situation and subject used to enhance understanding and enrich data interpretation. As well as observing participants the researcher is observing different selves and building interpretations of selves and these selves' interpretations of data into the final outcome of the research. How the researcher fits and is involved with the research is not simply recognised but becomes an element of the research; personal investment in the research becomes part of the analysis. However, reflexivity has limited validity as it asks the reader to take interpretations at face value as an authentic attempt to explore selves and be truthful and conscientious about the narrative accounts provided.

A reflexive attitude involves intensive scrutiny regarding how something is known and/or understood. Reflexivity incorporates an iterative and interactive dialogue about past experience in relation to present perspectives and future possibilities. A reflexive position is not simply reporting facts or truths but providing interpretations of data and issues raised in the field. 'The outcome of reflexive social science is reflexive knowledge: statements that provide insight on the workings of the social world and insight on how that knowledge came into existence' (Hertz, 1997: viii). Object and subject are brought back into the same space. Reflexivity may be perceived as the route to 'radical consciousness of self in facing the political dimensions of fieldwork and constructing knowledge ... Reflexivity becomes a continuing mode of self-analysis and political awareness' (Hertz, 1997: viii). Reflexivity permeates the whole research process through continually challenging the researcher to be aware of ideology, culture and politics of the situation and self. Researchers should be aware of their own self, interests and social standing as these will direct and influence the research process. The impact of the researcher on the situation and individual being investigated needs to become part of the analysis. Previous experience should be assessed in relation to the research process. Reflexivity requires awareness of self that can only be partial, however it is important that this be made clear in the research text. The influence of previous work on individual perspectives should be openly acknowledged (Charmaz, 2000). Such awareness may be realised through memo-writing as this provides a discourse or conversation between the researcher and the data.

Reflexivity involves the double hermeneutical idea concerning the interpretation of the interpreting subject; this can be intensified through employing further levels of interpretation but the core of reflexivity incorporates reflection of interpretation and the self analysis of the person undertaking interpretation. Reflexivity provides ways of seeing or different lenses that act introspectively on data interpretations. Theory and abstraction are part of reflexivity and interaction between theoretical analysis and practical situations a necessary element of the process. Reflexivity is a two-way process of reflection or a primary concept reflecting on other secondary levels; fundamentally levels of interpretation are reflected in each other. Levels include involvement with data in terms of observations, focus groups and interviews, interpretation of materials through producing meanings, critique of interpretation through theoretical perspectives such as power, politics and ideological positions, reflection regarding the production of texts regarding selection of voices, claims of authority and self within the levels of interpretation. There is an incremental shift through levels of interpretation:

- direct involvement with the data and low level interpretation of this data;
- identification of relationships between theory and practice (praxis) or theoretical interpretation;
- relationships between self data and theory or reflective interpretation.

The ideal situation incorporates theory being re-moulded by the data; norms, accepted values and personal perspectives should be challenged and reconstructed. Obviously, the extent of the interpretations will be curtailed by access to theory, consequently some comprehension of theoretical frameworks is required. A reciprocal relationship is needed between theoretical frameworks, the individual researcher and the data. The theories and individual researchers order the data and deal with anomalies and uncertainties in the early stages of the study.

Important aspects of interpretation include:

- creativity;
- depth of theoretical knowledge;

- breadth of theoretical knowledge;
- variety of theoretical knowledge.

If the researcher has dedicated their career to a particular area or the student concentrated on a specific theory, then the research will be restricted to this area and reflexivity reduced. One may become emotionally attached to a theory and attempt to prove or confirm this. Consequently, knowledge of at least two theories will assist multiple interpretations and reflexivity. Controlled theories enable possible interpretations, the juxtaposition and synthesis of theories in relation to data delivers and enhances creativity. Fundamentally, wide reading is required as the sound theoretical knowledge engenders diverse interpretation and reflective capability.

Validity and Trustworthiness

For positivism, validity involves the extent to which measurement is accurate and what is supposed to be measured is actually being measured; how far can we be sure that a test measures the phenomenon we expect it too. Whereas, for phenomenological approaches the main emphasis regarding validity relates to whether access to knowledge and meaning has been realised. Questions relating to validity that require attention when evaluating the findings of research include:

- Are the findings authentic?
- Can the research be trusted?
- Can the research be acted upon?

| Definition Box |

Validity

- Face validity: the measure should reflect the concept in question and be plausible.
- Concurrent validity: the recognition that criteria on which cases are based are different and require comparison with other measurement procedures.
- Predictive validity: the use of future measurement criteria with predictive capability.
- Construct validity: the deduction of hypotheses from a relevant theory.
- Grouping validity: comparison with different groupings that differ from the phenomenon in question.

Validity involves different understandings and interpretations of individual positions and it is important to identify whether the research acknowledges the interpretation of the researched in relation to the researcher while undertaking data collection and analysis. For phenomenology, multiple voices are included in the research process and the individual voice of the positivist position is challenged.

This involves reflexivity and reflection regarding ultimate and ongoing interpretation. Validity involves the extent to which research undertaken has integrity and includes measurement, internal, external and experiential validity.

Measurement validity is closely related to reliability (measurements must be reliable) and mainly involves statistics or quantitative research; it is mainly concerned with the extent that a mode of measurement regarding a given entity does actually reflect the that which it purports to be measuring. If not, then the research results are questionable, for example, if an entity or idea fluctuates and this is not taken into consideration then the measurement could be said to be unreliable. Internal validity is concerned with the causal relationship between separate variables. If we consider that lack of education rather than the media causes deviancy and criminality, then evidence to support this relationship is required. Questions relating to levels of certainty between and *independent variable* (the cause or affect) and *dependent variable* (the outcome or effect) become apparent. Can we definitely say that a lack of education (*independent variable*) produces criminality (*dependent variable*)? External validity concentrates on the extent the outcomes of the research can be generalised; that is the extent that the specific findings can provide a more general explanation and/or understanding and involves close attention to sampling (how organisations or individuals are chosen to participate in the research). Experiential validity incorporates the level to which the research environment reflects real life experience. How far do research outcomes identify the real life situation and experiences of those being researched? This questions the level that the research captures or reflects people's everyday lives. This validity is expressed when the research is undertaken in the field or natural settings rather than those setup by the researcher. Furthermore, participation is not recommended and non-participatory observation and a positivistic stance (distinction between subject and object) deemed more appropriate.

These forms of validity testing, with the exception of a weaker approach to experiential validity (one where participatory observation is recognised), primarily adhere to positivist and post-positivist notions of research. Consequently, Guba and Lincoln (1985) proposed alternative terms for non-positivist approaches that directly related with the validity and reliability objectives of quantitative research projects. Indeed, in many instances the holy trinity of validity, reliability and generalisation failed to deal with the vagaries of qualitative research. 'Many qualitative researchers have struggled to identify more appropriately how we do what we do. So, rather than take terms from the quantitative paradigm, qualitative researchers have ... offered alternative ways to think about descriptive validity and ... case study work' (Janesick, 2000: 393). Rather than validity, phenomenological and more qualitative analysis should pursue trustworthiness. 'Terms such as credibility, transferability, dependability and confirmability replace the usual positivist criteria of internal and external validity, reliability and objectivity' (Denzin and Lincoln, 2000: 21).

Credibility is similar to internal validity because it wishes to determine the extent that findings can be believed. Credibility stresses triangulation (or multiple perspectives and accounts of the situation under analysis). As noted in Chapter 6, for action research, credibility may be determined by the 'willingness of local stakeholders to act on the results of the action research' (Greenwood and Levin, 2000: 96). Credibility recognises the 'standards and proof that are favoured by clients and stakeholders' (Chambers, 2000: 863). Credibility can be assessed through the presentation of evidence regarding the phenomena under investigation.

Transferability mirrors external validity and the extent to which findings can be generalised to other settings and/or situations. Phenomenological research entails in-depth study of groups and pursues depth of understanding regarding unique situations. 'Thick descriptions' (Geertz, 1973: 6) are pursued through a selection of interpretive methods that will in turn become 'thick interpretations' (Vidich and Lyman, 2000). Such thick interpretations will provide a database that will allow judgements about transferability of findings to other situations. Again triangulation may be sought but in this case the triangulation of methods, such as interviews, focus groups and observations. As with reliability, dependability pursues replication, all parts of the research should be audited because through this audit, trust in the research process will emerge. It involves keeping records relating to development of the research question and problems in terms of data collection procedures, analysis and transcripts. These would then be assessed or reviewed by colleagues regarding correct procedures for theory development. This of course creates problems in terms of the amount of data a qualitative study appropriates and the time this would take to assess. A good example of dependability may be found in grounded theory coding procedures and memo writing. Finally, confirmability investigates the axiological perspectives and subjective biases the researcher brings to the research project and the relationship between the researcher, research setting and individuals within the research process.

Furthermore, as well as trustworthiness, Guba and Lincoln (2000) suggested that for phenomenological inquiry *authenticity criteria* should be developed. The criteria suggested included; fairness, ontological authenticity, educative authenticity, catalytic authenticity and tactical authenticity (Guba and Lincoln, 2000: 180). Fairness in a research project or programme should ensure that all voices have equal status, it should encourage inclusion and deter marginalisation. Fairness involves inclusion of all voices in an equal and equitable manner.

Ontological and educative authenticity provides empathy regarding the participants involved in the research process and those who interact with them in a personal, organisational or social context. This necessitates a sound knowledge of the situation and an empathetic stance regarding those under investigation; this means that the researcher is required to put themselves in the place of those being researched; being-in-the-world is clearly recognised. Catalytic and tactical authenticity builds on the previous requirements and incorporates an assessment of the extent to which the research has led to social action and/or empowerment in relation this. With regard to empowerment tactical authenticity may include, 'the involvement of the researcher/evaluator in training participants in specific forms of social and political action if participants desire such training' (Guba and Lincoln, 2000: 181).

Conclusion

Even though one may argue that certain methodologies and methods may be more conducive for undertaking research on social phenomena and humanity, no specific approach provides a panacea in the pursuit of ultimate knowledge. Indeed, discourse relating to validity and reliability was initially developed for use in positivist and more quantitative research. That said, validity and reliability are useful mechanisms that should ideally be carried out at the pilot stage of the research project. Initial responses may then be measured against each other and correlations determined and reliable indications of accuracy assessed. Once it is accepted that the characteristics of meanings can transform we have no way of determining that what we find involves the truth or not; 'there is no way of finding the true Cinderella ... There is no dependable glass slipper we can use as a test, since the old slipper will no longer fit the new Cinderella' (Hirsch, 1967: 46)

Alternatively, one may take a phenomenological stance which moves beyond the positivist concern with social experience from which generalisation may be drawn but rather concentrates on single experience or individual situation, moment of discovery and feeling and emotion. On occasion, in the phenomenological tradition there is a little reluctance to use notions such as validity, reliability and generalisation because they imply acceptance of positivist ontology. This of course undermines the pursuit of objectivity and re-defines validity in terms of subjectivity and interpretation. Whether or not validity exists, an individual piece of research relates to the extent that data has been rigorously collected triangulated and interpreted. Indeed, validity may be conceived of as absurd if no single, correct interpretation exists. However, if the research project is undertaken in such a way that it ensures faithful description of the ideas, interpretations and understandings of those researched, validity, reliability and generalisation can provide useful tools for rigorous analysis. Overall, sound methods based in paradigms of inquiry and methodology identify how an investigator can satisfy others to the extent that they trust that what has been seen has been accurately described and that the conclusions that have been drawn are valid. As noted when assessing both positivist and phenomenological approaches certain difficulties emerge. One major difficulty is that of identifying truth (or reality)

Table 12.1 Research criterion

Positivism	Phenomenology
Validity	Credibility
Reliability	Transferability
Generalisation	Fairness
Stability	Trust
Consistency	Reflexivity

and in this context one may question all methodological approaches and methods. However, notions regarding levels of reliability, validity and generalisation, as with trustworthiness, fairness and credibility provide a yardstick by which levels of rigour and measurement in research projects can be gauged and assessed. As human beings we may not be able to ascertain a perfect reality or a general theory that explains existence but this should not divert us from attempting to understand ourselves and the world in a reflective manner. Indeed, a fuller picture of the world and other human beings in relation to self may be better conceived if a range of measurements and approaches are used. That is, both positivist and phenomenological approaches and the techniques used in each have something to tell us about human endeavour and existence. It does not follow that a valid interpretation is correct, but it is more likely to be the case given existing evidence at our disposal. Acknowledging that for some studies mixed methodologies may be appropriate, in the following chapter I overview methods of data collection and describe how these may be used to develop greater validity, reliability and/or trustworthiness in the pursuit of different types of generalisation.

Further Reading

Alvesson, M. and Skoldberg, K. (2009) *Reflexive Methodology*. London: SAGE Publications.
Denzin, N. and Lincoln, Y. (1994) *The Handbook of Qualitative Research*, 1st edn. Thousand Oaks, CA: SAGE Publications.
Denzin, N. and Lincoln, Y. (2000) *The Handbook of Qualitative Research*, 2nd edn. Thousand Oaks, CA: SAGE Publications.
Denzin, N. and Lincoln, Y. (2005) *The Handbook of Qualitative Research*, 3rd edn. Thousand Oaks, CA: SAGE Publications.
Hertz, R. (1997) *Reflexivity and Voice*. Thousand Oaks, CA: SAGE Publications.
Kuhn, T.S. (1970) *The Structure of Scientific Revolution*. Chicago, IL: University of Chicago Press.
Popper, K. (2002) *The Logic of Scientific Discovery*. London: Routledge.

THIRTEEN

Methods of Data Collection

Introduction

No matter what philosophical position or paradigm of inquiry is used in a research project, it is always possible to use a combination of research methods when collecting data. The rationale for the balance between these methods will depend on the objectives of the research and the extent to which qualitative or quantitative techniques are to be utilised. This said, when undertaking positivist and post-positivist approaches the likelihood will be that quantitative methodologies and surveys and structured interviews will predominate. For phenomenological studies, incorporating critical theory, constructivist and participatory paradigms of inquiry, it is likely that qualitative data will be collected through interviews, focus groups and observations. Quantitative data collected through surveys allow quick, clean and relatively inexpensive modes of data collection. However, such requires sampling techniques that ensures the data is representative of the population the study proposes to analyse. If the sample does not correspond with the population then generalisation and the ability to predict will be negated; that is, statistical techniques will be undermined.

Definition Box

Sampling

Sampling is usually confined to positivism, post-positivism and the quantitative methods involved with these approaches. Samples involve certain groupings incorporated within a population, for example, a set of companies within a sector or number of individuals within a company or department. The *sampling frame* involves a record or listing of the total population from which the samples are drawn (a list of the companies in a sector or record of individuals within a company or department). On occasion it may be possible to use the entire population. However, in a large positivist or post-positivist study a representative sample of the population will be required that should be objective, random and as large as possible. That said, sampling techniques are used by grounded theorists and especially by those who follow the Strauss and Corbin variant (see Chapter 9 for further information).

Surveys usually provide quantitative data and allow reliability, aspects of validity and clear non-disputed generalisation. However, the thick description and richness of the data along with the context of the research can be lost when using surveys or structured interviewing; one is left with narrow explanation rather than in-depth understanding. This said, even though they provide a more in-depth comprehension of complex situations, qualitative methods of data collection can be time consuming and expensive. Furthermore, as we have discussed in previous chapters, issues relating to subjectivity and rigour require attention when dealing with meaning and interpretation of qualitative data.

Data can be collected through a number of different methods that include:

- surveys or questionnaires;
- interviews (structured, semi-structured and unstructured);
- observations (participatory and non-participatory);
- focus groups.

However, when one undertakes a piece of research one is faced with conflicting demands regarding data collection in terms of levels of validity, reliability and trustworthiness.

Surveys

Survey research came to prominence during the Second World War (especially in the USA) where surveys were undertaken to measure experiences of US soldiers (GIs) during combat. In the post-war period, surveys became the norm in the social sciences and these predominated as the main research method for over 30 years. However, there was some dissent to the preponderance of survey research with academics considering that this had become obsessive. Indeed, C. Wright Mills considered that the survey inhibited research and nothing could be said unless it had been through the statistical ritual. He argued that the scientific method expressed in post-positivist studies inhibited the social sciences. Wright Mills considered that because of the scientific method 'the kinds of problems that will be taken up and the way in which they are formulated are quite severely limited' (2000: 57). This is because the scientific method 'has been largely drawn with expedient modifications, from one philosophy of natural science' (Wright Mills, 2000: 57). Today other methods challenge the dominance of the survey but until the 1990s the dominance of the survey method continued unabated. During the 1950s governments saw the benefits of survey research and funding followed; consequently, universities and research centres that required funding became very interested in this approach. More qualitative methods co-existed with the survey method but these were also expected to comply with the narrow rigour set out by quantitative analysis.

Surveys

- Contact by letter and ask people to complete and return. Problem: reaches many but few returned. Also, the questions need to be clear because they cannot be explained.
- Researcher picks up the completed survey. Problem: very expensive, still no certainty that they will be completed.
- The survey may be completed by a group of people under the supervision of the researcher. Problem: how are the groups selected.
- A trained interviewer asks the questions and records the responses. Problem: Very reliable but expensive.
- Consider the problems identified and suggest how they may be overcome.

A broad analysis is accomplished through surveys because a full range of the phenomena needs to be understood. However there is also the need to be sufficiently well acquainted with each particular case. The more the former is satisfied the more the latter is frustrated. Surveys can be used for positivist, post-positivism and phenomenological studies; however, for the latter, questions normally remain open-ended and for both forms of positivism they would usually be closed. Closed questions can be coded quite easily especially if a Likert scale is used, whereas open questions will require further procedures following the data collection process. Consequently, for large-scale research projects, which involve large amounts of data, the use of closed questions is advised. One major difficulty with closed questions is ensuring respondent comprehension of the questions being asked; if the researcher is not on site (and this would be very difficult with a large-scale survey) then clear straightforward questions are imperative. For this reason it is necessary to undertake a pilot study (a smaller study that tests comprehension) before the main survey is despatched. The pilot study will provide some evidence regarding levels of respondent comprehension. For positivist and post-positivist studies, surveys are ideal methods of data collection; they are the least expensive and have proved the easiest means of collecting large amounts of information. However, there are a number of issues that should be guarded against when designing the survey. Surveys should only ask questions that are relevant and keep these to a minimum. Remember people are busy and if presented with a long onerous questionnaire it is highly likely to end up in the bin. Ensure the questions are clear and understandable and include a covering letter that gives clear instructions and explanation of the research project. Be very clear regarding methods of distribution and identify strategies for following up non-returned questionnaires (this may be done through numbering or coding). Funnel the questions, which means moving from the general to the specific and be sure of the mode of analysis.

There is some disagreement regarding the best place for personal information, that is, age, gender, education and so forth. However, it is necessary for this information to be collected and should be requested either at the beginning or end of the individual questionnaire. Number each questionnaire (this will help with analysis and tracking non-respondents), as noted funnel questions and where necessary filter the questions (as the government does in the Census) 'If No go to question 8.'

When formulating questions always keep the audience in mind; how well educated are they; are they specialists or generalists regarding the area of study? Good questions will provide superior data so developing the questions is fundamental to survey methods. Qualify your questions in terms of temporality or space, for example, over the past month or provide the institutional or organisational location. It is also useful to insert 'normally' or 'usually' when asking questions relating to daily experience such as 'do you normally travel to work on the 9.00 a.m. train'?

Definition Box

Likert Scale

A Likert scale was devised to automatically code data through a numerical scale. The survey requires respondents to agree or disagree with given statements on a scale of usually 1–5:

1 = strongly agree
2 = agree
3 = don't know
4 = Disagree
5 = strongly disagree

When assessing the reliability of responses to surveys (especially in positivist and post-positivist investigations), they need to be looked at in terms of the extent that the questions are unclear or contain discrepancies and that the respondents dealt with the questionnaire in a fair and honest manner. Indeed, the researcher may employ a number of strategies when dealing with these issues which may include:

- asking questions of the same individuals at different times; through correlation these can identify a means of measuring reliability;
- dividing the survey in half through distinct variables (odd and even questions) and again undertake correlation;
- correlate every question with every other across the sample; the inter-item correlation becomes the given index of reliability.

Overall, the survey should request that individuals describe and explain behaviour and attitudes through a set of questions or statements (Likert Scale), which is normally analysed through statistical techniques. It is important to understand what you intend to investigate as well as the theoretical framework that hypotheses and null hypotheses are based in, only then can the theory as well as practice be part of validation or falsification; the theoretical element as well as the practical needs to be captured in the questions. Consequently, a good knowledge of the theoretical literature is required when developing hypotheses. Questions should be closely attended and formulation should incorporate simplicity and straightforward unambiguous language. Pilot test all questions before the main survey is despatched.

Reflection Box

Formulating Questions

- Clear explanation of the research.
- Use jargon and specialised language.
- Use clear, simple, straightforward language.
- Ensure multiple meanings.
- Ask more than one question at a time.
- Use vague adjectives and descriptive words such as limited and large.
- Ask negative questions.
- Include concept questions that can clarify comprehension.
- Ask obnoxious, insensitive questions.
- Keep the number of questions to a minimum.
- Ask for only the information required.

Use a Likert scale to deal with these statements, then consider the reasons for your responses.

Interviews

Examples of data collection through interviews may be observed in studies undertaken by Charles Booth in the late 19th century *Life and Labour of the People of London* (1902–1903). Booth mainly used surveys but triangulated his study through unstructured interviews and observations. Following this initial study, further work on other UK as well as US cities were undertaken using similar methods (Converse, 1987). Investigation through questions and answers involves ambiguity; interpretations of answers will always involve a level of subjectivity. However, how else are we to accumulate understanding unless we ask questions of ourselves and other human beings? This involves questioning ourselves when observing or reflecting or others when interviewing or being involved with focus-groups. Interviews involve a wide variety of forms and can either be face-to-face individual or group (this could be perceived as a type of focus group), structured, semi-structured or unstructured. Positivist and phenomenological research both rely on interviewing as a method of data collection; both quantitative and qualitative techniques are employed. Interviews can either give an in-depth comprehension of the area under analysis or give the basis for a numerical study through a scale or matrix. Indeed, the interview is used well beyond the bounds of social science and social research and is generally perceived as a means of developing an accurate interpretation and understanding of a given situation. Fundamentally, the interview has become an intrinsic aspect for gathering data in general and may be encountered in all walks of life.

Interviews provide data collection mechanisms that enable description, interrogation, evaluation and consideration of personal accounts or biographical and historical data; interviews can be confrontational and allow an environment for storytelling. The interview has become institutionalised and the norms embodied within it second nature for individuals in society, consequently minimal training is seen to be needed for conducting them; they are considered technical constructs that can be conduct by anyone. 'Interviewing has become a routine technical practice and a pervasive taken for granted activity in our culture' (Mishler, 1986: 23). However, contextual situations do exist as do different personnel within the interview situation; it is not purely a technical matter. Interviews incorporate relationships between the interviewer and interviewee and reflects this dynamic as well as the more technical accounts and reporting of questions and answers. That is, interviews involve social dynamics and these will determine and mould the knowledge and understanding accrued. Indeed, knowledge of such dynamics provides the social scientist with further capability for interpretation and knowledge construction when dealing with questions and answers in an interview setting.

QUESTION

INTERVIEWS

- Job applications
- University applications
- Housing applications
- Social security eligibility
- Research project
- News items
- Biography
- Interrogation
- Media.

Are all of these types of interviews? How would these different situations affect the type of interview employed? What sort of data would be sought?

Using Interviews

- Structured interviews: uses fixed questions and attempts to standardise the interview in an attempt to reduce the effect that the interviewer's biases or personal approach may have on the results. Problem: Constrains the interview and omits data that may be useful to the research project.
- Semi-structured interviews: uses fixed questions which may be adapted as the interview progresses. This allows for some flexibility in the outcomes. Problem: Necessitates a capable interviewer and allows subjective influences.
- Unstructured interviews: uses open conversation on a given topic. Problem: Needs a trained interviewer or at least one that is capable of keeping the conversation going. The interviewer must also be sensitive to what is being disclosed. Furthermore the researcher may observe unseen or participate and observe. The former approach has ethical implications and the latter acknowledges that individuals react differently when they know they are being observed (Hawthorne Effect).

Consider the strengths and weaknesses of the above techniques and determine the most appropriate for the research project you are considering.

└───┘

As noted, for positivist and post-positivist studies the most appropriate form of interview involves structured interviews with closed questions. In a structured interview all respondents are asked exactly the same pre-defined set of questions; the expectation is limited variation, clear means for coding in a pre-established format. In this context the interview takes the form of a questionnaire and there is little difference between this method of data collection and the closed questionnaire directly administered by the researcher or researcher's assistant. More phenomenological approaches would involve unstructured and semi-structured interviews. Unstructured interviews require the researcher to enter the research with no pre-conceived questions and the interview should take the form of a discussion or conversation. The unstructured interview is able to produce in-depth data and relates closely with observation (especially participatory observation). Also labelled ethnographic interviewing, this form of informal interview involves collecting and collating data in the field. The objectives of the unstructured interview is to understand social and behavioural complexities in an inductive manner whereas the aims of structured interviews is to generate specific data explaining human behaviour that can easily be coded in pre-determined categories. The latter uses a priori categorisation which may stifle discovery and impose constraints on the investigation. Semi-structured interviews provide a set of pre-conceived questions but these are not closed and allow for deviation and more open discussion; as the label suggest these are a hybrid of structured and unstructured interviews. That said, for the inexperienced interviewer they provide a useful method because they ensure that the interview remains on the right track while at the same time enables opportunity for wider discussion. It can sometimes take a great deal of work to enable access and an unstructured interview with a government official or managing director may be interesting but deviate from the research project objectives. With a semi-structured interview it is likely that the researcher will leave with some information relevant to the study. Unstructured interviews are for the more experienced interviewer and/or ethnographic participatory observer. Semi structured and unstructured interviews are useful when:

- the underlying rationales for beliefs and attitudes are necessary;
- a comprehension of worldviews, culture and norms are required;
- the process or research methodology is inductively driven;
- in-depth understanding of the situation and the individuals position within this context is imperative for the analysis.

Reflection Box

Positivist Structured Interviews

- Ask questions exactly how they are worded and ordered; never improvise.
- In each case use similar intonation, emphasis and body language.
- Record responses exactly.
- Refrain from interpreting the questions.
- Do not give personal views or show agreement.

Consider these recommendations for the structured interviewer and think about the effects on the data that would be accumulated.

Unstructured and semi-structured interviews evolve as individual interviews proceed and information accrued in each interview adds to the next. There is a process of inductive open discovery within and between interviews. This is a fundamental strength of these methods but the emergence of ideas must be tracked and as they are incorporated noted explicitly in the research process; such may identify patterns and illustrate rationales for why such issues emerged in a certain way. Interviews used in this way should adhere closely with transferability.

In any interview the interviewer will have some impact on the interview and interviewee; bias in terms of sexuality, gender, race or class may exist. Furthermore, expectations from the research may overshadow what is discovered or emerges. Bias and subjectivity are difficult to negate in all interviews but even more so in unstructured or semi-structured situations e.g. what is said pre-interview could influence responses. However, these are difficulties for social science research in general and should be given thought no matter what methods of data collection are employed. Some reflexivity regarding these issues pre-interview and during the interview may assist and inform the researcher at the analysis stage of the research project. In general, interviews are one-to-one but sometimes can involve others and become group interviews. Group interviews involve more than one and usually several people in a hybrid formal/informal situation. Indeed, the idea of the group interview has evolved into the idea of the focus group, which will be covered in more detail in the next section.

Focus Groups

There are numerous texts identifying how to construct and facilitate focus groups (Fern, 2001; Krueger, 1988; Stewart and Shamdasani, 1990; Templeton, 1994;). Focus groups encompass elements of two main techniques used by qualitative researchers (observations and interviews). Focus groups allow access to individual opinions and life stories, however it overcomes the problem of dealing with the 'self–other' divide in the research process. Indeed, focus groups provide the most suitable method for dealing with discourse in 'which images of research subjects as Other are constantly reproduced' (Madriz, 2000: 840).

Focus groups can be used to explore a specific set of issues and explore individual experiences, opinions and concerns. Respondents can formulate and pose their own questions and pursue issues they considered paramount. They can use their own vocabulary and provide social situations within which individuals and group interaction can be observed. Group interaction can generate data and encourage participants to speak with one another through exchanging anecdotes, questioning one another and commenting on different points of view. Indeed, participants can create an audience for one another and facilitators can encourage group discussions. The focus group can encourage multiple lines of communication and a safe environment for people to share ideas, beliefs and attitudes between individuals from similar professional backgrounds. However, 'compared with participant observations focus groups have the disadvantage of – sometimes – taking place outside of the setting where social interaction typically occurs' (Madriz, 2000: 836). Ideally focus groups should be undertaken in the field however, this may be difficult to achieve and artificial settings will be required. Focus groups incorporate an evolving method of data collection, which is continually being adapted and expanded, for example, political scientists using focus groups to assess public perceptions regarding policies and reform. Focus groups have enormous potential but like any research method they may be open to careless or inappropriate usage as results can be manipulated and subjects of research exploited.

As a method of data collection focus groups are a means of dealing with the dominant role of the interviewer and the closed question approach within the one to one interview. Focus groups were perceived as a mechanism for overcoming the interviewer's bias and subjectivity in terms of beliefs and values directing the interview. Through attempted negation of interview bias and power the focus group can provide a more accurate perspective of social constructions of those participating. Acceptance of this has been slow given the positivistic insistence for quantitative validity when measuring or explaining reality. Indeed, with new paradigms of inquiry the positivistic perception is challenged as opinions, attitudes and daily interaction become ever more important for research projects.

Focus groups have the potential to transform the researcher/researched relationship. Indeed the balance of power shifts to the participants as they provide the environment for them to define their own questions and even involve them in the writing of projects. Focus group research is participatory and is a cycle of interaction between researchers and participants that begins and ends in shared activities and understanding. There is a distinction between working on and working with people. However, this is not inherent to focus groups and if the full potential regarding the change between researchers and researched is to be reached practical exercises need to be utilised. The dynamics of focus groups have been identified as a means of developing a new knowledge through accessing raw un-codified data through stimulating the imagination of both researchers and participants (Johnson, 1996).

Focus groups are similar to other methods in that they enable access to individual opinions and life stories, they also allow means of dealing with the 'self/other' divide in the research process. Through the multi-vocal make-up of the group and their unstructured character. The control of the researcher is minimised in focus groups. Furthermore, focus groups allow horizontal as well as vertical interactions and even though power relations may surface among the participants, these will be more authentic than the artificial relationship between the researcher and participants. Moreover, observing these natural hierarchies and their development within the group can provide some very rich data. Focus groups provide an environment that encourages plurality in the construction of knowledge. Precedence is given to what the participants consider important. Understanding is constructed through the participant's language and frameworks; consequently, a sensitive comprehension of people's lives and shared symbols is required (this could be labelled theoretical sensitivity).

Through asking questions and challenging each other, focus group participants enter conversations and group interaction that accentuate empathy and commonality regarding each other's experiences and this fosters self-disclosure, self-understanding and self-validation. Communication allows the participants to build on each other's thoughts and opinions and provides evidence that certain opinions are valid and legitimate. It becomes clear that, rather than belong to the individual, problems are structural and reside with society in general. In this way focus groups can become an empowering experience as it gives voice to those without power. Indeed, through their own frameworks participants can become change agents in their own communities.

Focus groups are used to explore a specific set of issues. They are group discussions that focus on some form of collective activity, for example, viewing a video or discussing sets of questions. Focus groups are different from group interviews in that they explicitly use group interaction to generate data. Focus groups encourage participants to speak with one another through exchanging anecdotes, questioning one another and commenting on different points of view. Furthermore, they provide multiple lines of communication and a safe environment for people to share ideas and beliefs. Fundamentally, focus groups provide a situation where people can learn, educate others and provide an explorative environment.

Focus groups can be made up of strangers, friends or colleagues and consist of lay people or professionals who attempt to undertake diverse tasks within the group setting. These may include:

- brainstorming;
- ranking exercises;
- discussion, compromise and consensus.

Used correctly focus groups can explore individual experiences, opinions and concerns. The method can allow people to formulate and pose their own questions and pursue issues they consider to be paramount. Furthermore, the method allows this process to occur through the group using its own vocabulary while at the same time providing a social situation within which individuals and the group can be observed. Indeed, the group allows insight into articulation as issues are opposed and compromised through interaction, communication and the implementation of group norms. Focus groups provide an environment where the construction of points of view may be explored and are adept for studying attitudes and experiences based around specific topics. Overall, focus groups allow the situation for the researcher to observe and examine how ideas, understanding, knowledge, storytelling and self-presentation operate in a cultural context. Focus groups can provide fertile soil for the collection of anecdotal material. Fundamentally, they do not automatically need to be statistically representative and usually employ less positivist style sampling. Indeed, in order to ensure diversity focus groups rely on flexibility rather than sampling guided by a set of questions relating directly to issues the research is addressing. A flexible approach to the sampling frame should be built in at the planning stage.

The size of focus groups is flexible; however, some commentators argue that groups should incorporate 8–12 people, while others consider as few as 3 will be acceptable. Another difficulty revolves around whether they should be homogenous or heterogeneous in terms of group design. Homogeneity can be more productive whereas heterogeneity can provide deeper insight. One may also identify advantages and disadvantages regarding access and recruitment of focus groups; although some individuals may be intimidated by the prospect of group discussion the group environment may offer reassurance to others. Focus groups are ideal for individuals whose views you wish to draw on but protest that they have little to say. There are also practical considerations in terms of organisation, for example, most focus groups rely on a number of individuals travelling to a designated venue in coordination with others. Furthermore, there is also increased dependency on gatekeepers, who may screen participants to show the best side of a given institution/organisation. The other point on recruitment is ethical. Should participants know they are part of a research programme? There is also the question of confidentiality in relation to participants. Unlike interviews, focus groups cannot assure confidentiality. Furthermore, the researcher has a responsibility to provide accurate information for the group so that discussion can concentrate on actuality rather than myth. Such issues can be dealt with by setting ground rules prior to the participation and debriefing and supplying outcomes reached by the group.

Facilitation Techniques

Facilitators should approach the group discussion with a set of key questions and employ specific group exercises and provide participants with pens, flip charts and stimulus material, such as video, newspaper clippings, advertisements, leaflets and cartoons. Indeed, this could take the form of developing exercises such as vignettes and the use of pictures to stimulate group discussion. Furthermore, participants should be presented with key statements to be collectively assessed and that during collective tasks the participants concentrate on one another rather than the facilitator. Those participating should explain and defend their positions and discussion focused on key points of interest. Overall, those involved in discussions should not feel uncomfortable with the situation and each person be given equal opportunity to participate.

Facilitators should avoid being judgemental and refrain from making assumptions that close down further exploration. Intervention requires balance and should be undertaken mainly to clarify ambiguity, encourage participation and pursue unexpected avenues and ensure interaction between research participants is encouraged. Overall, understanding of separate cultural meanings and knowledge of the group's language is important as is the ability to lose control and allow the group to lead the discussion. However, strategies for reaching safer ground should be considered and employed when necessary.

Positivism would encourage the researcher to be objective or pursue an anonymous position within the research process. However, this is difficult for the facilitator and certain stances will be more appropriate to certain topics or research participants. Fundamentally, it is paramount to consider how facilitation persona or position will affect data collection. If a group is brought together on the basis of shared characteristics or experiences, how is the facilitator to fit with the situation? Is the facilitator an insider (one of us) or an outsider (one of them)? How will identity, dress, accent and behaviour influence how the facilitator is perceived? Obviously close proximity between the researcher and the researched is required, however some theorising regarding this proximity and participatory perception is an integral part of the research process.

Focus groups are capable of generating large amounts of rich dynamic data. However, such richness and dynamism can make the data difficult to manage so consequently sufficient time must be set aside for analysis. The researcher needs to reference the group context (this means starting from the group rather than the individual) and provide a balance between the picture provided by the group as a whole and the recognition of the individual voices within it. The researcher should try to distinguish between opinions expressed that oppose the group and identify the emergence of consensus and compromise constructed through group interaction. In addition, the facilitator should identify how discourse, anecdotes and jokes are used in group discussions and interactions.

Analysis can be undertaken through presenting large chunks of transcripts to illustrate the context in which they were made. One may also include a sense of dynamism and change during the course of the focus group, that is, people shifting positions, challenging one another and accommodating arguments. There is some debate in academic circles regarding how data should be used, for instance some complain that data should not be tallied or taken out of the context in which actual comments are made (Ashbury, 1995). However, others consider that tallying can be useful in some situations (for example, the number of groups that remember a specific case or situation). Indeed when there is persistent reference to a specific case then this needs to be noted as a historical reference point or conceptual template.

Overall, focus groups enable research environments where researcher's assumptions may be assessed and common problems relating to the group identified. Furthermore they encourage full explanation of issues under investigation and provide fora for sharing common experiences and development of solutions for existing and emergent problems. However, the other side to focus groups is that they are a powerful, public relations mechanism in that they are easily presented as consultation exercises or for findings to be manipulated to justify decisions that have already been taken. They may also be used in a political context and insights used to provide a veneer for unpopular government policies rather than question and change policies. Furthermore, some academics question whether focus groups are empowering and suggest that this is an exaggerated claim. That said, given these deficiencies researchers continue to use focus groups and are engaged in creating critical ways of unlocking their full potential.

In general, focus groups intensify the opportunity for the participants to decide the direction of the research and in this way it offers much to constructivist and participatory paradigms of inquiry. The control of the researcher is minimised and an environment that encourages plurality in the construction of knowledge provided. Precedence is given to participants and what they consider important issues relating to the research area. Multi-vocal participants limits the control of facilitators. Indeed, participants enter conversations and group interaction that accentuates empathy and commonality regarding each other's experiences and encourages self-disclosure, self-understanding and self-validation. Communication allows the participants to build on each other's thoughts and opinions and provide evidence that certain opinions are valid and legitimate. Focus groups involve vertical interaction between moderator and interviewees but enable richer data through horizontal interaction among participants.

Observations

Most studies and methods of data collection are based on some form of observation. For example, interviews and focus groups take into consideration body language and gestures that lend meaning to the interviewees discourse. In general, social scientists make observations of people interacting and acting in social situations. Observation can be either participatory or non-participatory and used for both positivist and phenomenological studies. In a positivist context the researcher attempts objective distance from where the actions of participants are either covertly or overtly observed in a natural or constructed setting. Phenomenological, especially constructivist and participatory, paradigms encourage interaction with respondents in natural settings. As noted, observation can take place in natural settings normally labelled the 'field' or controlled situations, or example, a clinic or laboratory. However, one may argue that some so-called natural settings are actually unnatural and the product of colonial or class based relationships, such as studies of the developing world or inner-city depravation. That said, the demarcation between controlled and natural settings exist in the literature with the latter predominating in non-positivistic research projects.

Definition Box

Observation

Structured/systematic observation (most appropriate for positivist studies) behaviour here is recorded through a definitive observation schedule that informs researchers about what should be looked for when observation takes place. The observation schedule involves a set of directives that enables systematic recording of each person's behaviour and the emergence of an aggregate of all those involved in the research.

Non-participatory observation: structured observation is best employed by non-participatory observation; the researcher is part of the situation under investigation but remains external to activities undertaken by the group. Again a useful method for positivist and post-positivist paradigms of inquiry.

Participatory observation: primarily associated with constructivist and participatory paradigms of inquiry, this method requires researchers to immerse themselves in the activity of the groups being researched. The rationale for this approach is to provide

---

detailed information and in-depth understanding regarding motives, values of those under investigation. Levels of participation will obviously vary.

Unstructured observation: this approach does not utilise an observation schedule but records as much varied data as possible; all behaviour is monitored and an account of this behaviour is described in a narrative. Unstructured and non-participatory observations are usually used in conjunction with each other.

Simple/contrived observations: in both simple and contrived observation the observer is concealed and the observed is unaware that observation is taking place. In the former the observer has no control over the observed whereas in a contrived situation the observed can make changes to the environment and track behavioural change in relation to these changes.

Observing people in controlled settings can make demands on individuals and force them to act differently or act as they think the researcher requires them to act. A good example of this was the Illumination Experiment in the Hawthorne Studies where production continued to improve when lighting in the workplace was both increased and decreased; eventually it was determined that the reason for increased production was the fact that the women in the experiment were being observed. The women in the Hawthorne Study changed their behaviour in relation to the expectations of the researchers and continued to increase production no matter how the variables changed. Such identified the 'Hawthorne Effect' (people act differently when being observed) and demand characteristics (demands are made of those being researched). One way around this is to be opaque about the rationale for the research and not state that the research is to assess productivity increases but changes in ergonomics or satisfaction in the workplace. However, certain determinants regarding the research may be implicitly conveyed; this may be dealt with by using a secondary researcher that does not know the rationale but this does create problems in terms of understanding nuances in the data while being collected and ongoing or later capability regarding interpretation. Obviously, in accordance with ethical imperatives the rationale for the study should be clarified once the research is completed. That said, eventually individuals become less aware of being observed and this can be perceived in reality television programmes and in natural settings such as the Bank Wiring Observation Room (another experiment in the Hawthorne Studies), the workplace or home.

Reflection Box

Observation Schedule

- Who or what should be observed?
- Clarify the research problem, project and questions.

(Continued)

(Continued)

- Categorise behaviour into mutually exclusive and inclusive variables.
- Develop a simple straightforward recording system.
- Nuances will require observer interpretation.

Identify the difficulties in developing an observation schedule that involves these considerations. Give an example of an observation schedule (see Mintzberg, 1973).

So as noted above, observations can involve both non-participatory and participatory forms; this given, it has been accepted for some time that even in a non-participatory context (as with the Hawthorne Studies) investigators can affect the research process. However, whether non-participant or participant observers, researchers are still expected to undertake rigorous objective modes of reporting to overcome subjective tendencies when writingup findings. Even though participant observers immerse themselves in the cultural environment of those under investigation and embrace a level of subjectivity in data collection when it comes to reporting results, a certain objective or scientific style is still required. If a scientific style or objective stance is not provided then research may be viewed as suspect and the researcher is seen to have 'gone native'. That said the postmodernist position questions whether such a scientific position exists when interpreting data and identifies the importance of understanding the nuances or position of the researcher (gender, social class, ethnic background) when interpreting data. Researchers are not the founts of all knowledge within specific situations or cultures analysed and their results can be challenged by those whom the research presumes to speak for; versions of truth conflict so objective absolute knowledge will be an unlikely outcome. Truth is varied, dislocated, has multiple parts and no one authoritative privileged position exists; truth is multi-voiced and contested.

For positivistic approaches, observation in a natural setting does not allow much control of the research environment and even with an observation schedule different interpretations of similar situations will emerge. Mintzberg (1973) devised a schedule which included a distinction between scheduled meetings and unscheduled meeting; scheduled meetings are straightforward however how does one define an unscheduled meeting e.g. is it a chance conversation by the photocopier or something more formal and substantial? Triangulation and clear definition is a means of dealing with these problems but again issues relating to ethics and observation (should the observed be informed?) have impacts on the validity of the method. Overall for a positivist study, observation requires other methods to substantiate objectivity and even if a phenomenological approach is undertaken a triangulated reflective approach is recommended.

Definition Box

Secondary Data

Secondary data can be collected from a number of sources:

- Statistical sources, particularly census or statistics produced by industrial or commercial firms, trade unions or relevant organisations. Problems with this data include: What is relevant for official statistics may not be for the research being undertaken and /or the data may not be presented in a form that is useful for the researcher.
- Historical documents including records and accounts of a qualitative nature relating to beliefs and values (such records may be historical or contemporary). Problems with this data include: problems of interpretation and exactitude.

Conclusion

This chapter has discussed a number of different methods of data collection which includes surveys, interviews, focus groups and observations. Overall, a clear distinction is made between methodologies and methods; this said, there exists a clear relationship between these areas. For example, the way data is collected and the mode of analysis will be determined by the methodological approach and the philosophical position that guides the methodological approach. Surveys and structured interviews predominate in positivist and post-positivist positions whereas observations, especially participatory observations, have greater usage in the constructivist and participatory paradigms of inquiry. Obviously, when it comes to methodologies, action research would incorporate greater participation than scientific method. However, different methodological approaches can display disparate philosophical positions and adhere to specific paradigms of inquiry. For example ethnography can either display a positivist or constructivist demeanour. Fundamentally, the philosophical position and paradigm of inquiry will identify the best methodology and consequent stance when methods of data collection are employed; there is a direct relationship between the philosophical position and best means regarding methods of data collection for a specific research programme or project. In the main, surveys will pursue verification and/ or falsification whereas focus groups or observations will be more likely involved with knowledge development. However, as noted in the introduction to this chapter, one may always employ numerous combinations of research methods when undertaking data collection. However, in general the phenomenological positions will use qualitative data and positivist quantitative, the methods of data collection deployed will reflect this.

Surveys and structured interviews enable quick, clean, inexpensive data collection and allows greater reliability and validity as well as generalisation. Other methods of data collection are more time consuming and raise issues regarding reliability, validity and generalisation. Surveys provide thin data and repeatable explanation whereas other methods enable thick data and in-depth understanding. However outside of the survey method and structured interview when using other methods repetition is problematic. That said, rather than adhere to positivist criteria such as reliability, validity and a certain interpretation of generalisation, researchers who use methods of data collection beyond surveys have developed criteria of their own. As discussed in Chapter 11 these include, trustworthiness, credibility, transferability dependability and confirmability. Overall, issues regarding objectivity and subjectivity continue to resonate in the social sciences and it is the role of the methodology to inform the methods used and provide logical rationales regarding the trustworthiness, reliability or validity of the truth or knowledge developed or tested and reflected through theory.

Further Reading

Bryman, A. and Bell, E. (2007) *Business Research Methods*. Oxford: Oxford University Press.

Cresswell, J.W. (2007) *Qualitative Inquiry and Research Design: Choosing Among Five Approaches*. Thousand Oaks, CA: SAGE Publications.

Denzin, N. and Lincoln, Y. (1994) *The Handbook of Qualitative Research*, 1st edn. Thousand Oaks, CA: SAGE Publications.

Denzin, N. and Lincoln, Y. (2000,) *The Handbook of Qualitative Research*, 2nd edn. Thousand Oaks, CA: SAGE Publications.

Fern, E.F. (2001) *Advanced Focus Group Research*. Thousand Oaks CA: SAGE Publications.

Hertz, R. (ed.) (1997) *Reflexivity and Voice*. Thousand Oaks, CA: SAGE Publications.

Mishler, E.G. (1986) *Research Interviewing: Context and Narrative*. Cambridge, MA: Harvard University Press.

Saunders, M., Lewis, P. and Thornhill, A. (2007) *Research Methods for Business Students*. Oxford: Pearson Education.

FOURTEEN
General Conclusion

Each chapter in this book constructs a framework for undertaking research projects, programmes or underpinning research funding proposals. This study deals with a number of different, disparate and complementary issues as it investigated ontology, epistemology and methodological approaches as means of enabling greater understanding and explanation of the relationship between theory and practice (praxis). This work explains how certain paradigms of inquiry may be synthesised, identifies levels of theory and outlines how they may best be utilised when explaining or understanding social phenomenon. Disagreement existed between rationalists and empiricists regarding the foundations of knowledge or truth; both argued that knowledge requires sound foundations that could be directly intuited. Empiricism involved an idealised term coined in the 19th century to illustrate distinctions between those thinkers who considered experience as the route to knowledge and those who considered the mind as the starting point. However, rationalists considered that that truth or knowledge was intuited through reason without the assistance of sensory experience. Kant and Schopenhaur combined the rationalist and empiricist positions and argued that experience and thought were involved in the formation of knowledge and truth. Indeed, they identified the relationship between internal and external worlds and how understanding, truth, reality, theory and knowledge involved a synthesis of the two.

For Hegel, truth and knowledge involved the whole that must then be present in each of its moments. If a single material fact cannot be reconciled then the proposition or entity is not true knowledge and theory is disproved. For William Pierce truth, knowledge and theory were fallible and always incomplete, partial approximations. John Dewey argued that truth was incomplete and identified through experience but he also indicated that it was self-corrective through being tested by the community. Truth is confirmed through application to concepts and practice. Indeed, such an approach moves toward a historical realism and the development of reality through historical and social formulations. Each necessitates metaphysical objectivism where truth exists independently of beliefs.

Knowledge, truth reality and theory are considered contingent and based on human perception and experience. *Verum ipso factum* 'truth in itself is constructed' (Vico, 1999). Truth, or the basis of reality and knowledge are agreed through democratic processes and discussion. The dilemma regarding the constitution of knowledge, truth, reality and theory relates to broad perspectives of ontology and epistemology outlined by positivism and phenomenology. The former considers that a truth is consistent; that it is observable, understandable and exists in an external context (of course the post-positivist would consider a truth as such until it was displaced and question whether humanity is able to fully understand truth). The latter, to varying degrees, considers that because interpretations of truth are intrinsically tied to the subject externality is difficult to establish, consequently truth and knowledge and the theories that reflect these are transitory and flexible.

Phenomenology may be considered an element of the continental philosophy movement that begins with a certain perspective of Kant and Hegel and includes Husserl, Nietzsche, Heidegger, Merleau-Ponty, Sartre, Foucault, Derrida among others. Kant tried to legitimise the idea of human knowledge through identifying the relationship between the object and subject which leads to numerous dualisms which also includes distinctions within the individual and investigates the extent that the mind is non-physical. Such dualisms question the relationship between mind and body or the individual and society. Hegel attempts to overcome dualism and through dialectic of spirit argued that rationality is not simply about individuals but communities and historical process. However, some continental philosophers cast doubt on Hegelian optimism that freedom and fully rational human beings may be realised through dialectical processes. Indeed, through nihilism Nietzsche argued that his philosophy brings the process back to earth; that he is realistic about the human condition. Nietzsche considered that Enlightenment thought and human culture were superficial and groundless because morality was firmly based in the values of science rather than the Greek values of art and myth. He identified three metamorphoses of spirit in the realisation of new values in the camel, lion and child. The weight-bearing spirit kneels like the camel and with much weight trundles into the desert where the spirit transforms into that of the lion. The lion pursues freedom and values and struggles with the great dragon it no longer wishes to worship. However, the great dragon is called 'thou shalt' and the lion wilfully obeys. The lion is incapable of creating new values but is able to achieve a level of freedom and is a necessary step in the development. The great dragon argues that 'all the values of things – glitter on me. All values have already been created, and all created values are in me' (Nietzsche, 1969: 15). Subsequently, the lion transforms into the spirit of a child which following reverence of 'thou shalt' and dragon values forgets and provides a new beginning. In other words, initially the word of God is taken as gospel then challenged through scientific revolution and Enlightenment which produce a set of meaningless values that are then written in stone. Fundamentally, if we are to discover new values then re-birth or renaissance is required. Such sentiments may also be found in the work of phenomenologists and critical theorists that have been covered in this text.

The term continental philosophy was coined by analytical philosophers in the 1950s and did not really embody one central idea but revolved around issues relating to problems of existence. Analytical philosophy emerged through ideas outlined by logical-positivism, which argued that we should or could achieve levels of detachment through simplification. Analytical clarity is sought, problems relating to individuals nullified and logical rigour emphasised. Indeed, for analytical philosophy no distinction between natural and social science existed. As we have noted, the main objectives of both positivism and post-positivism is explanation, control and prediction; positivism pursues verification of hypotheses, facts and laws whereas post-positivism is critical and concentrates on falsification. Consequently, knowledge or truth for the former involves verified laws and for the latter non-falsified laws that were probably true. Post-positivism identified further difficulties for research and phenomenology forms criticisms of both positivism and post-positivism. Indeed, even though phenomenology was defined by Hegel (1977) and more specifically for our purposes by Husserl in the 19th century, it is not until Heidegger, Sartre and Merleau-Ponty in the 20th century that the phenomenological approach began to challenge the (by then) dominant position of post-positivism.

That said, in 1931 Moritz Schlick argued that two distinct approaches to the pursuit of truth and knowledge may be identified; the approach of the historian and the approach of the philosopher. The historian will look at the thinkers given epochs or eras and their activities in relation to these times. However, the philosopher will concentrate on whether or not truth has been realised. Philosophers will disassociate themselves from the numerous philosophers and philosophies and the variations in opinion that such will create. It would be impossible to ascertain truth in relation to many separate philosophical positions and opinions advanced in different historical periods. For the philosopher the extent of truth within the different systems is paramount but because of different positions unlike progress in science, advances in the history of philosophy are at the best difficult and at worst impossible. Consequently, Schlick (2002) asks whether the chaotic situation that has reigned so far will continue into the future or will a final truth be discovered. Fundamentally, he explores the future role of philosophy in the pursuit of truth. Is philosophy about the discovery of an ultimate truth presented by one philosophical system or is philosophy the history of ideas? Eventually, philosophy is considered as a means of clarifying thought, not a theory but an activity. Philosophy is not about setting up propositions but making propositions clear. The philosopher will not need to be a scientist but a human being with deep understanding; a wise-man. In such a way the distinction between the positivist and phenomenological position begins to breakdown with in-depth understanding is required for both approaches.

Phenomenologists understand human beings as finite entities that suffer loss and pain and more importantly our very nature made us aware of this. Indeed, finitude and self-awareness allows humanity to ask questions relating to being, that no other entity on the planet (as far as we know) is capable of. We are part of the questioning and incorporate existential beings; that is we do not assess analyse or study ourselves from a detached point of view because through our very being we are intrinsically linked with the entity under observation. In the act of observing we become an element of the observed. The general methodologies for proponents within the continental school involved contextual understanding through historical conditions and social criticism. There was a challenge to natural science methods in that it was not that these were wrong but they failed to understand the inside and personal issues such as, anxiety, depression, happiness; they developed understanding of the individual in relation to social situations and uncovered problems that could be rectified. Consequently they became critical of socially accepted norms and suggested improvements and change.

Overall, this text has identified relationships between a number of different paradigms of inquiry identified by Denzin and Lincoln (1994, 2000, 2005). The traditional paradigms included positivism and post-positivism and the later critiques of positivist ontology and epistemology involved critical theory, constructivism and participatory paradigms of inquiry. Overall, the first two have been discussed under the heading of positivism and the last three, phenomenology

Positivism ascertained an external reality which may be perceived in an objective manner, whereas phenomenology considered that 'reality … is the result of that something and the mind's percipient activity' (Mairet, 1973: 13) and that any explanation of humanity has to begin from the subjective (Sartre, 1973). Positivism takes up an external position whereas phenomenology attempts to understand and construct an inner view. However, when we started to investigate and analyse the nuances in phenomenology and post-positivism similarities began to emerge. Phenomenology does not expect to provide an understanding of humanity and the cosmos from any starting point other than facticity. On the one hand, this involves a transcendental subjectivity, while, on the other hand, the world already exists before reflection begins. In this way, the dualist perspective leans toward the post-positivist perspective while at the same time the transcendental involves relativism. Phenomenology pursues a philosophy that attempts to provide comprehension of space, time and the world in which we live. Indeed this text has identified, investigated and outlined phenomenology and the three distinct paradigms of inquiry related to it: critical theory, constructivism and participatory. The paradigms of inquiry incorporate more specific mechanisms for undertaking research and through ontological and epistemological positions directly relate with different methodological approaches.

Critical theorists argued that ontology or reality developed through historical process and findings and theoretical perspectives are discovered through historical values. This involves historical realism and a epistemological approach that leads toward a specific methodology, which identifies a dialogic and dialectical approach. Dialogue is needed between the researcher and the researched as well as past and present. Structures are changeable and actions affect change.

In this context, truth, knowledge and the theory that reflects these are change-able in relation to historical circumstance. Understanding is developed through human endeavour in historical and cultural circumstances as the interaction between researcher and researched and historical values influence the analysis. Constructivism identifies 'relativist realisms' and even though it is not histori-cally based it has an epistemology similar to critical theory; findings are cre-ated and develop as the investigation progresses. Results are co-created through consensus and theory is relative and changeable. Furthermore, we have a new emerging paradigm or the participatory paradigm which incorporates co-creation of the world through mind and cosmos through both subjectivity and objec-tivity. The epistemology involves critical reflexivity and subjectivity through transactions between self and world. Findings are co-created through practical and theoretical knowledge in the context of becoming. Methodologically, this involves action research in its numerous forms and collaboration in terms of a practical and shared experience. Closely linked to this emerging paradigm is action research which returns social research to the objective of 'knowing how'. Knowledge is cogenerated and aimed at developing strategies for social action and social change; knowledge generation through action research is closely related to action. Theory and practice become intimately related to one another, they interact, are iterative and provide an in-depth comprehension of specific situations.

Constructivist and participatory paradigms are closely related to postmodernist and post-structuralist positions; that is, a criticism of Occidentalism and specifi-cally Enlightenment thought. Post-structuralists consider that language is unable to give meaning in a literal and unequivocal manner and language becomes uncertain, metaphorical and evasive. Truth is not fixed and is discovered either historically or relatively constructed through the reflexivity of communities. The theorist and practitioner or researcher and researched become interchangeable within the research and theory generation process. Rather than pure reflection, language provides a prism through which the observed may be understood or interpreted. Language outlines theories that reflect multi-faceted perceptions of truth. Furthermore, discourse analysis, which is similar to post-structuralism, also considers that individuals are inconsistent and language is contingent. Obviously this has implications for truth and generalisation and directs the researcher toward understanding and analysing what people say in relation to the specific situation. In this context, interviews or focus groups become part of the research rather than simply means of data collection. Foucault outlines the problem of the unity and discontinuity of discourse. Foucault argued that discourses construct meaning in specific situations and temporalities and that the everyday, usual or normality is captured. Consequently the researcher should concentrate on a genealogy of epistemé and discourse to uncover true meaning of experience and lifeworlds. However, while concentrating on epistemés and discourse the researcher continually needs to recognise the power/knowledge relations beneath the immediate surface. Self is central to the method pursued by Foucault; the central question becomes who am I? And the active creation of the subject occurs within the research process. However, the self is not a primarily a social construction but a construction of self through self reflexivity in an attempt to oppose the imposition of accepted power/knowledge norms. Postmodernism and post-structuralism also identify difficulties relating to the way theories claim a certain authority, assumptions that exist within them, the way they are constructed and how the language used validates their supremacy.

As a methodological approach ethnography may be understood from a postmodern, critical theory or post-positivist perspective. Based on the phenomenological perspectives, the critical theory and postmodern constructivist ethnographic approaches consider human understanding to be subjective and relative. Ethnographic studies should define humankind and provide social scientific descriptions of people and their cultural bases; in such a way we can develop comprehensions of 'self' in relation to 'other' in terms of becoming. Critical ethnography argues that conventional ethnography describes micro-based situations in a common sense manner that fails to take into consideration wider political and social frameworks. Glaser and Strauss requested that readers use grounded theory flexibly and in their own way (1967: 9). Theory is seen as being discovered as it emerges through the data. Charmaz (2000, 2006) argued that neither theories nor data are discovered but part of the same world as ourselves and offer an interpretive portrayal of the world under study and analysis, not an extant picture. Substantive theories are ontological constructions and grounded theory involves phenomenological, interpretivist positions with pragmatist underpinning. Hermeneutics negates naïve realism and the idea that immutable laws can be realised or that a final interpretation can be reached. Meaning is negotiated and in a continual state of becoming. In this way understanding is a practical experience. It is existential, it is who we are in the world in relation to our historical situation.

Even though one may argue that certain methodologies and methods may be more conducive for undertaking research on social phenomena and humanity, no specific approaches provide a panacea in the pursuit of ultimate knowledge. One may take a phenomenological stance which moves beyond the positivist concern with social experience from which generalisation may be drawn but rather concentrates on single experience or individual situation, moment of discovery and feeling and emotion. This of course undermines the pursuit of objectivity and re-defines validity in terms of subjectivity and interpretation. Whether or not validity exists, an individual piece of research relates to the extent that data has been rigorously collected, triangulated and interpreted. Indeed validity may be conceived of as absurd if no single correct interpretation exists.

This said, in understanding the beliefs of a person we need to locate tradition or culture or some such generality that forms a social context. However, discourse, ideology, and culture only exist in the context of individuals and once aggregation is accepted individual difference is undermined. Recognition of this difficulty forces the researcher to decentre aggregated positions such as culture and make explicit diversity within the concept and unpack specific individual beliefs and actions of those that make up the general aggregation. Indeed, such an approach requires different epistemological and ontological positions than those offered by positivist or modernist perspectives. The positivist perspectives argue that simplification and abstract facts (divorced from contexts) provide the basis of knowledge or truth. Phenomenological positions consider that all facts and understanding derive within a set of beliefs or theoretical frameworks. Knowledge is not neutral but constructed through interpretation, it is 'created not discovered because evidence is not evidence until it makes something evident' (Collingwood, 1965: 99). Knowledge and truth are constructed through concepts and theories, as such resulting interpretations are always incomplete and challengeable. Overall, sound methods based in paradigms of inquiry and methodology identify how an investigator can satisfy others to the extent that they trust that what has been seen has been accurately described and that the conclusions that have been drawn are valid.

Glossary

a priori/a posteriori – In the 17th century a priori involved the mind reasoning from cause to effect and a posteriori from effects to causes. Overall, a posterior knowledge is developed through experience and closely linked with empiricism. A priori knowledge emanates from thought and is closely related to rationalism. Kant considered that a priori knowledge was clear and independent of experience.

Adorno, Theodor Wiesengrund (1903–1969) – A critical theorist and member of the Institute of Social Research (Frankfurt School); his work is based in Hegelian thought and concentrates on the dialectical relationship between the individual and society.

anti-foundationalism – Challenges the very grounds of belief systems; postmodernists and post-structuralists are anti-foundational. Any system that makes a judgement requires some starting point (foundation) anti-foundationalists argue that the very starting point needs some a priori unfounded assumption.

archaeology – The study of the past through excavated artefacts; Michel Foucault uses this term to identify the excavation of the epistemé or the unconscious assumptions, beliefs and values of a social order of a historical time or epoch. Archaeology in this context attempts to uncover the rules and regulations of a system at a given point in time.

case study – A case study can be seen as either a methodology that draws together numerous methods of data collection (observations, interviews, focus groups) or as itself a method for collecting data.

communicative action – Requires interaction between speaker and hearer; identifies the distinction between the written word and speech. Speech is immediate and has richer meaning than the written word. Discourse takes place in a public context and meaning conveyed to society in general.

Comte, Augustus (1798–1857) – French philosopher and sociologist who coined the term positivism in his work *Philosophie Positive* (1830–42) translated into English by Harriet Martineau as *The Positive Philosophy of Augustus Comte* (1896).

critical realism – Reality exists independent of humanity but cannot be perfectly apprehended. Critical realism was further developed by Roy Bhaskar and involves transitive and intransitive forms of knowledge.

critical theory – A paradigm of inquiry closely linked with the Frankfurt School; there is no overall approach but it is underpinned by a criticism of the status quo and an inclination to bring about emancipation and change. Closely associated with neo-Hegelianism and Marxism there is a general criticism of capitalist society. Critical theory also criticised the dominance position held by positivism and post-positivism in the social sciences. It also disagrees with the perceived economic determinism apparent in the work of Karl Marx.

deconstruction – Involves dealing with the multiple meanings in texts and is a way of reading that identifies the internal contradictions of texts and illogicality of language in relation to the author's claims. The term was used by Jacques Derrida to examine the extent to which or why one term should be elevated above another and how the preference of one term subordinates or excludes the other.

Derrida, Jaques (1930–2004) – Developed deconstruction and identified the relationship between thought and language. Derrida questions the certitudes of consciousness and rationality as well as the idea that meaning can be traced to an original intention. It is imperative to question whether language or the word in general and cosmos or world correlate or coincide. His main concern involved questions regarding the extent to which action coincided with the word.

discourse analysis – Refers to the study of discourse as it unfolds through usage; when individuals involve themselves in discourse, pre-conceptions (a body of knowledge) informs the extent to which meaning and understanding is perceived as truth.

empiricism – Knowledge is rooted in experience and developed through the senses, for example, sight, smell, touch. Experience provides the basis for knowledge development and how we understand the world. Empiricism provides a common sense measure for knowledge in that all knowledge should be tested through experience and if it fails, then rejected. This has problems for more abstract concepts such as authority, responsibility and morality. The main mode of testing through experience involves the scientific method which incorporates induction, experimental procedures and for post-positivism, statistical techniques. Criticisms of empiricism can be identified in mathematics and metaphysics: mathematics cannot be verified through experience but obviously cannot be rejected and even though empiricists would like to reject metaphysics they themselves make certain assumptions.

Enlightenment – Normally the Enlightenment is perceived as a European movement that took place between the Glorious Revolution (1688) and the French Revolution (1789). The Enlightenment encompassed an awakening for humanity and a period from which many new ideas and philosophical positions emanated. Populated by French intellectuals, British empiricists and German philosophers, the Enlightenment provided a period of fervent debate and human self-discovery. The Enlightenment challenged religion and the state and dispelled darkness and superstition embedded in traditional institutions. It was a time of re-examination and the emergence of doubt.

ethnomethodology – Ethnomethodology is more interested in the interaction between people than what is actually debated. Concerned with the recognition that a person is saying something and how this was said rather than what was said and what was spoken about

falsification – A central part of post-positivism and was developed by Karl Popper who considered that a good hypothesis was one that was constructed in such a way that it could be falsified. If a theory was to be considered true then it would have been tested many times in such a way that it could be deemed false; in this way theories only remain true until they are shown to be untrue. For example the statement all swans are white could be falsified if/when a black swan was discovered.

Foucault, Michel (1926–1984) – French philosopher who developed the idea of archaeology and his own distinct form of discourse analysis. Foucault investigated numerous institutions through a form of historical analysis e.g. insanity and the asylum in his initial work *Madness and Civilisation* (2001). He also outlined how disciplines of knowledge were demarcated during the Enlightenment and how this ordered the world and our comprehension of it. Furthermore, through his idea of archaeological study and analysis he proposed an extension of the idea regarding historical discontinuity; that is, the past is formed through innumerable instances that the historian moulds into a narrative. Foucault argued that following periods of relative stability, discourse regarding knowledge about humanity undergoes major transformation when not only discourse changes but the very basis of knowledge itself.

Frankfurt School – Founded at the University of Frankfurt, the Frankfurt School developed the notion of critical theory that sought to uncover power relations that existed in capitalist societies.

genealogy – Associated with Nietzsche and looks to trace the origins of phenomenon.

grammatology – A term used by Jacques Derrida to illustrate the inconsistency between signifier and signified.

Habermas, Jurgen (1929–) – Initially undertook an analysis of historical materialism and concentrated on a means of freeing social science from the positivist straitjacket constructed during the 19th century. Habermas has been criticised for his highly theoretical constructions that lean toward grand narratives regarding human nature and social evolution. Most agree that Habermas is directly connected to the Enlightenment programme.

hegemony – Concept initially used by Antonio Gramsci to illustrate power relations between the bourgeoisie and proletariat. Ideology and belief systems provide the basis for class domination.

Heidegger, Martin (1889–1975) – German phenomenologist who considered that becoming and being-in-the-world (Dasein) provided the very basis for understanding human existence. He underpins much postmodern thought and that the objective of knowledge was the very looking or seeking itself. Seeking is becoming.

historical realism – This ontological position is the basis of the critical theory paradigm of inquiry and considers that reality is formed through historical processes, for example, the concept of democracy or democratic existence was very different for antiquity than it is today. The theory that reflects democracy has changed and developed through to the present day and it is still transforming through dialectical or evolutionary process.

intransitive knowledge – Intransitive knowledge incorporates knowledge that exists beyond humanity, for example, gravity, evolution and discovered by scientists and philosophers as opposed to transitive knowledge which is brought to the analysis of intransitive knowledge and developed by humanity.

Kant, Immanuel (1724–1804) – Kant argued that the way we understand the world is determined by the structures and categories of cognition. Object is based on the perceiving subject; that is there exists a relationship between the two. He considered that universal categories involved an aspect of human nature and that through this objective knowledge existed. Critique was central to Kantian philosophy; Enlightenment thought provided the basis for human confidence in their own analysis, thought and understanding.

Kuhn, Thomas (1922–1996) – In *The Structure of Scientific Revolutions* (1966) Kuhn argued a radical method of theoretical transformation; for Kuhn transformation was sporadic and chaotic and involved revolutionary paradigm shifts.

Indeed during these revolutionary changes previous knowledge or truths are swept away and replaced by emerging knowledge and theory.

Marxism – A philosophical position developed by Karl Marx and Friedrich Engels that uses the dialectical method to understand history and social change. The world did not encompass a collection of entities but involved a process of change. Dialectical method rejects empiricism and appearances as the base of knowledge and seeks to identify patterns from which such appearances evolve. Through dialectical materialism Marx pursued what he termed a complete science of history and society with economic variables determining (or interacting with super-structure) historical process and change.

metaphysics – A branch of philosophy that asks questions such as: What is being? What exists and what is existence? Metaphysics incorporates philosophical speculation beyond the present situation that exists within science and stands in direct opposition to the empiricist viewpoint that all knowledge is derived from experience. It attempts to provide abstract theoretical systems that explain mind, matter and the place of humanity in a complicated world.

modernism – Involves grand ideas or theories and is linked to intellectuals that came to prominence based on Enlightenment thinking. For example the Marxist idea of the proletariat overthrowing the bourgeoisie through some form of determinism incorporates a modernist vision.

naive realism – Reality exists independent of the mind and this reality may be clearly understood and accurately reflected through theory.

Nietzsche, Friedrich (1844–1900) – Nietzsche questioned the notion of truth and argued that two separate kinds existed; interpretations, illusion and lies arrived at through metaphysics and scientific truths which provide practical knowledge. Primarily truths are pretentious social illusions. In the *Gay Science* (1882) Nietzsche explores the idea of a science that recognises its inconsistencies and biases.

objectivity – One must ensure research is free of bias. Distance is required between the researchers and researched so that a bias free non-interference perspective can be reached. Objectivity is mainly pursued in natural sciences through measurement of variables and notions of cause and effect.

ontology – Stems from an Enlightenment metaphysical concern with reality or what exists. Empiricists and rationalists have different ontological positions, which become apparent in positivism, phenomenology and each paradigm of inquiry discussed in this text.

paradigm – A paradigm involves a framework of ideas, procedures and outcomes within which a piece of work is structured. Unlike the scientific method a paradigm is flexible and moves away from the rigidity of positivism. Science is not considered an abstraction but exists in concrete historical situations and is developed through preceding antecedents; paradigms are only upset or changed when an accumulation of anomalies forces transformation.

phenomenology – Phenomenologists divide knowledge into indirect (aspects) and direct (essences) knowledge. Essences can be presented in their entirety whereas individual things can only be presented through aspects of themselves. Consciousness is known directly as an essence and certain memories or the act of hearing is not given as aspects but as wholes. Consequently, there is a difference between objects in the world and those of consciousness; the former are never given whole and the latter always complete.

positivism – Closely linked with empiricism, in its initial stages positivism was an attempt to understand the development of thought. Augustus Comte considered that thinking had evolved through three stages labelled the religious, metaphysical and scientific. For Comte the scientific was the most useful but he considered that the earlier stages had intrinsic value as well. In later years the main emphasis was placed on the scientific element of positivism and the religious and metaphysical dimensions were lost. That said, there emerged a more critical approach to science and greater self examination in terms of its presuppositions and procedures. Science required observation; consequently phenomenon that could not be observed should be omitted from scientific explanation.

post-positivism – Developed through positivism and involves falsification rather than verification. There are variants of post-positivism which exist on a continuum; some variants are closer to positivism and others to phenomenology and critical theory.

postmodernism – Postmodernism involves a sceptical perspective of knowledge and truth and disputes modernist ideas such as rationality, originality and progress.

rationalism – Rationalism is distinct from and critical of empiricism. It considers that the only way knowledge can be gained is through rational reflection and reasoning and not simply through experience.

realism – Realism considers that reality exists independently of the human mind, thought and experience.

relativism – Relativism argues that objective universal truths do not exist.

relativist realism – Reality is formed through specific situations; it is frequently changing.

subjectivity – Of the mind and stands in direct opposition to objectivity. Reality is of the mind.

transitive knowledge – Transitive knowledge is apparent in the social sciences; this is opposed to intransitive knowledge, which is mainly found in natural phenomenon.

Vico, Giambattista (1668–1744) – Vico disagreed with the Cartesian idea that knowledge had been sourced and that physical science underpinned truth. He argued that greater emphasis was required in identifying historical and social knowledge.

References

Adorno, T.W. and Horkheimer, M. (1997) *Dialectic of Enlightenment*. London: Verso.

Adredt (1982) *Lectures on Kant's Political Philosophy*. Chicago, IL: University of Chicago Press.

Alvesson, M. and Skoldberg, K. (2009) *Reflexive Methodology*. London: SAGE Publications.

Annells, M. (1996) 'Grounded theory method: philosophical perspectives, paradigm of inquiry, and postmodernism', *Qualitative Health Research*, 6 (3): 379–93.

Ashbury, J. (1995) 'Overview of focus group research', *Qualitative Health Research*, 5 (4): 414–20.

Ayer, A.J. (1946) *Language, Truth and Logic*. London: Gollancz.

Bauman, Z. (1978) *Hermeneutics and Social Science*. New York: Columbia University Press.

Benton, T. and Craib, I. (2001) *Philosophy of Social Science: The Philosophical Foundations of Social Thought*. Houndmills Basingstoke: Palgrave MacMillan.

Berlin, I (1979) *Against the Current: Essays in the History of Ideas*. Oxford: Oxford Paperbacks.

Bernet, R. (1999) 'Husserl in a companion to continental philosophy', in S. Critchley and W.R. Schroeder (eds), *Blackwell Companion to Philosophy*. Oxford: Blackwell. pp. 198–207.

Bhaskar, R. (1975) *A Realist Theory of Science*. London: Version.

Blau, J.L. (1952) *Men and Movements in American Philosophy*. New York: Prentice Hall.

Blumer, H. (1962) *Symbolic Interaction in Human Behaviour and Social Process,* (ed.) A.M. Rose. Boston, MA: Houghton-Mifflin. pp. 179–84.

Blumer, H. (1969) *Symbolic Interaction*. Englewood Cliffs, NJ: Prentice Hall.

Bryant, A. (2002) 'Re-grounding grounded theory', *Journal of Information Technology Theory and Application*, 4 (1): 25–42.

Bryant, A. and Charmaz, K. (2007a) 'Grounded theory research: methods and practices', in A. Bryant and C. Charmaz (eds), *The Sage Handbook of Grounded Theory*. Thousand Oaks, CA: SAGE Publications. pp. 1–28.

Bryant, A. and Charmaz, K. (2007b) 'Grounded theory in historical perspective: an epistemological account', in A. Bryant and C. Charmaz (eds), *The Sage Handbook of Grounded Theory*. Thousand Oaks, CA: SAGE Publications. pp. 31–57.

Caputo, J.D. (1999) 'Heidegger', in S. Critchley and W.A. Schroeder (eds), *A Companion to Continental Philosophy*. Oxford: Blackwell. pp. 223–33.

Chambers, E. (2000) 'Applied ethnography', in N.K. Denzin and Y. Lincoln (eds), *Handbook of Qualitative Research*. Thousand Oaks: SAGE Publications. pp. 981–99.

Charmaz, K. (1983) *The Grounded Theory Method: An Explication and Interpretation* in *Contemporary Field Research: A Collection of Readings*, ed. R.M. Emerson. US: University of California.

Charmaz, K. (2000) 'Constructivist and Objectivist Grounded Theory', in N.K. Denzin and Y. Lincoln (eds), *Handbook of Qualitative Research*. Thousand Oaks, CA: SAGE Publications. pp. 509–35.

Charmaz, K. (2006) *Constructing Grounded Theory: A Practical Guide Through Qualitative Analysis*. London: SAGE Publications.

Clarke, A.E. (2002) *Situational Analysis: Grounded Theory after the Postmodern Turn.* Thousand Oaks, CA: SAGE Publications.

Coase, R.H. (1995) *Essays on Economics and Economists.* Chicago, IL: University of Chicago Press.

Conrad, J. (1995) *Heart of Darkness.* Harmondsworth: Penguin.

Converse, J.M. (1987) *Survey Research in the United States: Roots and Emergence 1890–1960.* Berkley, CA: University of California Press.

Corbin, J. and Strauss, A. (1990) 'Grounded theory method', *Qualitative Sociology,* 13: 3–21.

Cresswell, J.W. (2007) *Qualitative Inquiry and Research Design: Choosing Among Five Approaches.* Thousand Oaks, CA: SAGE Publications.

Deleuze, G. (1999) *Foucault,* ed. and trans. S. Hand. London: Continuum.

Denzin, N. (1989) *Interpretive Interactionism.* London: SAGE Publications.

Denzin, N. (1997) *Interpretive Ethnography: Ethnographic Practices for the 21st Century.* Thousand Oaks, CA: SAGE Publications.

Denzin, N.K. (2007) 'Grounded theory and the politics of interpretation', in A. Bryant and K. Charmaz (eds), *The SAGE Handbook of Grounded Theory.* Thousand Oaks, CA: SAGE Publications. pp. 454–71.

Denzin, N. and Lincoln, Y. (1994) *The Handbook of Qualitative Research,* 1st edn. Thousand Oaks, CA: SAGE Publications.

Denzin, N. and Lincoln, Y. (2000) *The Handbook of Qualitative Research,* 2nd edn. Thousand Oaks, CA: SAGE Publications.

Denzin, N. and Lincoln, Y. (2005) *The Handbook of Qualitative Research,* 3rd edn. Thousand Oaks, CA: SAGE Publications.

Derrida, J. (1976) *Of Grammatology.* Blatimore, MD: The Johns Hopkins University Press.

Derrida, J. (1982) *Differance, Margins of Philosophy.* Chicago, IL: University of Chicago press.

Descartes, R. (1968) *Discourse on Method and Meditations.* London: Penguin.

Dewey, J. (1950) *Art as Experience.* New York: Capricorn.

Diesing, P. (1972) *Patterns of Discovery in the Social Sciences.* London: Routledge and Kegan Paul.

Dilthy, W. (2002) *Formation of the Historical World in Human Sciences.* Princeton, NJ: Princeton University Press.

Dreyfus, H.L. (1991*) Being-in-the-World: A Commentary on Heidegger's Being and Time, Division One.* Cambridge, MA: MIT Press.

Dryseck, J.S. (1995) 'Critical theory as research program', in S.K. White (ed.), *The Cambridge Companion to Habermas.* Cambridge: Cambridge University Press.

Edkins, J. (1999) *Poststructuralism and International Relations: Bringing the Political Back In. Critical Perspectives and International Relations.* London: Lynne Rienner Publishers.

Faulconer, J.E. (2000) 'Appropriating Heidegger', in J.E Faulconer and M.A. Wrathall (eds), *Appropriating Heidegger.* Cambridge: Cambridge University Press. pp 1–5.

Fern, E.F. (2001) *Advanced Focus Group Research.* Thousand Oaks, CA: SAGE Publications.

Foucault, M. (1980) *Power/Knowledge,* ed, C. Gordon. Brighton: Harvester.

Foucault, M. (1981) 'The order of discourse', in R. Young (ed.), *Untying the Text: A Post-structuralist Reader.* London: Kegan Paul. pp. 48–79.

Foucault, M. (1983) 'Structuralism and post-structuralism: an interview with Michel Foucault by Raulet, G.', *Telos,* 55: 53–8.

Foucault, M. (1992) *The History of Sexuality.* Volume Two. Harmondsworth: Penguin.

Foucault. M. (1998) *The Will to Knowledge: the History of Sexuality, Volume One.* Harmondsworth: Penguin.

Foucault, M. (2002a) *The Archaeology of Knowledge.* London: Routledge

Foucault, M. (2002b) *Madness and Civilization.* London: Routledge.

Foucault, M. (2003) *The Order of Things*. London: Routledge.

Foucault, M. (2004) *Society Must Be Defended; Lecture Jan 7th 1976*. Harmondsworth: Penguin.

Foucault, M. (2007) *Security, Territory, Population. Lectures at the College De France 1977–78*, ed M. Senellart and trans. G. Burchell. Houndsmill: Palgrave MacMillan.

Fromm, E.T (1997) *To Have or To Be?* New York: Continuum.

Gadamer, H.-G. (1970) *On the Scope and Function of Hermeneutical Reflection, trans.* G.B. Hess and R.E. Palmer. London: Continuum.

Gadamer H.-G. (2004) *Truth and Method*. London: Continuum Press.

Gadamer, H.-G. (2008a) *The Universality of the Hermeneutical Problem in Philosophical Hermeneutics*. Berkeley, CA: University of California Press.

Gadamer, H.-G. (2008b) *Philosophical Hermeneutics,* trans. D.E. Ling. Berkeley, CA: University of California Press.

Garrison, J. (1996) 'A Deweyian theory of democratic listening', *Education Theory*, 46: 429–51.

Geertz, C. (1973) *The Interpretation of Cultures*. New York: Perseus Books.

George, S. (1976) 'The Reconciliation of the "classical" and "scientific" approaches to international relations', *Millennium: Journal of International Studies*, 5: 28–40.

Gergen, K.J. (1994) *Realities and Relationships: Soundings in Social Construction*. Cambridge, MA: Harvard University Press.

Giddens, A. (1977) *New Rules of Sociological Methods*. London: Hutchinson and Co.

Glaser, B. (1978) *Advances in the Methodology of Grounded Theory: Theoretical Sensitivity*. Berkeley, CA: University of California.

Glaser, B. (1992) *Emergence vs Forcing: Basics of Grounded Theory Analysis*. Mill Valley, CA: Sociology Press.

Glaser, B. (1998) *Doing Grounded Theory: Issues and Discussions*. Grounded Theory Institute, Mill Valley: Sociology Press.

Glaser, B. (2001) *The Grounded Theory Perspective I: Theoretical Coding*. Grounded Theory Institute, Mill Valley: Sociology Press.

Glaser, B. (2005) *The Grounded Theory Perspective III: Theoretical Coding*. Grounded Theory Institute, Mill Valley: Sociology Press.

Glaser, B. and Holton, J. (eds) (2007) *Grounded Theory Seminar Reader*. Grounded Theory Institute, Mill Valley: Sociology Press.

Glaser, B. and Strauss, A. (1967) *The Discovery of Grounded Theory*. New York: Alpine.

Goulding, C. (2002) *Grounded Theory: A Practical Guide for Management, Business and Market Researchers*. London: SAGE Publications.

Gramsci, A. (2005) *Selections from the Prison Notebooks*. London: Lawrence and Wishart.

Greene, J.C. (2000) 'Understanding social programs through evaluation', in N.K. Denzin and Y. Lincoln (eds), *Handbook of Qualitative Research*. Thousand Oaks, CA: SAGE Publications. pp. 981–99.

Greenwood, D.J. and Levin, M. (2000) 'Reconstructing relationships between universities society', in N.K. Denzin and Y. Lincoln (eds), *Handbook of Qualitative Research*. Thousand Oaks: SAGE Publications. pp. 85–106

Guba, E.G. and Lincoln, Y.S. (1985) *Naturalistic Inquiry*. London: SAGE Publications.

Guba, E.G. and Lincoln, Y.S. (1989) *Fourth Generation Evaluation*. London: SAGE Publications.

Guba, E.G. and Lincoln, Y.S. (1994) 'Computing paradigms in qualitative research', in N. Denzin, and Y.S. Lincoln (eds), *Handbook of Qualitative Research*. Thousand Oaks, CA: SAGE Publications. pp. 105–17.

Guba, E.G. and Lincoln, Y.S. (2000) `Paradigmatic controversies, contradictions, and emerging confluences', in N.K. Denzin and Y.S. Lincoln (eds), *Handbook of Qualitative Research*. Thousand Oaks, CA: SAGE Publications.

Gubriem, J.F. and Holstein, J.A. (2000) 'Analyzing interpretive practice', in N.K. Denzin and Y. S. Lincoln (eds), *Handbook of Qualitative Research*. Thousand Oaks: SAGE Publications.

Gurwitsch, A. (1967) 'On the intentionality of consciousness', in J.J Kockelmans (ed.), *Phenomenology: The Philosophy of Edmund Husserl and its Interpretation*. New York: Doubleday and Company. pp. 118–37.

Habermas, J. (1971) *Knowledge and Human Interest*. Boston, MA: Beacon Press.

Habermas, J. (2004) *Theory and Practice*. Cambridge: Polity Press.

Habermas, J. (2007) *Moral Consciousness and Communicative Action*. Cambridge: Polity press.

Hajer, M.A. (1995) *The Politics of Environmental Discourses: Ecological Modernization and the Policy Process*. Oxford: Clarendon Press.

Hall S. (ed.) (1997 *Representation: Cultural Representations and Signifying Practices*. London: SAGE Publications.

Hammersley, M. (1992) *What's Wrong with Ethnography?* London: Routledge.

Hammersley, M. and Atkinson, P. (2007) *Ethnography: Principles in Practice*. Abingdon: Routledge.

Hampsher-Monk, I. (1992) *A History of Modern Political Thought*. Oxford: Blackwell.

Harre, R. (1987) 'The positivist-empiricist approach and its alternative', in P. Reason and J. Rowan (eds), *Human Inquiry: A New Sourcebook of New Paradigm Research*. Chichester: Wiley and Sons. pp. 3–17.

Hegel, G.W.F. (1977) *Phenomenology of Spirit,* trans. A.V. Miller, foreword J.N. Finlay. London: Clarendon Press.

Heidegger, M. (1962/2004) *Being and Time*. Oxford: Blackwell.

Heidegger, M. (1994) *Basic Questions of Philosophy: Selected Problems of Logic*, trans. R. Rojcewicz and A. Schuwer. Bloomington, IN: Indiana University Press.

Heron, J. (1996) *Cooperative Inquiry: Research into the Human Condition*. London: SAGE publication.

Heron, J. and Reason, P. (1997) 'A participatory inquiry paradigm', *Qualitative Inquiry*, 3: 274–94.

Heron, J. and Reason. P. (2000) 'Co-operative inquiry: research with rather than on people', in P. Reason and H. Bradbury (eds), *Handbook of Action Research*. London: SAGE Publications. pp. 179–88.

Hertz, R. (1997) *Reflexivity and Voice*. Thousand Oaks CA: SAGE Publications.

Hess, G.B. and Palmer, R.E. (1970) *Function of On the Scope and Hermeneutical Reflection*. London: Continuum.

Hirsch, E.D., Jr (1967) *Validity in Interpretation*. New Haven, CT: Yale University Press.

Hood, J.C. (2007) 'Orthodoxy vs. power: the defining traits of grounded theory', in A. Bryant and C. Charmaz (eds), *The SAGE Handbook of Grounded Theory*. Thousand Oaks, CA: SAGE Publications. pp 1–28.

Hofstede, G. (2007) *Culture and Organisations: Software of the Mind*. NewYork: McGraw Hill.

Howell, K.E. (2000) *Discovering the Limits of European Integration: A Grounded Theory Approach*. New York: Nova Science Publishers.

Howell, K.E. (2004) *Europeanization, European Integration and Financial Services: Developing Theoretical Frameworks and Synthesising Methodological Approaches*. Basingstoke: Palgrave MacMillan.

Horkheimer, M. (1972) *Critical Theory: Selected Essays*. New York: Continuum.

Husserl. E. (1969) *Ideas: General Introduction to Pure Phenomenology*, trans. W.R. Boyce Gibson. London: George Allen & Unwin.

Husserl, E. (1992) *The Crisis of European Science and Transcendental Philosophy*. Evanston: Northwestern University Press.

Husserl, E. (1997) *Things and Space: Lectures of 1907*. Boston, MA: Kluwer.

Husserl, E. (1998a) 'The Vienna lecture', in R. Kearney and M. Rainwater (eds), *The Continental Philosophy Reader*. London: Routledge. pp. 7–14.

Husserl, E. (1998b) 'Phenomenology', in R. Kearney and M. Rainwater (eds), *The Continental Philosophy Reader*. London: Routledge.

Huxley, A. (1994) *Brave New World Revisited*. London: Flamingo.

Janesick, V.J. (2000) 'The choreography of qualitative research design', in N. Denzin and Y. Lincoln (eds), *The Handbook of Qualitative Research*. Thousand Oaks, CA: SAGE Publications. pp. 379–99.

Johnson, A. (1996) 'It's good to talk: the focus group and the social imagination', *The Sociological Review* 44: 517–38.

Kant, I. (1952) *Critique of Judgement*, trans. J.C. Meredith. Oxford: Oxford University Press.

Kant, I. (1992) *Critique of Pure Reason*, trans. N.K. Smith. Houndmills: MacMillan.

Kant, I. (1995a) *Political Writings*, ed. H. Reiss and trans. N.B. Nisbet. Cambridge Texts in the History of Political Thought. Cambridge: Cambridge University Press.

Kant, I. (1995b) 'On the common saying: this may be true in theory but it does not apply in practice', in H. Reiss (ed.), *Political Writings*. Cambridge: Cambridge University Press.

Kant, I. (1997) *Critique of Practical Reason*. Cambridge: Cambridge University Press.

Kemmis, S. and Mctaggart, R. (2000) *The Action Research Planner*, 3rd edn. Geelong, Victoria: Deakin University.

Kidder, P. (1997) 'The hermeneutic and dialectic of community in development', *International Journal of Social Economics*, 24 (11): 1191–202.

Kojeve, A. (1980) *Introduction to the Reading of Hegel: Lectures on the Phenomenology of Spirit*. Ithaca, NY: Cornell University Press.

Krueger, R.A. (1988) *Focus Groups: A Practical Guide for Applied Research*. Newbury Park, CA: SAGE Publications.

Kuhn, T.S. (1996) *The Structure of Scientific Revolution*, 3rd edn. Chicago, IL: University of Chicago Press.

Kuhn, T.S. (1970) *The Structure of Scientific Revolution*. Chicago, IL: University of Chicago Press.

Lakatos, I. (1970) 'Falsification and the methodology of scientific research programmes', in I. Lakatos and A. Musgrave (eds), *Criticism and the Growth of Knowledge*. Cambridge: Cambridge University Press.

Lewin, K. (1946) 'Action research and minority problems', *Journal of Social Issues*, 2: 34–6.

Lincoln, Y.S. and Guba, E.G. (1985) *Naturalistic Inquiry*. Thousand Oaks: SAGE Publications.

Longino, H. (1993a) 'Essential tensions – phase two: feminist, philosophical and social studies of science', in L.M. Antony and C. Witt (eds), *A Mind of One's Own: Feminist Essays on Reason and Objectivity*. Boulder, CO: Westview. pp. 257–72.

Longino, H. (1993b) 'Subjects, power and knowledge: descriptions and prescriptions in feminist philosophies of science', in L. Alcott and E. Potter (eds), *Feminist Epistemologies*. New York: Routledge. pp. 101–20.

Lyotard (2004) *The Postmodern Condition: A Report on Knowledge*. Minneapolis, MN: University of Minnesota Press.

Madison, G.B. (1988) *The Hermeneutics of Postmodernity*. Bloomington, IN: Indiana University Press.

Madriz, E. (2000) 'Focus groups in feminist research', in N.K. Denzin and Y. Lincoln (eds), *The Handbook of Qualitative Research*. Thousand Oaks, CA: SAGE Publications.

Mairet, P. (1973) *Introduction to Existentialism and Humanism*, ed. J.P. Sartre. London: Methuen.

Makkreel, R.A. (1999) 'Dilthy', in S. Critchley and W.R. Schroeder (eds), *A Companion to Continental Philosophy*. Oxford: Blackwell. pp. 425–32.

Malinowski, B. (1922) *Argonauts of the Western Pacific: An Account of Native Enterprise and Adventure in the Archipelagoes of Melanesian New Guinea*. New York: E.P. Dutton.

Marcuse, H. (2004) *One Dimensional Man: Studies in the Ideology of Advanced Industrial Societies*. New York: Routledge.

Margolis, S. (1989) 'Postscript on modernism and postmodernism, both', *Theory, Culture and Society*, 6: 5–30.

McCarthy, T. (1999) 'Habermas', in S. Critchley and W.A. Schroeder (eds), *A Companion to Continental Philosophy*. Oxford: Blackwell. pp. 397–406.

McFarlane, J. (1976) 'The mind of modernism', in M. Bradbury and J. McFarlane (eds), *Modernism*. Harmondsworth: Penguin.

Mead, G.H. (1962) *Mind, Self, and Society*. Chicago, IL: University of Chicago Press.

Merleau-Ponty, M. (1968) *The Visible and Invisible*. Evanston: Northwest University Press.

Merleau-Ponty, M. (1999) *Phenomenology of Perception*. London: Routledge.

Merleau-Ponty, M. (2004) *The World of Perception*. London: Routledge.

Mintzberg, H. (1973) *The Nature of Managerial Work*. New York: Harper and Row.

Mishler, E.G. (1986) *Research Interviewing: Context and Narrative*. Cambridge, MA: Harvard University Press.

Moran, D. (2008) *Introduction to Phenomenology*. London: Routledge.

Navon, D. (2001) 'The puzzle of mirror reversal: a view from Clockland target article on mirror-reversal', *Psycoloquy*, 12 (17): 1–19.

Nietzsche, F. (1969) *Thus Spoke Zarathustra*. London: Penguin.

Nietzsche, F. (1984) *Beyond Good and Evil*. London: Penguin.

Norris, C. (1987) *Derrida*. London: Fontana Press.

Norris, C. (1993) *Deconstruction: Theory and Practice*. London: Methuen.

Patton, P. (1999) 'Foucault', in S. Critchley and W.R. Schroeder (eds), *A Companion to Continental Philosophy*. Oxford: Blackwell. pp. 537–48.

Pippin, R.B. (1997) *Idealism as Modernism: Hegelian Variations*. Cambridge: Cambridge University Press.

Pippin, R.B. (2005) *The Persistence of Subjectivity*. Cambridge: Cambridge University Press.

Plato (1976) *The Phaedrus*. London: Penguin.

Polkinghorne, D.E. (1989) 'Changing conversations about human science', in S. Kvale (ed.), *Issues of Validity in Qualitative Research*. Lund: Studentlitteratur. pp. 13–46.

Popper, K. (1992) *Unended Quest: An Intellectual Biography*. London: Routledge.

Popper, K. (1969) *The Open Society and its Enemies*. London: Routledge and Kegan Paul.

Popper, K. (1994) *The Myth of the Framework: In Defence of Science and Rationality*. London: Routledge.

Popper, K. (2002a) *Conjectures and Refutation: The Growth of Scientific Knowledge*. London: Routledge.

Popper, K. (2002b) *The Logic of Scientific Discovery*. London: Routledge.

Potter, J. (1996) *Representing Reality: Discourse Rhetoric and Social Construction*. London: SAGE Publications.

Rabinow, P. (1991) *The Foucault Reader*. Harmondsworth: Penguin.

Reason, P. and Bradbury, H. (eds) (2001) *The SAGE Handbook of Action Research. Participative Inquiry and Practice*. London: SAGE Publications.

Reinharz, S. (1997) 'Who am I? The need for a variety of selves in the field', in R. Hertz (ed.), *Reflexivity and Voice*. Thousand Oaks, CA: SAGE Publications. pp. 3–20.

Ricoeur, P. (2004) *The Conflict of Interpretations: Essays in Hermeneutics*. London: Continuum Press.

Ricouer P. (2008) *From Text to Action*. London: Continuum Press.

Rorty, R. (1979/2009) *Philosophy and the Mirror of Nature*. Princeton, NJ: Princeton University Press.

Rorty, R. and Engel, P. (2007) *What's the Use of Truth?* New York: Columbia University Press.

Rosenau, P.M. (1992) *Post-Modernism and the Social Sciences: Insights, Inroads and Intrusions.* Princeton, NJ: Princeton University Press.

Russell, B. (1980) *Our Knowledge of the External World.* London: George Allen & Unwin.

Sartre, J.P. (1973) *Existentialism and Humanism*, trans. and intro. P. Mairet. London: Methuen.

Sarup, M. (1993) *An Introductory Guide to Post-Structuralism and Postmodernism.* Chichester: Harvester Wheatsheaf.

Saussure, de. F (1974) *Course in General Linguistics.* London: Fontana/Collins.

Scheffler, I. (1974) *Four Pragmatists: A Critical Introduction to Pierce, James Mead and Dewey.* London: Routledge and Kegan Paul.

Schlick, M. (2002) 'The future of philosophy, Vol 2', in Y. Balashov and A. Rosenberg (eds), *Philosophy of Science: Contemporary Readings.* London: Routledge. pp. 8–21.

Schon, D. (1983) *The Reflective Practitioner: How Professionals Think in Action.* New York: Basic Books.

Schopenhaur, A. (1966) *The World as Will and Representation Vols One and Two*, trans. E.F.J. Payne. New York: Dover Publications.

Schwandt, T.A. (2000) 'Three epistemological stances for qualitative inquiry: interpretivism, hermeneutics and social constructionism', in N.K. Denzin and Y. Lincoln (eds), *Handbook of Qualitative Research.* Thousand Oaks: SAGE Publications. pp. 85–106.

Schutz, A. (1970) *On Phenomenology and Social Relations: Selected Writings*, ed. H. Wagner. Chicago, IL: University of Chicago Press.

Scott-Jones, J. (2010) 'Origins and ancestors: a brief history of ethnography', in J. Scott-Jones and S. Wat (eds), *Ethnography in Social Science Practice.* London: Routledge. pp. 13–27.

Silverman, D. (1985) *Interpreting Qualitative Data.* Thousand Oaks CA: SAGE Publications.

Sim, S. (1998) 'Postmodernism and philosophy', in S. Sim (ed.), *The Icon Critical Dictionary of Postmodern Thought.* Cambridge: Icon Books. pp. 3–14.

Skrbina, D. (2001) 'Participation, organization, and mind: toward a participatory worldview'. Doctoral thesis, Centre for Action Research in Professional Practice, School of Management, University of Bath.

Stern, N.P. (1994) 'Eroding grounded theory in critical issues', in J.M. Morse (ed.), *Qualitative Research Methods.* Thousand Oaks, CA: SAGE Publications. pp. 212–22

Stewart, D.W. and Shamdasani, P.N. (1990) *Focus Groups: Theory and Practice.* Newbury Park, CA: SAGE Publications.

Strauss, A. (1987) *Qualitative Analysis for Social Science.* Cambridge: Cambridge University Press.

Strauss, A. and Corbin, J. (1990/1998) *Basics of Qualitative Research: Techniques and Procedures for Developing Grounded Theory.* Thousand Oaks, CA: SAGE Publications.

Strauss, A. and Corbin, J. (1994) 'Grounded theory methodology: an overview', in N.K. Denzin and Y.S. Lincoln (eds), *Handbook of Qualitative Research.* Thousand Oaks, CA: SAGE Publications. pp. 273–85.

Tedlock, B. (2000) 'Ethnography and ethnographic representation', in N. Denzin and Y.S. Lincoln *Handbook of Qualitative Research.* Thousand Oaks, CA: SAGE Publications. pp. 455–86.

Templeton, J.F. (1994) *The Focus Group.* Chicago, IL: Irwin.

Torbert, W.R. (2001) 'The practice of inquiry', in P. Reason and B. Bradbury (eds), *The Handbook of Action Research.* Thousand Oaks, CA: SAGE Publications. pp. 250–60.

Toulmin, S. (1953) *The Philosophy of Science.* London: Hutchinson.

Vedder, B. (1999) 'Schleiermacher', in S. Critchley and W.R. Schroeder (eds), *A Companion to Continental Philosophy*. Oxford: Blackwell. pp. 417–24.

Vico, G. (1744/1999) *New Science*. London: Penguin Classics.

Vidich, A.J. and Lyman, S.M. (2000) 'Qualitative methods: their history in sociology and anthropology', in N.K. Denzin and Y.S. Lincoln (eds), *Handbook of Qualitative Research*. Thousand Oaks, CA: SAGE Publications. pp. 37–84.

Watzlawick, P. (1984) *The Invented Reality: How Do We Know What We Believe We Know? Contributions to Constructivism*. New York: Norton.

Weber, M. (2004) *The Protestant Ethic and the Spirit of Capitalism*. London: Routledge.

Williams, B. (2004) *Truth and Truthfulness*. Princeton, NJ: Princeton University Press.

Willis, P. (1977) *Learning to Labour: How Working-Class Kids Get Working-Class Jobs*. Farnborough: Saxon House.

Winch, P. (1991) *The Idea of a Social Science and its Relation to Philosophy*. London: Routledge.

Woodruff Smith, D. (2007) *Husserl*. London and New York: Routledge.

Wright Mills, C. (2000) *The Sociological Imagination*. Oxford: Oxford University Press.

REFERENCES

Index

Page numbers in *italics* represent tables.

empathy 158
empirical knowledge *36*
empirical science 2–3
empiricism 32–54, 211; definition 34
Engel, P.: and Rorty, R. 16
Engels, F.: and Marx, K. 79
Enlightenment 11, 215
epistemés (Foucault) 168, 172–3
essence 59–61, 72
ethical issues 124
ethics 12
ethnography 117–30; definition 118;
    history 120–2; types *119*
European colonialism 121
evolution 123
evolutionary process 123
existence 59–61
experience 38

facilitation 204–6
faisification 44–6, *47*
fiction 120
focus groups 201–4
formal theory 145–7
Foucault, M. 168–81; *epistemés* 168, 172–3;
    History of Sexuality 172; *Madness and
    Civilization* 170
foundationalism: definition 91
anti-foundationalism 103
Frankfurt University 75
Fromm, E.T. 76

Gadamer, H.-G. 162
genealogy 174
generalisation 184–5
Gergen, K.J. 91–2
Glaser, B. 136, 138, 147–56;
    and Strauss, A. 126, 145, 216
global structure 157
Greek Enlightenment 13
Greenwood, D.J.: and Levin, M. 96
grounded theory 131–53; definition 151;
    disputation 147–56; surveys 144–5;
    usage 135–41
group interaction 201
Guba, E.G.: and Lincoln,
    Y.S. 90, 189

Habermas, J. 26; critical theory 83–4
Hammersley, M.: and Atkinson, P. 118
Hawthorne Effect 207
Heart of Darkness (Conrad) 121
Hegel, G.W.F. 8–9, 55, 211
Hegelian optimism 212
hegemony 78–80; definition 79–80
Heidegger, M. 15, 64–8
hermeneutical phenomenology 64–8

hermeneutics 154–67; alethic *159*,
    161–2; objectivist 159–61, *159*;
    phenomenological 64–8, *159*, 162–5
heuristic model 49
historical consciousness 164
historical context 161
historical process 48
historical realism 85
Hobbes, T.: *Objections* 36
homogeneity 204
Horkheimer, M. 77; and Adorno, T.W. 77
human behaviour 199
human beings 165
human existence 168
human interests 84
human mind 35, 72
human nature 39
human science 39, 68, 180
human understanding 216
An Inquiry Concerning Human Understanding
    (Hume) 38–9
An Essay Concerning Human Understanding
    (Locke) 37–8
humanity 36, 77, 86, 173
Hume, D. 38–40; *An Inquiry Concerning Human
    Understanding* 38–9; and Locke, J. 5–6
Husserl, E. 56, 60
Huxley, A.: *Brave New World* 82

idealism 5, 6–7
identifying theory 19–31
ideology 78–80, 84
Illumination Experiment 207
immanence: rule of 178
immutable laws 35, 46
inalienable presence 69–70
inductive procedure 42–3
industrial action research (IAR) 99
inquiry 24–30; knowledge 95; paradigms *29*,
    88–100
intransitive knowledge 52
intentionality 57–9, 175
interaction: symbolic 89, 133
interpretation 187–8
intertextuality 111
interviews 197–201; positivist structured
    200; unstructured 199; usage 199

judgement 10–14, 61–2

Kant, I. 7, 12; *Critique of Pure Reason* 3;
    theory and practice 23–4
knowledge 25, 174–9; accumulated 113;
    accumulation 34; construction 198;
    intransitive 51; posteriori 3; priori 3;
    transitive 51, 52
Kuhn, T.S. 47

Lakatos, I. 50
language 63
Levin, M.: and Greenwood, D.J. 96
Lewin, K. 88
liberation 82
Life and Labour of the People of London
    (Booth) 197
lifeworld 63
Likert scale 195; definition 196
Lincoln, Y.S.: and Denzin, N. 128; and
    Guba, E.G. 90, 189
Locke, J. 37–8; *An Essay Concerning Human
    Understanding* 37–8; and Hume, D. 5–6
logocentricism 109
Longino, H. 92
Lyotard 101, 112–13

Madness and Civilization (Foucault) 170
Malinowski, B. 120
Margolis, S. 102
Marshall, A. 43, 152–3
Marx, K. 12, 75; and Engels, F. 79
Marxism 41, 75
master–slave relationship 9
materialism 6–7
meaning 81, 163, 166
measurement validity 189
mechanistic worldviews *95*
Merleau-Ponty, M. 68–71
microanalysis 139
Mintzberg, H. 208
misinterpretation 114
modernism 32, 101, *115*
postmodernism 32, 101–15, *115*
modernity 171
moral stance 65

narrative knowledge 112–13
narratives 102
National Socialism 76, 82
natural science 40, 214
negation 126
Newton, I. 21–2
Nietzsche, F. 104
norms 187
Novum Organum (Bacon) 35

object and subject *8*
Objections (Hobbes) 36
objective truth 55
objectivist hermeneutics 159–61, *159*
objectivity 134
observation 43, 206–9; participant 128–9
observation schedule 208
Occidentalism 215
oppression 171
Oxford English Dictionary 106

paradigm norms 48
paradigm shifts 46–50, *47*
participant observation 128–9
participatory paradigm 88, 94–6
participatory worldview *95*
perception 22
personal information 195
phallocentricsm 109
phenomena 66
phenomenological hermeneutics 64–8,
    159, 162–5
phenomenology 55–74, 86, 212; theory 28;
    transcendental 56–64; types 73
philosophical position 28
philosophy 12, 30; continental 213
phonocentricism 108
physical confinement 170
Pierce, W. 16, 211
Popper, K. 42, 44–6
population control 178
positivism 32–54, 80–3, 136, 214
post–positivism 32–54
A General View of Positivism
    (Comtè) 40
post–positivist approaches 43–6
positivist ethnography 122–4
positivist notions 30
positivist structured interviews 200
positivist study 208
positivistic perception 202
Potter, J. 91
power 174–9
power balance 202
pragmatism 132
preconceptions 165
prediction 123
presence 111
public relations 205

question formulation 197

rationality 80–3, 169
realism 91; relativist 215;
    transcendental 3
reality 2, *17*, 52
reason 82
Reason, P.: and Bradbury, H. 94
recognition 9
reflexivity 81, 182–92
reliability 183–4; definition 183
representation 7
research 113
researchers 196
retrospection 156
Ricoeur, P. 160
Rorty, R. 161; and Engel, P. 16
Russell, B. 46